Lluís Domènech i Montaner

Man of the *Renaixença*
Architect of *Modernisme*

Table of Contents

5 **Foreword**
Mireia Freixa

Man of the *Renaixença*

7 **The civic-minded, inquiring and political sides of Domènech i Montaner's personality**
Lluís Domènech Girbau

15 **Domènech i Montaner's architecture, at a prudent distance from art nouveau**
Mireia Freixa

23 **In the architect's studio. Domènech's associates**
Teresa-M. Sala i Garcia

31 **Domènech i Montaner and the graphic arts**
Pilar Vélez

39 **Domènech and Barcelona: architect and "town planner"**
Enric Granell and Antoni Ramon

49 **Canet de Mar, Comillas and Reus.
Lluís Domènech i Montaner's creative triangle outside Barcelona**
Gemma Martí, Xavier Mas i Gibert and Carles Sàiz i Xiqués

Architect of *Modernisme*

- 59 **The most significant buildings**

- 61 **Montaner i Simon: the publishing house that resembled a bullring (1879-1885)**
  Núria Homs

- 79 **Café and restaurant for the Universal Exhibition (1887-1892)**
  Rossend Casanova

- 97 **Palau Montaner (1889-1897)**
  Gemma Martí

- 123 **The marine cemetery: Domènech i Montaner's funerary architecture in Comillas (1893-1899)**
  Antonio Sama

- 135 **Casa Thomas (1895-1912)**
  Gemma Martí

- 169 **Castell de Santa Florentina (1896-1912)**
  Carles Sàiz i Xiqués

- 185 **Institut Pere Mata (1897-1912)**
  Jordi March Barberà and Clàudia Sanmartí Martínez

- 219 **Refurbishment of the Fonda España (1900-1903)**
  Maria Manadé Palau

- 237 **Gran Hotel in Palma (1901-1903)**
  Mireia Freixa

- 251 **Casa Navàs (1901-1907)**
  Jordi March Barberà

- 279 **Hospital de la Santa Creu i Sant Pau (1902-1920)**
  Clàudia Sanmartí Martínez

- 319 **Casa Lleó i Morera: the integration of the arts (1903-1905)**
  Pilar Vélez

- 353 **Palau de la Música Catalana (1905-1909)**
  Lluís Domènech Girbau

- 383 **Casa Consol Fabra de Fuster (1908-1911)**
  Ramon Anglada Lara and Teresa-M. Sala i Garcia

- 401 **Can Rocosa (1905-1906) and Casa Domènech (1919) de Canet de Mar**
  Carles Sàiz i Xiqués

- 412 **Chronology and catalogue of works**

- 422 **Bibliography**

Foreword

Mireia Freixa

Lluís Domènech i Montaner (1849-1923) was one of the most influential figures during the time of the Catalan cultural revival, the *Renaixença*, and the homegrown art nouveau movement, *modernisme*. He played a prominent role in Catalonia's cultural and social life and was a member of political organisations, including Jove Catalunya, the Lliga Catalana, the Unió Catalanista and the Lliga Regionalista. He was a deputy in the Spanish parliament and worked on important publications such as *La Renaixensa*, *La Veu de Catalunya* and *El Poble Català*. He also served several times as president of the Ateneu Barcelonès, which was a meeting place for the city's intellectuals, and produced a vast body of work as a historian and heraldic expert.

He had a long and prolific life that was not free from social and political strife, which was reflected in his work and personal life. In 1875, he married Maria Roura Carnestoltes, who hailed from the seaside town of Canet de Mar. One of his sons, Pere Domènech i Roura, also studied architecture and was one of his main collaborators towards the end of his life. Another son, Fèlix Domènech i Roura, studied heraldry, and one of his closest associates, Francesc Guàrdia, married his daughter Dolors.

The Taula Lluís Domènech i Montaner was set up in 2017 to organise the wide range of events to commemorate the centenary of his death in 2023 and to bring his work to a wider audience. The book you are holding in your hands is part of this project and is a collective work that focuses on his architectural landmarks as well as other aspects of his long, productive career.

The book is divided into two parts. The first comprises six articles that give a broad overview of the civic-minded, enquiring and political sides of Lluís Domènech i Montaner, and then moves on to his work as an architect in the context of the international art nouveau movement. It describes the architects and craftsmen who worked with him; his work in the fields of the graphic arts and heraldry; his contributions as a "town planner"; and examines the creative triangle of Reus, Canet and Comillas, outside Barcelona.

The second part consists of fifteen articles which look individually at the architect's most significant buildings in the most accurate chronological order possible. For obvious reasons, his two UNESCO World Heritage buildings – the Palau de la Música Catalana and the Hospital de Sant Pau – are covered more extensively due to their extraordinary value.

The book ends with a chronology and catalogue of his works, which brings together the most significant aspects of his life and also features his projects that do not have a dedicated chapter of their own, such as the monument to Doctor Robert (1903) in Barcelona and the mausoleum and pantheon of Jaume I (1906) in Tarragona.

We would like to give special thanks to the sixteen authors of the articles who are the leading authorities on the different facets of the architect and his buildings, as well as the public and private institutions that have made this book possible, particularly the Col·legi d'Arquitectes de Catalunya, which houses the Lluís Domènech i Montaner archive.

We hope you enjoy reading this book and that it gives you a better understanding of Lluís Domènech i Montaner's architecture and his outstanding achievements.

← Hospital de Sant Pau (1902-1920). Detail of a mosaic in the great hall of the administration pavilion.

The civic-minded, inquiring and political sides of Domènech i Montaner's personality

Lluís Domènech Girbau

Domènech i Montaner's civic-minded personality through his education and membership of political and cultural institutions

Lluís Domènech i Montaner's education was fundamental to developing apersonality with a great civic sense: his father, Pere Domènech Saló, trained him from a very young age as an assistant in his bookbinder's workshop, where he became an accomplished craftsman with regards to rigorousness and the achievement of technical excellence (Domènech Girbau, 2018, pp. 45-55). With his father, Lluís made his first trip to Paris to acquire printing presses and breathed in the atmosphere of the cultural capital of the world, where the Haussman reform had begun (1853) under the reign of Napoleon III and the influential Eugenia de Montijo.

The classes given by the philosopher and university professor, Xavier Llorens i Barba, were another essential ingredient in Domènech's training. Llorens played an important role during his twenty-five year tenure at Barcelona University and also worked at the Galavotti School to bolster his salary (Vilagrassa, 2006, pp. 144-145). He was a leading authority in his field and a man of ideas and great integrity. His temperament and teachings, which brought together different disciplines, made him a kind of "guru" for Domènech's generation.

Domènech acquired a love of history – and ancient civilisations in particular – from Llorens, who also influenced his interdisciplinary approach to work. Both qualities are what distinguished Llorens' classes from those of other professors. Llorens stated that each human environment, each geography provided its inhabitants with their own worldview, which, at the time of the *Renaixença*, lent coherence to the discourse of recovering the language and historical events of the Crown of Aragon. Llorens was interested in the legacy of the past, in the philosophies of both Joan Lluís Vives and Ramon Llull, trying to make the official discourse of the Church compatible with positions that were clearly heterodox and related to the European thought of the time. A certain Gnosticism tinged his analysis of reality, studying the limits of human capacity in terms of knowledge and consciousness. He liked to consider human psychological characteristics as a core part of philosophy. In his philosophy classes, he advocated thinking based on common sense, coexisting with "*seny*", a Catalan word meaning common sense, which is the basic element to arrive at the truth, in contrast to "*rauxa*", or impulsivenes. Llorens' philosophy proposed a synthesis between empiricism and rationalism, relying on psychology. Obviously, the balance provided by "*seny*" was well-suited to the temperament of the conservative thinking of the time. Seen from today's perspective, Llorens' philosophical position is not strange, but at the time it was difficult to rise above historical and religious prejudices.

The third element that caused Domènech to acquire a civic conscience early on, in 1871, was his participation in the Jove Catalunya (Young Catalonia) association, the starting point of his friendship with Àngel Guimerà, Pere Aldavert, Antoni Aulèstia, and Ramón Picó i Campamar, which also marked the beginning of their regular gatherings to discuss political matters at the Cafè Suís (Domènech Girbau, 2018, pp. 74-78). There, the world of the *Renaixença* matured in successive stages, and allowed Domènech to meet and become friends with Valentí Almirall and to work on Jove Catalunya's weekly jour *La Gramalla*, as well as the campaign in favour of Catalan Civil Law.

These circumstances would lead to an optimistic temperament – at least until 1900 – founded on friendship and

← *Portrait of Lluís Domènech i Montaner.* Ramon Casas, c. 1903-1908. Museu Nacional d'Art de Catalunya.

the openness of ideas stemming from the professional diversity of the members of the Jove Catalunya club. In an overall reckoning of Domènech's political activity, perhaps the Jove Catalunya stage did not have major practical repercussions, but it was fundamental as a formative phase for the architect.

Constant activity at the Ateneu Barcelonès

Lluís Domènech i Montaner's long-standing presence as a member (1877-1923) of the Ateneu Barcelonès (Barcelona Athenaeum) and his repeated terms as president of this institution, although they may not seem an essential part of his multiple creative activities, must be seriously taken into account because Athenaeum-related activities were connected to political practice (Domènech Girbau, 2018, pp. 78-81). Moreover, the opportunity for presidents to deliver the opening speeches or lectures each academic year led Domènech to investigate the history of relations between Spain and Catalonia. We are thus witnessing another example of the multiple interests in the architect's life, fostered by the powerful networking hub that was the Athenaeum.

Lluís Domènech i Montaner joined in April 1877, shortly after Àngel Guimerà and just before Narcís Oller. In May, Jacint Verdaguer agreed to read, at a session for members, excerpts from *L'Atlàntida*, the epic poem that the Montaner i Simon publishing house would later put out with a cover drawn by Domènech.

Domènech first presided over the Ateneu in the 1898-99 academic year and was subsequently re-elected in 1903-04, 1904-05, 1905-06, 1911-13 and 1913-14. During his first term, accompanied by Prat de la Riba and Verdaguer i Callís, he took an approach that would have enabled the pro-Catalan movement to come to an agreement with General Polavieja, an option that failed, sowing the first seeds of doubt in Domènech's mind about Catalonia's chances of reaching an agreement with the State about a less burdensome fiscal system than the one in force at that time.

On 14th November 1898, a message was delivered to Queen Regent Maria Cristina in which two requests were made: the establishment of the corporate vote in the elections of City Councils, Provincial Councils and the Senate and the decentralization of the State in matters of education, public works, health, etc. Both were denied.

Domènech's research activity

From a very young age, Domènech sensed that research was the most direct source for acquiring the scholarship and critical spirit that knowledge entailed.

One of his first research channels arose when he took charge of the *Historia General del Arte* project, commissioned by the Montaner i Simon publishing house. When his uncle Ramón Montaner asked him to be the editor of this work, the architect set about it, planning the eight volumes and presenting the collection in a luxurious brochure explaining the aim of the encyclopaedia and indicating the subscription price at the end. The history of art imagined by Domènech was an attempt to go beyond the commission itself: in addition to having the photographic reproductions provided by the publisher, with high-precision chromolithography techniques in the subsequent engravings, he himself provided fifteen hundred drawings he interspersed in the text, many made by the architect himself, as indicated by the characteristic L and D stamp.

Domènech edited the first volume on ancient cultures, a theme he explored at length and in depth, making the connection between their artistic aspects and the anthropological contents that explain them. One noteworthy aspect is that, in the first chapter dedicated to "human dwellings", he studies in depth the cultures of the Palaeolithic (Solutrean, Aurignacian, etc.) and, in addition to describing them, draws the various sections of the caves (dwelling prototype) according to their location, lending importance to defensive topography, the existence of rivers, etc., thus increasing the study's interest. It is curious how he references, among others, the findings of Marcelino Sanz de Sautuola in the cave of Altamira. Domènech draws the elongated floor plan and the section, detailing elevation lines and useful passage heights in his characteristic handwriting. But he makes no mention whatsoever of paintings on the rock walls... Sanz de Sautuola's paper is dated 1880, and perhaps Domènech had not yet discovered the paintings or thought it best to conceal them.

This volume describes Egyptian architecture and the entire Asian panoply, with special emphasis on the Assyrians, Chaldeans, Persians, Babylonians, etc. Here, too, the accuracy of the description and illustrations is surprising. Each site map of a city details topography, constructions, graphic

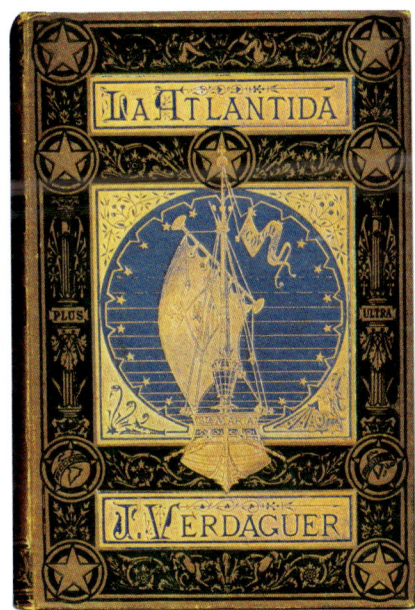

L'Atlàntida by Jacint Verdaguer, published by Montaner i Simon (1878) with a cover designed by Lluís Domènech i Montaner.

scale and orientation. There is a general map of Babylon, for instance, with roads, walls, the Euphrates canals, vegetation, which looks like a modern guide. Also, the Nineveh map, according to Oppert's discoveries, is approached with a care that reminds me of my fascination with *Gods, Graves, and Scholars*. In this archaeology bestseller, one of the heroes is the Frenchman Layard, and Domènech does not forget to mention him, analysing the elevation of the Nineveh plan by this archaeologist and comparing it to a spatial sequence of the Alhambra but explaining the differences according to the technology available in each culture. Many of the illustrations in this part are by Domènech himself, drawn in India ink with a very fine pen, and numerous originals have been preserved. (Domènech Girbau, 2018)

The other fundamental episode in Domènech's life was the publication of his article "In Search of a National Architecture", in *La Renaixensa* in 1878. This text was unique and unprecedented on the Spanish architectural scene at the time, but it had a great deal in common with the contributions to architecture that had beenappearing for some time in France, England, Germany, based on criteria of how to adapt to the changing circumstances of modernity. Cèsar Daly, Viollet-le-Duc, Thomas Hope, James Ferguson and others wrote texts that reflect on functionality, form, industrialisation, craftsmanship, symbolism, rationalism, etc., and Domènech wrote a Catalan version.

The article's title is deceptive, as it seems to be indicating the existence of a national architecture that needs to be found, when the conclusion will be the opposite: the existence of a national architecture is impossible, whether Catalan or Spanish, because architecture has become international thanks to new construction technologies adapted to a modern way of life, with new needs throughout the world. While waiting for a language to materialise that expresses these new requirements, the "eclectic" spirit re-examines the past in order to take a step towards the future.

In a rhetoric very much of the time, Domènech declares that: "The final word of every conversation about architecture, the capital question of all criticism, comes to revolve unwittingly around an idea, that of a national modern architecture", but inquiry into this new architecture needs "the energy of a productive idea, a moral environment in which to live (...). Whenever an organising idea dominates a people, whenever a new civilization emerges, a new artistic era appears".

He thus extrapolates: "Modern architecture, daughter and heir of all past architectures, will rise above all, bejewelled with the treasures of the latter and with those of industry and science, acquired on her own", and concludes: "Architecture, given the current conditions of modern society, cannot retain a truly national character... the powerful manner of assimilation of modern Instruction will nullify efforts to create a national architecture".

All in all, however, he qualifies this statement by admitting the singularities of place due to geography, climate, traditions... and he finally has an outburst: "How could we obey the extremely rational economic and constructive laws, which force us today to accept iron in new mechanically determined forms? Why not prepare a new architecture, since we cannot shape it? Let us be inspired by the traditions of our homeland, but let us not use them to the detriment of the knowledge we have or can acquire".

Eventually, after re-analysing the positive stages of history, he decides to take a stance: "Perhaps we will be told that this is a new form of eclecticism. If attempting to practise all good doctrines is to be eclectic, if assimilating the elements that are needed to live a healthy life, like plants do with air, water and earth, is considered eclecticism; if believieg that all generations have left us something good to learn and wish to study and apply makes the same mistake WE DECLARE OURSELVES CONVINCED OF ECLECTICISM".

The conflictive word has appeared: "eclecticism"; and if we wish to understand what Domènech is trying to say, going beyond the ambiguous meanings of the term, we can focus on his work – in the Palau de la Música Catalana, Casa Fuster or Hospital de Sant Pau, for instance – to grasp that, in his use of historical styles, the quotations of the elements are not literal, but rather in the development of the work that reinterprets them, the basic factor of syntax intervenes, which is the way in which they interrelate, transgressing academic norms and introducing the characteristics of a new architecture through surprise, adaptation to an invented function, irony and formal ingenuity.

Domènech devoted his practical life to architecture and politics, which meant dedication, relations with others, participation in city affairs, in short, thinking and doing. But his more personal dedication to heraldry and Romanesque art was also intense. Intentionally interrelating these double contents allowed me to make a discovery. In reality, the second pair, Romanesque art and heraldry, constituted in Domènech's activity a kind of "double" of the first, a reflection on a more ethereal and conceptual plane than the one in which he practised architecture and politics. His research on Romanesque art – in which he delved into the Carolingian and monastic origin that went from north to south from France, opening paths and creating inhabited centres – describes the territorial structure of Catalonia, anticipating the role of today's towns and of their architecture, whether religious or civil. And it was also a way of making a political reading, since it reveals the evolution of the Catalan territory from the 13th to the 19th centuries, with the loss of the territories incorporated into present-day France.

At the same time, it is also true that heraldry, cultivated with rigour as Domènech does, is the representation – through its identifying codes of lineages, estates and families – of the economic, social and political matrix that would powerfully shape the evolution of Catalan society, and would determine, for all intents and purposes, Politics with a capital. We are thus dealing with an enriching mechanism of cross-disciplinary interaction. We hypothesise that there are enough arguments to demonstrate that the interaction between the four components cited constitutes Domènech's life project, which was none other than investigating "the original structure of Catalonia", divided between the search for a nation and an architecture.

Politics: a vivid, contradictory activity in Domènech i Montaner

Domènech became involved in politics based on the ideology he held during the *Renaixença*, in this movement's attempt to recover Catalan national identity, primarily regarding culture. Preserving the language, getting to know the territory and conserving its artistic heritage were some of the expressions of this awareness. We shall focus on a very specific, decisive period in his political activity, i.e. the one stretching from 1890 to 1904:

1890. Catalan civil law lost much of its validity following the reforms to the Spanish civil code enacted by the Ministry of Mercy and Justice. This brought about greater awareness of Catalan identity across the region and strengthened the relationships between the pro-Catalan groups from Barcelona and the rest of Catalonia, particularly those in Tarragona, Reus and Girona (Duran Tort, 2002). In the face of this situation, the League of Catalonia (Lliga de Catalunya, 1887-1901), with Domènech at the head, promoted the foundation of the Catalanist Union (Unió Catalanista, emerging in early 1891) as a federation of all possible groups willing to work for the realisation of the programme of Catalanism. They were also joined by the young university students who had founded the Catalanist School Centre (Centre Escolar Catalanista, 1886-1901). They contributed a clearly political type of discourse in which the young Enric Prat de la Riba excelled, who in a speech delivered in 1890 defined the "Catalan homeland".

1891. It was agreed to convene an Assembly of all Catalanist groups in Manresa on 25th March. There, the *Bases per a una Constitució Regional Catalana* (Groundwork for a Catalan Regional Constitution) document was approved. A Board was appointed, chaired by Domènech i Montaner, with other members being Pau Font de Rubinat, from Reus, Joaquim Vayreda, from Olot, Pau Colomer, from Sabadell, and Enric Prat de la Riba acting as Secretary: a perfect articulation of the territorial structure and academic institutions. The law professor Joan Josep Permanyer was the theoretician of the *Bases*, which aimed to make the reform of the State of Spain compatible with the autonomy of Catalonia, and the lawyer Narcís Verdaguer i Callís founded the weekly *La Veu de Catalunya*, which would become a daily in 1899 with a masthead designed by Domènech i Montaner.

Els nostres diputats (Our deputies), Joan Llaverias. Published in the magazine *¡Cu-Cut!*, 1903.

La gloria mes llegítima (The most legitimate glory), caricature by Ramon Miró. Published in the magazine *L'Esquella de la Torratxa*, 1904.

The four presidents: Sebastià Torres, Albert Rossinyol, Doctor Robert and Domènech i Montaner. Anonymous photograph published in *La Costa del Llevant*. Arxiu Històric del COAC.

Un concert económich al Tívoli (A cheap concert at the Tivoli). Caricature by Ramon Miró published in *La Campana de Gràcia*, 1901.

1895-1896. In line with the strategy of the Unió Catalanista to try to exert influence by occupying positions in institutions and cultural organisations, Domènech went on to preside over the Floral Games of which he had already been a supporter and, at the same time Àngel Guimerà was elected president of the Ateneu Barcelonès, accompanied by Joan Maragall as secretary. On 10th December 1895, Guimerà gave his inaugural speech in Catalan, causing great uproar and indignation among the petty local bosses and economic powers. From that point on, the Ateneu became a powerful platform for Catalanism. Almirall, Permanyer, Domènech, Abadal and Maragall succeeded one another as presidents of the organisation. It was quite true that the intellectual origins of the *Renaixença* provided a truly enviable cast of characters for a time.

1898. Domènech was president of the Ateneu; his friend and collaborator Antoni Gallissà became president of the Unió Catalanista and interest revived in presenting a manifesto to Queen Regent Maria Cristina calling for administrative autonomy for the regions and the transformation of the parliamentary system to ensure the participation of all social classes. Domènech entrusted Bartomeu Robert, known as Dr Robert, to draw up the manifesto. At the same time, General Polavieja, a colonialist military man who had been in Cuba and the Philippines, burst onto the scene. When he returned to Spain, he had certain vague aspirations to power and sought out various allies, among them, the Catalanist parties. He addressed a letter to Lluís Domènech raising the possibility that Catalonia could have an economic agreement, reorganise the municipal administration to prevent *"caciquisme"* (petty local bosses), unite the four Provincial Administrations into one, guarantee full university autonomy and ensure respect for Catalan Civil Law.

1899. Negotiations with the general were progressing and, although he felt that all the Catalanist objectives had not been met, Domènech, who was a realist, decided to initially accept the proposal. However, the press and politicians in Madrid expressed such "indignation" that, at the end of September, Polavieja replied to Domènech by significantly watering down his first offer. This caused a crisis in Unió Catalanista that hurt Domènech. The newspapers *La Renaixença* and *La Veu de Catalunya* accused one another of colluding with Polavieja. The *Tancament de Caixes* (closing of the tills), the shopkeepers' protest against Gabinet Silvela's law, took place at the end of the year. The law raised taxes in Catalan industrial cities to higher levels than those in Madrid. A strike and refusal to pay taxes began. Robert, the mayor of Barcelona, committed to his citizens, resigned, and the Government declared a state of emergency in Barcelona and ordered arrests and imprisonments. Continued frustration in political relations with the State eroded his characteristic optimism. From 1897 to 1900, Domènech devoted a great deal of time to politics, time that he was unable to devote to his profession, something that displeased him and which he tried to compensate with an intense dedication to teaching at the School of Architecture, of which he would soon be appointed director.

1900. While Catalonia was being severely oppressed because of its refusal to pay taxes, the minister of government planned a visit during the first week in May. It was considered an act of provocation (Costa Martínez, 2018). He was loudly booed, also at the evening session at the Liceu opera house. The State's reaction was swift, *La Veu de Catalunya* was suspended and Domènech's friend Pau Font de Rubinat was deposed as mayor of Reus. The situation deteriorated so much that Dato himself resigned and the alternation system invented by Cánovas suffered a death blow.

1901. As a result of disagreements arising from Polavieja's unfortunate handling of the situation and the disappointment in the meagre results gained by the Catalanist Union, the Catalan National Centre (Centre Nacional Català, 1899-1901) was founded, joined by members of the Catalanist School Centre, among them Prat de la Riba and Puig i Cadafalch. This group would be joined by former active members of the League of Catalonia, including Domènech and Raimon d'Abadal, and a third group, known as the *"penya de l'Ateneu"* (Ateneu group), including Jaume Carner and Ildefons Sunyol. Domènech became a member of the new party's first executive committee. On 25th April, this party merged with the Regionalist Union to create a party that would be central to 20th-century political Catalanism, the Regionalist League (Lliga Regionalista). Finally, the confluence of Catalanist forces, the Regionalist League, decides to stand in the next elections, called for 19th May. A list of candidates, known as the Four Presidents, was drawn up with great haste: Bartomeu

Robert, ex-mayor of Barcelona and ex-president of the Barcelona Economic Society of Friends of the Country (Societat Econòmica Barcelonina d'Amics del País), Albert Rusiñol, ex-president of the Catalan employer's organisation National Employment Promotion (Foment del Treball Nacional), Sebastià Torres, ex-president of the Industrial and Commercial Defence League (Lliga de Defensa Industrial i Comercial), and Lluís Domènech i Montaner, former president of the Barcelona Athenaeum. Surprisingly, the candidacy won the elections, *caciquisme* (the local party boss system) was sunk and the people, especially in Barcelona, celebrated the victory.

1902. The Regionalist League, due to the diverse social background of its founders, began to show the different class interests of its members. This was exacerbated by the general strike decreed by workers and traders in response to the governor's disproportionate measures during the strike demanding a 9-hour work day. For a week, all the factories in Barcelona stopped and the city came to a standstill. The manufacturers demanded mass repression and the League was divided. Prat de la Riba was in favour. Domènech, in Madrid, responded to Prat de la Riba's letter in a way that explains the architect's political temperament: "I was surprised by your letter today. Our manufacturing friends have little wisdom and the Catalanists would have even less if we let them sound the bugle call of extermination. The government is forced into repression. Why take responsibility for it by inciting it publicly? How can we then make Catalonia a single body if we want to divide it into two enemy castes? Let's take advantage of the opportunity, dear Prat, since we won't have another more favourable one after the disappointment that the working class will now experience, left to their own devices in the streets by the government and republicans and pierced with sabres in those very streets by the ones who abandoned them".

1903. Domènech is re-elected deputy with Rusiñol, although the Catalanists suffer a loss to the radicals of Alejandro Lerroux. In an article, the architect attempts to clarify the crisis of Catalanism and the position of the League, but Raimon Casellas, acting director of *La Veu de Catalunya*, refuses to publish it and, moreover, accuses Domènech of doing a bad job as a deputy. The architect's position in the League is weakening, since while he is fighting in Madrid for Catalan interests, in Barcelona, the League is becoming a party with highly dubious interests.

1904. At the beginning of the year, the plan of Antonio≠ Maura, president of the government, to bring the king, Alphonse XIII, to visit Barcelona became known, a trip frowned upon by the monarchists of Madrid. Maura replied that it was the duty of a king to know the conflict zones. The League was mired in confusion when the trip was announced and they had to discuss the stance they were going to take. Apparently, the majority, including Domènech, thought that Catalans could not celebrate the arrival of a king so opposed to the aspirations of the Catalan people, and even interpreted the trip as a provocation. Regarding the meeting of the League, Domènech pointed out that "only a minority of these people were in favour of standing by the king and his government". The truth, however, is that in the voting, even if by a small margin, the supporters of going to the royal reception won. Francesc Cambó was entrusted with delivering the welcome speech, and Domènech, who had long since grasped this politician's determined individualistic rise, awaited the event on 7th April, in which Alfonso XIII responded evasively to Cambó's speech, postponing the Catalan question perpetually. After a few days, in the magazine *Joventut*, Domènech published an anonymous article entitled "*Fivellers de guardarropia*" ("Sham Fivellers"), alluding to the 15th-century Catalan councillor, a symbol of liberties in the face of royal power, and those who imitated him in an ambiguous way, calling them "cheap Machiavellians", while Cambó was treated an "ex-quasi-Regionalist councillor". At that point, Domènech realised that his break with the League was inevitable, and the split was consummated on 18th June.

This was how he bade farewell to his old friend Prat de la Riba: "Friend Prat, it seems to me that the movement pays too much attention to the insubstantial vanity of some and the adventurous and thoughtless cynicism of others... I'm leaving, but you know that I'll always be your friend. Lluís Domènech". Thus ended Domènech i Montaner's political career. There is yet another fact that further clarifies his image when, despite the invective against him in the pages of "his" *La Veu de Catalunya*, and entirely outside of the political struggle, he was elected president of the Ateneu in 1904-1905, at a time when it was considered the most prestigious institution. That same year he began building the Palau de la Música Catalana, showing his serene and at once courageous temperament, perhaps to demonstrate that in the field of architecture he could develop his thinking freely.

Domènech i Montaner's architecture, at a prudent distance from art nouveau

Mireia Freixa

Lluís Domènech i Montaner was a man of his time, fascinated by progress and modernity, and his architectural work would also necessarily reflect this reality. Many things were happening in Europe at the time and Domènech, like the Catalan architects who were his contemporaries, was aware of them and sought to reinterpret them with a home-grown approach. This is the defining characteristic of *modernisme* and what sets it apart from international art nouveau.

The different versions of what we define as art nouveau or *modernisme*

Current historiography has assumed that *Art nouveau, Modernisme, Modernismo, Sezessionstil, Liberty, Floreale* or *Jugendstil* are different languages or styles united by the will to search for a new art in and around 1900. They turned away from historical styles while nature became a formal resource, but also the foundation for a structural alternative. Art nouveau has been the predominant term since Stephan Tschudi-Madsen used it in the title of his book published in 1957. It was the first one to give a broad overview and analysis of the movement (Tschudi-Madsen, 1957). But art nouveau was not just a fashion; it incorporated other elements used since the mid-19th century, such as the integration between architecture and the applied arts, the unitary conception of interiors, the abundant – but at the same time rational – use of ornamentation, the Japanese influence and a taste for stylisation that came to create forms very close to abstraction.

Tschudi-Madsen established a coherent account of the movement, which he divided into two major trends. The first, in Brussels and Paris, was characterised by the use of sinuous and stylised forms, while the second, with the cities of Glasgow and Vienna as reference points, preferred straight lines and a rational sense of architecture. Two very different languages that were at the service of the same principle, since it did not depend on the use of a specific formal language, but on the application of theoretical approaches and the will to make a new, international art.

Catalan *modernisme*, on the other hand, went beyond being a movement linking architecture to the applied or industrial arts. It was a cultural trend that also imbued the visual arts, choral singing, opera, novels, drama or poetry, and lasted from approximately 1875 to 1915. Its early stages can be traced back to what we call proto-*modernisme* (Freixa, 2019), from 1875, when the Barcelona School of Architecture was fully recognised, until the Universal Exhibition in 1888. Architects and industrialists strove to find the relationships between new technology and design – eclectic models – based on the functional use of ornamentation, and a vibrant and creative language was developed with unusual textures and colours and a plethora of ceramic applications, very different from what was being done at the time in other parts of Europe. We have examples such as Gaudí's gatehouses of the Güell estate (1884-1887), or Domènech i Montaner's café and restaurant (1887).The period that followed the exhibition and continued throughout the 1890s was defined as early *modernisme*. It occurred in tandem with the wholesale modernisation of Catalan culture, and its defining events included the Casas, Rusiñol and Clarasó exhibitions at the Sala Parés, the founding of the Orfeó Català choral society and the *Modernista* Festivals in Sitges. They marked a return to the past for architecture and the applied arts, with the inclusion of medieval, archaic elements. Domènech i Montaner's Casa Roura in Canet de Mar (1889-1892) and Puig i Cadafalch's Casa Amatller (1898-1900) are examples of this. Finally, after the Paris International Exposition of 1900 and the Turin

← Casa Thomas (1895-1898).
Detail of the columns on the main balcony.

Castel Béranger (1894-1898).
Paris, Hector Guimard.
Entrance hall.

Hôtel Mme. Yvette Guilberg (1900).
Paris, Xavier Schoellkoff. *Arquitectura y Construcción*, no. 109.

Karlsplatz metro station (1895-1899). Vienna,
Otto Wagner. © C. Stadler/Bwag.

Decorative Arts Exhibition of 1902, the more international art nouveau taste began to spread, adding to the previous legacy and giving way to full *modernisme*, which incoporated the floral and abstract forms of art nouveau. The last stage would be determined by architects and industrialists, such as Rafael Masó or Josep Maria Pericas, who were looking towards the more regular and rational forms of the Viennese Secession. This aesthetic, despite being considered by European historiography as a variant of art nouveau, emerged in Catalonia as *noucentisme*, an alternative to *modernisme* connected with a new social and cultural attitude.

Domènech i Montaner and his large team of collaborators were working in the midst of these developments. In this text we aim to ascertain which architects or schools were Domènech's points of reference and to what extent his *modernisme* can be related to European currents and the more orthodox-style art nouveau. The architects conceived a total work of art, that is to say that construction – with the incorporation of new technology and materials – and ornamentation were a single thing, and had to be fully integrated. The structural organicism that came from the teachings of Eugène Viollet-le-Duc formed the basis of everything, further heightening the value of ornamentation. In fact, this latter aspect was fundamental, since architecture had to be lent *character* and this element – *character* – was what made it possible to "read" the architecture or make it comprehensible and allow its symbolic meaning to be grasped. Art nouveau forms could contribute to giving buildings a modern and cosmopolitan tenor. This is why the image repertoires and architecture and interior decoration magazines were so highly valued.

The architect's gaze: books, magazines and travel

Technical and theoretical books, architecture journals and interior design magazines, together with field trips abroad, enable us to ascertain the extent to which the European models had spread. In the specific case of Lluís Domènech i Montaner, even the earliest studies dedicated to him emphasise the importance of libraries and travel in his training (Domènech Girbau, 1989-1990, pp. 31-35). His cultural baggage can be specified in sufficient detail because his library and a significant part of his archive have been preserved at the archive of the Official Architects' Association of Catalonia (COAC) through a donation by his descendants. This material can be supplemented with the former bibliographic collection of the Barcelona School of Architecture, where he was a professor from the beginning of 1875 and the director for many years, and the materials held at the Ateneu Barcelonès, of which he was a member, as well as president on several occasions. In addition to his book collection, there were numerous illustrated magazines that he received by subscription.

The subject matter of his professional library is divided into books on the history of art and architecture, treatises and theoretical books and also works of a technical nature. Some 500 volumes have been preserved, in the different languages he spoke or read: French, German and English, as well as Spanish and Catalan. This material was analysed by Lluís Domènech Girbau in the biography he wrote (Domènech Girbau, 2018, pp. 89-102), which we refer to here, since there is not sufficient space to provide a more detailed description.

The repertoires that were so important in spreading the art nouveau taste deserve a separate chapter. By the mid-19th century, there were already basic repertoires such as Owen Jones' *Grammar of Ornament* (1856) or Albert Racinet's *L'Ornement polychrome* (1869-1873) and, locally, Lluís Rigalt's *Álbum enciclopédico-pintoresco de los industriales*, published only a year after Owen's book. By the end of the century, others were circulating that had already abandoned the historical models to seek inspiration in nature. We can cite those by Eugène Grasset, *La plante et ses applications ornementales* (1896), *Matériaux et documents d'architecture et de sculpture classés par ordre alphabétique* (1899-1900), *Art décoratif moderne: modèles nouveaux pour les industries d'Art* (1899); as well as the exhibition catalogues, such as *La Décoration et les Industries d'art à l'Exposition Universelle de 1900* (1901) and *L'Exposition Internationale des Arts Décoratifs Modernes à Turin* (1902).

But architecture journals, many of them illustrated, were the most common way to introduce new trends. Domènech undoubtedly followed the great journals that dealt with construction issues and were defenders of eclectic theory: the *Revue Générale de l'Architecture et des Travaux publics*, *La Construction Moderne* and *Zeitschrift für Bauwesen*. But he was also bound to know of the ones that were more geared towards promoting new art, such as *Art et décoration. Revue mensuelle d'Art Moderne* (first published in 1897), *L'art Décoratif. Revue Internationale d'Art Industriel et de Décoration* (since 1898), *Innen-Dekoration* (since 1890), edited by Alexander Koch, *Moderne Bauformen* (1906), *Deutsche Kunst und Dekoration* (1897), and the British magazine *The Studio* (which appeared in 1893).

The trips Domènech undertook during his formative period were another fundamental aspect. After all, it is one thing to interpret works through plans, photographs or descriptions and quite another to actually see them in the flesh. A first trip to Vienna, just after he had graduated, cannot be accurately documented. Some sources assume that he accompanied Josep Vilaseca i Casanovas (1848-1910), a fellow student in Madrid and a collaborator in his early professional work, but the critic Joaquim Bassegoda insists that Vilaseca went there "alone" (Bassegoda, 1911, pp. 242-249). Vilaseca's trip took place in the summer and autumn of 1873, when he toured England, France, Belgium, Germany, Austria, Italy and Greece (Bletter, 1977, pp. 13-14). Upon his return, when Domènech had finished his studies, collaboration between the two began (Bassegoda, 1911, pp. 242-249). However, their joint trip through France, Switzerland, Germany, Austria and Italy, when they had won the competition to design a building for the Provincial Education Institutions that was never built, can be documented with all certainty. They went "with the approval and under the auspices" of the Barcelona Diputació or Provincial Council (Domènech i Vilaseca, 1889, p. 17) with the aim of studying buildings that could serve as models for the new construction. This tour took place once they were definitively awarded the project; in other words, it must have been in 1879 or 1880 (Freixa, 2002, p. 119). The trip was fundamental from a formative point of view.

Despite not being able to build this great project, Domènech gradually garnered professional commissions of sufficient importance that they culminated in the 1888 Universal Exhibition. By then he was already a recognised professional and travel was a constant, both for tasks related to study and for pleasure. He concentrated on excursions or "pilgrimages" through the Pyrenees and Spain to research the work he was carrying out on Catalan medieval art, without excluding other options, such as his trip to London in 1906, which was documented by Domènech Girbau through the testimony of Ramon de Capmany (1899-1992), the architect's nephew. (Domènech Girbau, 2018, p. 87)

European references explained by the second generation of *modernista* architects

The article written by Puig i Cadafalch (1867-1956) in the journal *Hispania* (Puig i Cadafalch, 1902) is extremely useful in helping us ascertain the European references of the generation of architects with affinities to Domènech i Montaner. At the time, Domènech was at a high point, on a professional level and as a public figure. He was 52 years old, a professor and director of the School of Architecture, and a prominent figure in the newly created political party, the Lliga Regionalista, with the so-called "candidacy of the four presidents" having a resounding success in the legislative elections of 19 May 1901. As a professional, he had just been commissioned with the Hospital de Sant Pau project. Puig i Cadafalch, with whom he would later have profound differences, was one of his main collaborators at the time, as evidenced by the fact that he helped him write the architecture volumes of the *Historia General del Arte* for the Montaner i Simon publishing house (published between 1886 and 1901), and served as editor for the second volume (Freixa, 2020, pp. 11-27). The third consisted of plates and was signed by both. The relationship had started before 1886, when Puig was still a student.

Some of the ideas in the *Hispania* article had already been introduced, almost literally, in the *Historia General del Arte* (1901), as demonstrated by Ramon Graus (Graus, 2012, p. 39). In the last chapter, *El Renacimiento y las escuelas modernas derivadas*, an epilogue of just over two pages was added with the aim of "briefly stating what course contemporary architecture is taking" (Puig i Cadafalch, 1901, pp. 898-900). But this scant written reference contrasts with the abundant illustrations in the third volume that reveal Domènech's, and all Catalan architects', interest in Germanic and Austrian architecture, starting with Elies Rogent himself.

In *Hispania*, Puig argues that Domènech has turned Catalan architecture around, overcoming eclecticism based on copying or reinterpreting models from the past – and here there is an explicit criticism of

Maison Tassel (1892-1893) Brussels, Victor Horta. Staircase.
Photo G. Weyers. CIVA Collections, Brussels.

Glasgow School of Art (1897-1907).
Charles Rennie Mackintosh. Library.

neo-medievalism – to establish what he considers a "renewed eclecticism". The latter integrates form, models and ornamentation based on the previous option of typology selection and its inclusion within the urban fabric. On this basis, a solid foundation, new trends and fashions need to be established. He identifies this new art with *modernisme,* one of the first times we see this term written (Freixa, 1986, pp. 11-28) – both in the *Historia General del Arte* and in *Hispania* – and defines it as an ornamental art that has not managed to deal with the purely architectural elements, the structural ones. (Puig i Cadafalch, 1901, p. 899). In both texts, he uses a long quote about ornamentation with this phrase "the new is already realised in the decoration", but in the 1902 version he adds "but the *modernista* building remains to be built" (Puig i Cadafalch, 1902, p. 543), that is to say that the architectural synthesis had not yet occurred.

Also noteworthy are the references to foreign architecture because it helps portray what they had seen and understood. Puig, bringing the discourse to his particular terrain, held that none of the new models dispensed with tradition. The first architect cited is the Russian, Xavier Schoellkopf (1870-1911) who had settled in Paris and is erroneously cited in both texts as Schöllkopf. He was an architect of a distinctly art nouveau style who is little recognised today and who was remarkable for retaining the overtones of French rococo. In the journal *Arquitectura y Construcción,* on 3rd September 1901 (B.P., 1901, pp. 268-269), he published "Hôtel for Yvette Guilbert" (1865-1944), one of the performers drawn by Toulouse Lautrec. His dependence on this Louis XV style was specifically valued, a feature that can also be found in the French magazine *L'Art Décoratif* (Saunier, 1901, 191-195), which is undoubtedly the source. Other references were the cottages by Baillie Scott (1865-1945), which, according to Puig, were redolent of the English Middle Ages and Renaissance; the "art nouveau" of Victor Horta (1861-1947) and Henry van der Velde (1863-1957) – erroneously written as Van der Valle – , which he considered reminiscent of the typical Flemish house; Joseph Maria Olbrich (1857-1908) and the Darmstadt colony, where he saw the medieval-style German house; and Otto Wagner (1841-1918) and Ludwig Baumann (1853-1936) – transcribed as Haumann in the *Historia General del Arte*), a neo-Greek tenor and the Austrian tradition.

According to Puig i Cadafalch, Domènech's greatness resided in him having been the first to apply this principle of synthesis between tradition and modernity to Catalan architecture. But it is still surprising that there are no more references to the city of Paris, or to the interventions of Hector Guimard (1867-1942) for the 1900 Exposition.

In 1903, a year after the *Hispania* article, an even younger architect, Jeroni Martorell i Terrats (1876-1951), published a lengthy feature in *Catalunya* magazine, "La arquitectura moderna. La estética. Las obras", where he also reviews contemporary European architecture, which he simply calls "new". He was familiar with Vienna and cited Otto Wagner, but he was more interested in his disciple, Joseph Maria Olbrich (Martorell, 1903, pp. 562-566). He also provided a description of what he considered the most orthodox art nouveau, which he described by "th'use (sic) of the curve" and the use of a decoration based on "the study of beautifully transformed roots and leaves" (Martorell, 1903, pp. 566-567), quoting Victor Horta, but then goes on to deal with British domestic architecture by Hector Guimard, and the Italo-Turkish architect Raimondo d'Aronco, who designed the main pavilion for the 1902 Turin Exhibition, built the year before the article was written.

Martorell observed that an international language was being formed with a desire to overcome historical styles, but at the same time he saw the need not to forget tradition. We agree with Ramon Graus (Graus, 2012, p. 121) that the point of this article was to ratify the theories of Domènech i Montaner and Puig i Cadafalch on the need to define a modern art firmly rooted in tradition. Martorell clearly states that it is necessary to create a Catalan "school" that contains the parameters of "novelty and tradition" at once (Martorell, 1903, p. 577). This is the feature that was presented as typical of Catalan architecture on the basis of theory and practice.

"We have highly individual architects"; but at a prudent distance from art nouveau

With these words, Martorell described the Catalan architects of the time in the article cited above. He only mentions one building, Camil Oliveras' Casa de Maternitat (1840-1898), but there is a clear reference to Gaudí – and the Sagrada Família – and we understand that the phrase "there have been those who, in an admirable synthesis, have managed to harmonise the forms of the most different styles" (Martorell, 1903, p. 576), is a reference to Domènech i Montaner. This concept of synthesis would justify his entire production, a synthesis understood in two senses: knowing how to interpret the past through the present – including technique, knowledge of materials and ornamentation – and the wise interpretation of the innovations – and fashions – of the present. It is for this reason that we maintain he interprets international art nouveau, but keeping at a prudent distance. Gaudí received this influence directly, as of 1900, when projecting the furniture for Casa Calvet. The same was true for Puig i Cadafalch in his design for the Codorniu winery (Caves Codorniu, *c*. 1904) and the vast majority of Catalan architects.

This process of synthesis most likely began just after Domènech had completed his studies, with his interest in the work of Freidrich von Gartner (1791-1847) and Leo von Klenze (1784-1864) in Munich, Friedrich Schinkel (1781-1841) in Berlin and Gottfried Semper (1803-1879) in Dresden and Vienna, characterised by the search for unity between technique, form and ornament based on the prior choice of a typology and its inclusion within the urban fabric. In his more mature works, having abandoned the great masters of eclecticism, new perspectives opened up that also integrated an outlook on art nouveau, but the synthetic conception between technique, form and ornament was maintained, while incorporating a free interpretation of natural forms. Another feature would be that the most apparent aspects of art nouveau, the whiplash (*coup de fouet*) or rounded, sinuous shapes were mastered. But above all, what identifies the work of Domènech i Montaner is the fact that this synthesis was developed while intensifying its roots in tradition. The Palau de la Música Catalana, the Hospital de Sant Pau complex or the Casa Navàs in Reus are splendid examples. And this fact, which may seem like a contradiction, is what makes him more deeply *modernista*.

Palau de la Música Catalana (1904-1909).
Winged horse above the third tier.

In the architect's studio. Domènech's associates

Teresa-M. Sala i Garcia

The exhibition *Lluís Domènech i Montaner i el director d'orquestra* (Lluís Domènech i Montaner and the Orchestra Conductor - 1989) championed the architect's key role as someone who orchestrated, conducted, guided and set the tempo for his projects, involving a band of technicians, labourers, industrialists, artisans and artists. The musical metaphor is perfect when it comes to leading the performers playing in the architectural work, which requires a great rapport with the conductor in its execution. Hence, in order to resolve the planned ideas, it is essential to have finely tuned instruments that can interpret the form, the function and the symbolic and decorative programme.

Over time, Domènech expanded his portfolio of collaborators to include other architects, painters, sculptors, ceramicists., mosaicists, stained-glass artists, ironsmiths, metalworkers, carpenters, furniture makers and decorators. Some of them were involved in his projects throughout his career, from the very first to the very last buildings. They showed high levels of skill and attunement, defined by a desire to create projects of extremely high quality.

Fully in the spirit of the *Renaixença*

Domènech designed the tomb of the composer, poet and politician Josep Anselm Clavé (1876) with his architect friend Josep Vilaseca i Casanovas, who he also worked with on his first real, although unrealised, project: the schools run by Barcelona Provincial Council. Clavé became a cultural beacon who, under the slogan "progress, virtue and love", advocated and fostered the fraternal sentiment of belonging to a collective. In the field of architecture, the theoretical tenets of Eugène Viollet-le-Duc and the rationalism of Gothic buildings outlined the path to be followed.

← Portrait of Lluís Domènech i Montaner.
Cover of the magazine *Hispania: literatura y arte*, 1902.

Between 1880 and 1886, Domènech designed and built the premises of the publishers Montaner i Simon in Barcelona's Eixample neighbourhood. It became a shining example of the new architecture, a modern way for tradition. The ideal of collaborative work, defined by its ability to organise and find solutions to the application of art to industry, was the key characteristic of this fruitful and busy period. Domènech's projects, including his buildings in Comillas and for the 1888 Barcelona Universal Exhibition, reinterpreted the medieval past in a modern key. His project for the Hotel Internacional demonstrated an efficient approach to building and design, with a well-structured workforce that included Bonaventura Pollés i Vivó and Josep Forteza i Ubach as assistant architects. This vast, luxury building was built in just fifty-three days, with the labourers working day and night. Domènech came up with an ingenious solution using a grid made of railway tracks that underpinned inverted flat-brick vaults, which he produced in collaboration with Joan Torras i Guardiola, a professor at the Barcelona School of Architecture (Ramon, 2011). The city's most eminent industrialists also worked on the project, alongside the architect, contractor and workforce. A number of artisans and artists worked on the interior decoration and the façade. Saumell and Vilaró, who rendered Domènech's drawings in sgraffito work, and the artists, Joan Llimona, Dionís Baixeras and Alexandre de Riquer, were among the most notable.

The café and restaurant in the Parc de la Ciutadella became one of the most iconic buildings at the 1888 exhibition, although it had not been completed when the event opened. The building had picture windows and doors with leaded stained-glass panels made by Antoni Rigalt. From 1891 to 1892, Domènech set up an industrial arts workshop inside the building – which had been nicknamed the Castell dels Tres Dragons, or Castle of the Three Dragons – assisted by Antoni Maria Gallissà, who "would go hither and thither from our studio to the workshops, with samples and sketches, carrying out and overseeing tests" to try to "train (the makers) in architectural work" (Domènech; 1903, pp. 164-171). The idea behind the project was to create a series of small studios that could produce the elements required to finish the building, rather than a single workshop. It also involved converting the building into the city's history museum, the Museu de la Història (Casanova, 2000). Some of Domenech's collaborators had been entrusted with one-off commissions, whereas others worked with him on a more permanent basis. Some of them had well-established workshops or factories of their own, while others were just setting out on their careers. This meant that the architect's practice became a test bed for the available means and procedures as well as the research stages of the project. The sculptors H. Llàsser, Eusebi Arnau and Pere Quintana began their careers here, creating applied-arts sculptures. Collaborators from outside Catalonia worked on the decorative ceramics. They included Josep Ros, from Valencia, Cassany from the town of Manises, and Baldomero Santigós, a Catalan living in Madrid, who provided models in the ancient tradition and new techniques applied to the building's requirements. The ceramic coats of arms placed in a row around the outer walls of the café and restaurant building were made at the Pujol i Basus factory. They were designed by Alexandre de Riquer and Joan Llimona and feature motifs associated with its use.

The wonderful craftsmanship and skill shown at the seminary in Comillas involved the revival and reinvention of old techniques. Masriera and Campins, who ran a foundry, visited Domènech's workshop after being commissioned to cast the bronze door for the church. It was based on his drawing of Saint George and the dragon. Francesc Tiestos, a specialist in repoussé work, produced the reliefs on delicately hammered brass and iron sheets, while Bartolomé Domènech made the elaborate locks. The interior stained-glass windows were designed by Enric Monserdà, in the neo-Gothic style, and made at the Amigó studios in Barcelona, while the ones at the top of the building were produced at Antoni Rigalt's studio. He would use the same design in subsequent works. The sgraffito work decorating the walls of the seminary corridor was probably done by Eugeni Saumell and Jaume Vilaró. Domènech harked back to models with medieval-style and heraldic motifs for the mosaics used as decorative elements and on the floors and ceilings inside and outside the building, making them supreme examples of the evolution of mosaic as an art form (Saliné, 2015, pp. 207-378). Mario Maragliano and Lluís Bru's mosaic workshops made Roman-style mosaics from marble, stoneware and glazed tiles, based on Domènech's drawings.

Catalan art nouveau, or *modernista*, architects also had a keen interest in textiles and fabrics. Vilaseca, Gaudí and Domènech designed their first buildings to include awnings and flags. Indeed, "ornamental architectural motifs were taken from ancient fabrics to create bas-reliefs, grilles, ceramic and encaustic tiles, mosaics and sgraffito work..." (Carbonell-Casamartina, 2002, p. 59). Domènech worked with Benet Malvehy on the huge damask silk drapes in the great chamber, the Saló de Cent, in Barcelona City Hall, and Santa Floretina castle in Canet de Mar.

Working in close collaboration with Gallissà, Domènech i Montaner took over the project for the Palau Montaner, which had been begun by Josep Domènech i Estapà. The building was nearing completion, so their intervention focused on the decorative elements. These included the glazed ceramic panels on the façade, which refer to the owner of the publishing house, Montaner i Simon. The interior layout, which was drawn in detail by the architect, reveals a decorative style with a plethora of symbols alluding to his client. His regular collaborators produced the ornamental compositions, highlights of which include the magnificent staircase with stone carvings by Eusebi Arnau, which is lit from above by a stained-glass ceiling lantern with plant motifs made by Antoni Rigalt. Planas i Tort was responsible for the carpentry, and the lamps, in the shape of a mermaid, and the remaining woodwork were by Gaspar Homar i Mesquida.

Modernisme unfurled

Domènech found in the past a sense of identity rooted in tradition, as well as a useful form of reflection for his time, with a language that evolved towards the art nouveau ideal of a "total work of art". In this regard, the decorative arts were a means of expressing and transforming the possibilities offered by each technique or procedure in different fields. Some builders' suppliers, such as the Pujol i Bausis ceramics factory in Esplugues del Llobregat, regularly worked with the leading Catalan architects of the day. Escofet, Butsems and Orsolà were among the foremost manufacturers of the latest designs in encaustic floor tiles.

Marble letterbox (1895) outside the Casa de l'Ardiaca, Barcelona.

Many public and private organisations, as well as private clients, wanted to decorate the interiors and exteriors of new buildings in the latest styles, or to renovate the existing ones. One such example was the Barcelona Lawyers' Association, which had been housed inside the former archdeacon's house, the Casa de l'Ardiaca, since 1895. In 1902, it commissioned Domènech to decorate the building. By the main door, we can still see the letterbox designed by the architect and carved in marble by Alfons Juyol.

The refurbishment of the hotel, the Fonda España, which won Barcelona City Council's Architecture and Decoration Prize in 1904, is a superb example of the integration of the arts. The newspaper, the *Diari de Barcelona* (26/6/1900), mentions the creation of a decorative yet functional world, and names some of the craftsmen involved, putting particular emphasis on the grand dining room, the columns made of jasper marble from Tortosa, the coffered ceiling combined with Rigalt's mosaics, the woodwork by Martí, Alomar's decorative carpentry, and Pau Rabassa's marble and mosaic. The sgraffito work was probably done by the Paradís studio (Pifarré, 2015). Other highlights include the mermaids on the walls of the dining room known as *La Peixera*, or fish bowl, which, according to a news item published in *La Ilustració Catalana* in 1905, were drawn by Ramon Casas. They are swimming on a backdrop depicting the sea bed with motifs taken from the Japanese works of art Domènech collected. We can see prawns, lobsters, crabs, octopuses, fish and Hokusai's great wave off Karagawa (Bru, 2019). In the reading room on the ground floor, there is a monumental alabaster fireplace by Eusebi Arnau. It is an allegory of the family home and shows a mother and baby, and grandfather on either side of the fire, which also features dancing cherubs. An article in the journal *Arquitectura y Construcción* published in 1906 mentions that Arnau's sculptures could be found in almost all recent buildings.

Other sculptors, including Miquel Blay, Pau Gargallo, Francesc Modolell, Federico Bechini, Diego Masana and Alfons Juyol, were also involved in Domènech's decorative sculptural programme. The master woodworker and interior designer, Gaspar Homar, made a special contribution to the decorative programme inside

Castell dels Tres Dragons (1887-1893). Ceramic shields on the façade with designs by Joan Llimona and Alexandre de Riquer.

Fonda España (1900-1903). Sgraffito-work marine motifs in *La Peixera*.

the hotel, and catered perfectly to the demands of the architect and his clients. He achieved extremely high levels of quality in rendering the designs for the Casa Lleó i Morera and the Casa Navàs in the furniture and marquetry work – in association with artists of the calibre of Sebastià Junyent and Josep Pey –, the upholstery, embroideries and paintings for his furniture, and the curtains, rugs and lamps.

Equally important was Domènech's collaboration with his son-in-law and assistant, Francesc Guàrdia i Vial. One of the highlights was the extension of the Casa Thomas in 1912, a house and studio at 293 Carrer Mallorca, which successfully integrated the three storeys of the original building.

The Palau de la Música Catalana and Hospital de Sant Pau

These World Heritage buildings are defined by the unity in the repertoire of materials, the construction systems and decorative elements. Both are the result of a collaboration with an extraordinary team, where the details merge with an extremely beautiful composition and setting.

At the Palau, an orchestra of virtuosos interpreted the decorative repertoire: the stained-glass artists, Rigalt i Granell; the floor-tile manufacturers, Escofet; the mosaicists, Maragliano and Bru; the ceramicist, Josep Orriols; the sculptors, Blay, Arnau, Gargallo and Masana; and the painter, Miquel Massot. Miquel Blay's sculptural grouping, *La Cançó Popular* (Folk Song) creates a linking theme on the exterior of the building. It is made of stone quarried on Montjuïc and was produced at Frederic Bechini's workshop. Eusebi Arnau sculpted the busts of Palestrina, Bach, Beethoven and Wagner. Above the main entrance, a ceramic frieze by Lluís Bru celebrates Catalan music and includes mount Montserrat and the members of the Orfeó Català choir. Inside, a forest of columns leads to an area featuring Wagnerian motifs, with floral garlands that evoke the song of the Earth in springtime.

At Sant Pau, Domènech directed his team, comprising his son, Pere Domènech i Roura, Francesc Guàrdia, Francesc Julià, Enric Catà and Amadeu Llopart, and his regular collaborators, who specialised in the applied and decorative arts. The anonymous quarrymen who hewed out the stone from Montjuïc also made a vital contribution. It was combined with stone from quarries in Girona and Vilaseca, and the marble supplied by José Casals Comdor's company. The materials were chosen according to criteria of durability and hygiene. Exposed red brick, stone, pine and cedar, Arabic tiles, ceramics, mosaics, stained glass, metal work, iron and encaustic mosaic tiles were combined with great skill.

Eusebi Arnau's sculptural ensemble, an allegory of charity, pays tribute to the patron Pau Gil. His bust is placed above a sculpture of a woman and child with an old man. Highlights of Arnau and Pau Gargallo's richly crafted sculptures, which faithfully follow the iconographic programme for the building, are the four guardian angels, the virtues and other sculptures placed around the coat of arms of the city of Barcelona and the Hospital de la Santa Creu, with its figures of saints and illustrious figures throughout the history of the hospital until the time of Doctor Robert.

The sculptor Pau Gargallo's brother, Lluís, was hired to design the models for the ceramic panels, along with Francesc Madurell, who also designed the panels for the administration block. Francesc Labarta drew the friezes tracing the history of the hospital and Mario Maragliano transformed them into the mosaics on the exterior of the building. The Barcelona-based designers, Badia i Ferrer, landscaped the grounds.

The applied and decorative arts lend the interior spaces their unique appearance, with the tiles, cement and stucco work that were necessary to maintain standards of hygiene combined with decorative beauty. The ceramics factories, Pujol i Bausis in Esplugues and Elias Peris in Onda, made the ceramic elements that protect nearly all the spaces and make them even more beautiful. Cosme Toda in Barcelona and Mosaicos Nolla in Valencia were commissioned to produce the floor tiles, and the stained-glass was made by A. Rigalt i Cia. The Vilarós painted the surfaces and the Perpiñà workshop in Barcelona made the ironwork. Domènech used exposed brick – as he had done at the Castell dels Tres Dragons – to enrich the skin of the buildings and create different chromatic and textural effects. In a nutshell, the Palau de la Música and the Hospital de Sant Pau are the very epitome of the idea of a total work of art, or *Gesamtkunstwerk*, where music raises the spirits, and body and soul are healed in places that have been designed to be enjoyed.

Palau de la Música Catalana (1905-1909). Decoration inside the auditorium.

Hospital de Sant Pau (1902-1920). Sculptural grouping *Al·legoria de la Caritat* by Eusebi Arnau.

Domènech i Montaner and the graphic arts

Pilar Vélez

The Domènechs: a family associated with the graphic arts

Domènech i Montaner had a close, yet varied relationship with the graphic arts. He was born into a family who worked in bookbinding, which was considered an offshoot of printing. His father, Pere Domènech Saló (1821-1873), introduced industrial bookbinding to Barcelona and, at the same time, renewed artistic bookbinding with the use of gilding tools, which had fallen into decline at the time.

In 1840, he opened a workshop on Carrer de Gignàs, which became one of the city's most important industrial bookbinders. By 1860, it had moved to new premises at number 2, Carrer de Santa Mònica, just off La Rambla, which was equipped with modern machinery and tools imported from France. These were listed in a catalogue published in 1867 and printed by Lluís Tasso. The workshop provided a learning environment where future bookbinders honed their skills, among them Josep Ruiz and the publisher Hermenegild Miralles – the sales manager of Domènech's industrial bookbinding workshop – and also specialised in selling bookbinding machines. When Pere Domènech died in 1873, Lluís, who had recently qualified as an architect – he had graduated in December 1873 – took over the family business, together with his brothers Eduard and Enric. Eduard (1854-1918) continued with his father's work in the bookbinding workshop while Lluís and Enric took care of the publishing side, although it was not long before Lluís embarked on his career in architecture. (Trenc, 1977; Quiney, 2005)

← Montaner i Simon publishing house (1879- 1885). Shield on the upper part of the façade.

Domènech i Montaner, an architect at the service of the graphic arts: the Montaner i Simon publishing house and the Casa Thomas

Domènech had worked closely as an architect with the world of publishing and the graphic arts. Two of his most important Barcelona projects from the end of the 19th century (the Montaner i Simon publishing house and the Casa Thomas) were featured in a special edition of *Revista Gráfica* – the journal of the Institut Català de les Arts del Llibre – in 1900, dedicated to the Gutenberg press on the five-hundredth anniversary of the invention of the printing press.

Montaner i Simon was one of the most active and innovative publishing houses in Barcelona and, for many years, the main exporter of books in Spanish to South America (Bellver Poissenot, 2017). The company was founded in 1867 by Domènech i Montaner's maternal uncle, Ramon Montaner Vila, who had trained at Pere Domènech's bookbinding workshop, and his business partner, Francesc Simon Font. In 1879, Domènech i Montaner began working on the project for the new company headquarters on Carrer d'Aragó. This can be considered his first major project, and came just after the publication of his article "En busca de una arquitectura nacional" (In search of a national architecture) in 1878. He had previously worked on minor projects, such as the renovation of the Casa Maria Montaner, at number 6, Ronda de la Universitat, which was the block of family dwellings where Domènech and his wife lived during the early years of their marriage.

The façade features a series of symbolic motifs referring to the world of books and publishing. At the top of the central section are three terracotta busts by the sculptor Rossend Nobas, dedicated to Dante, Cervantes and Milton, classic authors from Italy, Spain and Great

Cover of *Historia General del Arte* (1886) published by Montaner i Simon.

Cover of the Bible (1871) published by Montaner i Simon.

Britain. The publishing house printed many of their works. Interspersed between the busts are a series of plaques bearing the names of prestigious contemporary authors whose books were also published by Montaner i Simon: the Danish geographer, Malte-Brun; the Spanish historian, Modesto Lafuente, who had written the *Historia General de España*, which was published by Montaner i Simon in six volumes; the astronomer, Angelo Secchi; and a fourth, whose name is missing. These elements were intended to show that the publishing house was involved in disseminating the ideas of the day. The three cogwheel-shaped carvings underneath symbolise the industrial era, and the eagle standing on an open book inside the central wheel, surmounted by a star, represents the success of the business. At the top of the façade, in the centre, a helmet and an angel playing a trumpet are symbols of Catalan identity.

The Casa Thomas was Domènech i Montaner's second project associated with the graphic arts. It was founded in 1880 and it was a major Barcelona printing workshop specialising in reproduction art prints produced using the most innovative technical processes of the day: collotype, autotype, lithography and chromolithography. By 1900, his was one of the most important photoengraving studios in Barcelona, and worked mostly for large publishing companies, such as Montaner i Simon and Salvat.

During this period of growth, Thomas commissioned Domènech, a friend of his, to design his workshop and his family home on the upper floor, at 375 Carrer de Mallorca (now number 291). It was built between 1895 and 1898, in Domènech's trademark neo-Gothic style. The building had a rectangular floor plan and a semi-basement, ground floor and upper floor. The façade is a compendium of the applied arts with an eye-catching segmental arch with mouldings on the façade which acts as a huge window providing the workshop and semi-basement with light and ventilation. It has wrought-iron railings which act as a balustrade and gate to the semi-basement. The are stone medallions in the spandrels above the arch bearing the owner's monogram (JT). In 1912, one of Josep Thomas' sons, who was married to Maria Domènech i Roura, the architect's eldest daughter, decided to extend the building and convert it into rental apartments. With Domènech i Montaner's consent, they commissioned Francesc Guàrdia to carry out the project. Francesc Guàrdia was one of Domènech i Montaner's assistants and was married to his daughter Anna. He respected the spirit of the original project but added three storeys with galleries on either side of the main façade. The original architrave, with its shields bearing the four stripes of the Catalan flag and the cross of Saint George – symbols of Catalan identity – arranged

Cover of *Sainetes* Volume I, by Ramón de la Cruz. Barcelona, 1882, published by Montaner i Simon. Fons antic del Museu del Disseny de Barcelona

Cover of *México*; engraver: Josep Roca i Alemany. Barcelona, c. 1900. Museu del Disseny de Barcelona.

in an alternating pattern, were placed on the top of the building in keeping with Domènech's original design.

As far as the materials and decorative elements are concerned, the Casa Thomas is a fine example of the integration of the arts that typified the *modernista* movement and Domènech i Montaner's designs, particularly ceramics, mosaics, stone and iron reliefs, which can be seen on the façade and the main staircase.

Domènech i Montaner: graphic designer and book illustrator

Domènech i Montaner worked extensively in the different fields of the graphic arts, and this is an aspect that has been studied in recent decades by a number of scholars. Firstly, Domènech illustrated books and magazines; and secondly, to use modern parlance, he was a graphic designer, creating mastheads, logotypes and typefaces. He later became an art director at publishing houses, including Montaner i Simon, or for collections of books, such as the illustrated library, the *Biblioteca Arte y Letras*. Of course, these different facets converged on more than one occasion, while he was working on his architectural projects.

We will begin by talking about Lluís Domènech i Montaner's role as art director of the *Biblioteca Arte y Letras*. The project was originally devised by Lluís and his brother, Enric, who was the manager. But what were these so-called illustrated libraries? They were collections of pocket-sized books, generally illustrated with zincographs, photogravures or galvanotypes, with very showy industrial bindings, both graphically and chromatically, heat-printed in relief onto percaline fabric and usually embossed in gold or silver. The compositions were usually produced by renowned illustrators. The books in the collection were mostly novels, but there were also volumes of poetry, biographies and extraordinary narratives by Spanish writers and foreign authors, which were translated into Spanish. They were sold at affordable prices.

A number of scholars (Vélez, 1987; Cotoner, 2002; Rodríguez Gutiérrez, 2016) have analysed the quality of the artwork and the graphic design of the collection, together with its socio-cultural impact and wide dissemination. The collection launched in 1881, after Enric Domènech had set up a partnership with Celestí Verdaguer, who was the printer. They published the first nine volumes, which were sold to subscribers. Some of Catalonia's most illustrious artists worked on the collection. They included Apel·les Mestres, who illustrated the first volume, Alexandre de Riquer, Josep

Pascó, Arturo Mélida, Francesc Jorba, and Domènech i Montaner himself. The architect became the art director of the collection, and chose the titles and illustrators. He also designed the covers of Vicente Espinel's *Marcos de Obregón* (1881), Josep Yxart's *Fortuny* (1882), Alphonse Daudet's *El Nabab* (1882), Ramón de la Cruz's *Sainetes* (1882), and *Tres poesías* (1883), featuring three poems by Wallin, Schiller and Andrada. He also drew the cover of *Odas de Horacio* (1882), and also produced the illustrations inside the book. The design of the decorative initials and the titles, which were usually placed inside a richly ornamented surround, are particularly striking.

But the library did not remain under the ownership of the Domènech brothers for long. In 1882, Verdaguer printed just three titles and died burdened with debts. After this, Enric Domènech started working with the printers Jaume Jepús and Fidel Giró, and they produced seven more titles. However, it seems that in 1883 he sold the collection to the printer Francesc Pérez, and the critic Josep Yxart took over as art director. Shortly afterwards Pérez sold the business to Daniel Cortezo, who continued until 1890. This would explain why Lluís Domènech i Montaner worked on the covers produced in 1881 and 1882 but only on one in 1883, because the collection was now under new ownership.

Domènech had also designed the endpapers and the logo for the collection, which always appeared on the back cover, with the classic Latin motto "Per angusta ad augusta" (Through difficulties to honours), which refers to the difficulties of meeting challenges, perhaps with the collection in mind. As far as we know, the business was not the one the Domènech brothers had dreamt about, probably because the printing processes and the binding in particular were too expensive for this type of project. Or it may have been because they also had to put their efforts into producing the monthly art and literature journal, *Arte y Letras*, which was a free gift for subscribers to the collection. It launched in July 1882 and lasted only five years until December 1883, when Cortezo closed it down. The project was the brainchild of Enric Domènech, and Josep Yxart was the editor. They had world-class contributors, including the Spanish novelists Pérez Galdós and Clarín, and, once again, Domènech designed the masthead in the distinctive neo-Gothic decorative style redolent of his 1880s' work. It seems that each issue came with two reproductions of photogravures produced by the great French printers, Goupil.

Lluís Domènech was also editor of the *Historia General del Arte*, the first major history of art in Spanish, which was published in Barcelona (Vélez, 2000). He designed the layout, which was extremely modern for the time, as is reflected in the way the contents were ordered and the illustrations produced using modern photomechanical processes, such as photogravure and phototypography. The texts are illustrated by 1,500 drawings, many of them by Domènech, along with full-page plates, which Domènech had found abroad, as was customary, and also commissioned from local artists.

The project consisted of eight volumes and the first one was published in 1886. The subject matter encompassed the fine arts and industrial arts, as specified in the advertising leaflet produced by the publisher. There were three volumes on architecture – two with texts and one with plates – by Domènech i Montaner and his former student, Josep Puig i Cadafalch, another leading light of *modernista* architecture; a volume devoted to painting and sculpture, by the art critic and historian Joaquín Fontanals del Castillo, which traced their history until the 18th century; a volume dedicated to ornamentation – in keeping with the eclectic tastes of the time – by Federico Cajal y Pueyo, professor of decorative arts and director of the Escola d'Arts i Oficis in Sant Martí de Provençals; two volumes on the history of clothing, by the German specialist Federico Hottenroth; and a final tome on the decorative arts by Francesc Miquel i Badia (furniture, weaving, embroidery and tapestries) and Antoni Garcia Llansó (metalwork, ceramics and glass) which was published in 1897. The last volume, which was steeped in the eclecticism of the time, raised the question of what the style of the 19th century had been and stated that none had been defined. In a nutshell, the architect edited a highly modern work that was up to the standards of the European studies of the day and was a fine example of historical and artistic thinking at the time. Domènech was also an artist and draughtsman – today we would have referred to him as a designer – of brands, logotypes and book covers, as described by a number of authors (Figueras, 1990; Sàiz, 2012). In addition to his designs for the aforementioned *Arte y Letras* collection, he also worked on the large-format

Bible, in two volumes, with gilded leather bindings by Fèlix Torres Amat, and illustrations by Gustave Doré. It was produced in 1871 by the Hermenegild Miralles workshop for Montaner i Simon. Its understated, sober design features a large cross in the centre and the symbols of the evangelists on the four corners. In 1878, the magazine *La Renaixensa* published the *Llibre d'Or de la moderna poesia catalana*, with an industrially produced cover designed by Domènech in gold and red, symbolising the four stripes of the Catalan flag. That same year he had designed the cover for the first edition of Jacint Verdaguer's poem *L'Atlàntida*, which was printed by Jaume Jepús. In 1883 he designed the cover of *Cristóbal Colón* published by Espasa. It had an industrially produced binding in blue and red with abundant gilding. He also created the unique cover for an edition of Don Quixote (1904-1906), which was produced in two volumes and cork-bound by the printers Octavi Viader in Palafrugell. Sketches of these designs survive that help us understand the architect's working process in the field of graphics. There is little record of his original designs for the cover of the book *México*. It was produced by the industrial bookbinders Roca, one of the leading companies of the time. There is only one known copy of the book. It is housed in Barcelona's design museum, the Museu del Disseny, and came from the collection of the engraver Roca i Alemany, once held at the now-defunct Museu de les Arts Gràfiques. It is a large-format, exotic and colourful composition, as befits the subject matter. Nevertheless, we have not been able to confirm that the book was published on a larger scale. (Vélez, 1989)

In addition to these series of publications, Domènech designed the covers for a number of books or albums paying tribute to eminent personalities, a widespread custom in the late 19th century. This is the case of the album dedicated to the former provincial governor of Barcelona, Antonio Gonzalez Solesio, which was made from noble metals and precious stones, and also featured his design of the Barcelona coat of arms, with the four stripes on a gilded background, with the crown of the Counts of Barcelona. He also designed three ornate missals. One for the bishop of Vic, Josep Morgades, in 1888, which won the gold medal at the 1888 Universal Exhibition; one for the bishop of Girona, Francesc de Pol, to mark his consecration in 1907; and a third that the Marquis of Comillas com-

Drawing for the masthead of the newspaper *La Renaixensa*. Barcelona, c. 1881. Arxiu Històric del COAC.

missioned him to make for the town of Bustiello in Asturias. The first two are masterpieces of silversmithing, made in ornate silver by some of the foremost silversmiths of the day. (Sàiz, 2012)

Reference must also be made to Domènech's collaboration in various illustrated magazines and newspapers from the last quarter of the 19th century. These included the mastheads for *La Renaixensa* (1879), *La Veu de Catalunya* (1881), *El Poble Català* (1904), Hermenegild Miralles' journal *Hispania* (1899), which featured a female figure seated on a throne, and *Ilustración cubana* (1885), printed by Lluís Tasso.

In conclusion, and as we have seen, Lluís Domènech i Montaner worked in almost every field of the graphic arts as an architect, draughtsman and artist. In fact, he fell short in only one aspect: he never theorised or wrote about the graphic arts, as he had done about other subjects, such as heraldry. Likewise, as strange as it may seem, there are no surviving examples of the exlibris he designed.

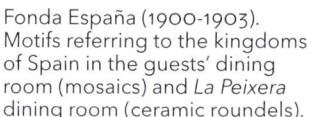
Fonda España (1900-1903). Motifs referring to the kingdoms of Spain in the guests' dining room (mosaics) and *La Peixera* dining room (ceramic roundels).

Heraldic shield, n.d., Arxiu Històric del Col·legi d'Arquitectes de Catalunya.

Domènech i Montaner and heraldry

Before we end, we wanted to refer briefly to another of the architect's many facets: his study of heraldry, which was also associated with the world of illustration, and his many contributions to the subject. Driven by his interest in historical and nationalist ideals, Domènech i Montaner came to master the aesthetics of heraldry. His vast body of work can be summarised in three titles. Firstly, *L'Armorial Històric de Catalunya. Des dels orígens fins al segle XVI*, for which he was awarded the Martorell Prize by the Institut d'Estudis Catalans in 1922. It consists of six large volumes illustrated with drawings of all manner of coats of arms and emblems, based on his study of stamps, coins, ceramics, manuscripts and the sculptural reliefs on a variety of monuments and landmarks. It was a painstakingly detailed work that took many years to complete and required a great deal of patience. He was able to trace the origins of ancient legends and clarify centuries-old misunderstandings, thereby contributing to the history of Catalonia and making the biggest contribution to the subject at the time.

His second magnum opus was the *Nobiliari General català de llinatges. Catalunya, València, Mallorca, Rosselló*, produced in collaboration with his son Fèlix and published in three volumes by Montaner i Simon (1923-1930). The third title, *Ensenyes Nacionals de Catalunya*, was published posthumously in 1936 by his son Fèlix, who was also the co-author. It was based on the exhaustive research carried out for *L'Armorial* and had a foreword by Pau Font de Rubinat. The Catalan government, the Generalitat de Catalunya, has produced a number of high-quality facsimile editions of the work since 1995.

There is no doubt that Domènech made major contributions to the field of heraldry. However, the three works also showcase his talents as a first-class illustrator, both historically and didactically.

The architect's interest in heraldry led him to include heraldic motifs in his buildings. Good examples include the publishing house, Montaner i Simon, which has a helmet and an angel playing a trumpet on the top of the façade, and the front of the Casa Thomas, which is surmounted by shields bearing the four stripes of the Catalan flag and the cross of Sant Jordi (Saint George), which are symbols of Catalan identity. The motifs he used on the mastheads he designed for newspapers and magazines, such as *La Renaixensa*, *El Poble Català* and *La Veu de Catalunya*, were also on a heraldic theme.

UN XANXES PROFETA

—¡Repara, Puig, si se 'ns en gira de feyna!
—¡No se engresquen tanto, hombres! ¿No ven que cuando este plan comience á realizarse, ni de ustedes ni de ninguno de los vivos se 'n cantará gallo ni gallina?

Domènech and Barcelona: architect and "town planner"

Enric Granell · Antoni Ramon

"His architectural works are well known and encompass all art forms, meaning that they do not fit into the limited framework of this journal. For this reason, we can only remember here the great master as the creator of valuable urban-planning projects, in which he deployed his inventive potential by creating true works of art."
(J. M. Barenys, "Luis Doménech y Muntaner", *Urbanización y edificaciones*, 1925)

Lluís Domènech i Montaner did not write any general urban-planning theories about the city, and this means that it is his singular interventions, be they individual buildings or joint projects, that allow us to understand that, for him, architecture and the city, were inextricably linked concepts. Understood as a whole, his projects – those that came to fruition and those that remained on the drawing board – bear witness to this.

It has been said many times that Domènech was a multifaceted architect. In addition to architecture, he also fell within the scope of historical research, the world of publishing, teaching and politics. But architecture formed the core of his wide range of interests: an architecture that had as its constant feature a certain idea of monumentality, which, just because it did not fit into what academicism understood as monumental, did not cease to be so. Whether we are dealing with private houses or large public buildings – restaurants, hotels, concert halls, universities or hospitals – this proposal is manifest.

Lluís Domènech qualified as an architect in 1874 and began his professional career working on Cerdà's urban expansion plan, the Eixample. It not only entailed the expansion of the existing city, but made it necessary to intervene in the old town as an inseparable part of the new city. It is in this context that we must understand how, in Barcelona, Domènech was as interested in building the new city as he was in redeveloping the old one.

The chronological arc we are covering in this text begins in 1877 with the project for the Provincial Institutions, moves on to the article "Reforma de Barcelona" written in 1879 and the important chapter about the project for the future Via Laietana in a section in "Reforma", and concludes with his preparatory studies for the 1929 International Exhibition, which Domènech was unable to see come to fruition because he died in 1923.

This timeline will help us understand how Lluís Domènech i Montaner redrew, redeveloped and remade the old city, and reread the Barcelona of Cerdà's expansion project, introducing variations that sought to break with the monotony of the grid layout. Embellishing the city by making it monumental is the main feature of the urban design of Lluís Domènech and his generation. For the so-called *modernista* architects, the city needed variety and to create new perspectives, according to the part-picturesque and part-*beaux arts* guidelines of the European civic art of Camilo Sitte and his school.

← Puig i Cadafalch and Domènech i Montaner in front of Jaussely's plan. Caricature by R. Miró in *L'Esquella de la Torratxa*, 1908.

1877. The Instituciones Provinciales and Barcelona's impossible ring

In 1877, Barcelona Provincial Council ran a call for entries for a *Competition for projects for a building to be used by the Provincial Institutions of Public Education*. Lluís Domènech i Montaner and Josep Vilaseca, who had just qualified as architects, were the winners. The large triangular plot where the building was to stand was located on a boundary between the old town and the new Eixample, between Carrer Bruc, Carrer Bailén, Carrer Ausiàs March and Ronda de Sant Pere. Some years earlier, the municipal architects, who wanted to build a monumental ring road on the site, had clashed with Ildefons Cerdà, who wanted to connect the Eixample with the old town, without any solution of continuity. Although Cerdà won the debate, it is nonetheless true that the monumental ring road never completely vanished, as is borne out by the presence of the Sant Antoni Market, the historic Barcelona University building and the law courts, the Palau de Justícia.

Domènech and Vilaseca's project must be understood in this context. Unlike the other submissions, and despite the fact that they used a *beaux arts*-style compositional structure, their design did not impose a building on the city; it let the city mould the building instead. The projects submitted by Narcís Josep Bladó and August Font were based on rigid rectangular floor plans with courtyards arranged symmetrically around a central core, like Elies Rogent's recently opened Barcelona University building, whereas Domènech and Vilaseca's plan recognised the irregular lines of the plot, while maintaining Cerdà's chamfered corners. Their project consisted of a complicated series of interlinking pieces that adapted to the old town and the Eixample. The architects understood the building not as an artefact that had been plonked on the site, but as an articulating piece of architecture that would engage in a dialogue with the two urban areas it was to be located in the middle of. (Freixa, 2000)

1879. "Reforma de Barcelona", an initial position

In 1879, Lluís Domènech i Montaner wrote a long article entitled "Reforma de Barcelona" in the newspaper *La Renaixensa* taking a position on the debate that had been ignited about the need to redevelop the old walled city. Although there are no plans to accompany the text, the author describes with sufficient clarity how to deal with the redevelopment.

The proposal had three objectives. The first was to reinforce the idea of a centre, designing a monumental core he called the agora, which would bring together the architectural relics of the city's historic past, from the columns of the Roman temple to the medieval cathedral and the Renaissance government building, the Palau de la Generalitat, which he presented as the city's crowning glory. The second interpreted a certain radiality in the medieval layout of the city, which would define and reinforce the layout of the streets that would connect the agora with the gates of the walled city.

The third objective, which reaffirmed the historicist character of the proposal, chose, somewhat arbitrarily, some historic landmarks over others, and either left them as standalone buildings, or added to them, to create urban scenes that, while looking historical, are actually modern. Like all the urban planning proposals of the time, this was not a conservation plan. Ultimately, it sought to modernise the city.

It appears that the "project for a square in Barcelona's acropolis" designed by Domènech's former student Francesc de Paula Nebot i Torrens in 1911, returned to the ideas set out in the eminent architect's article (Domènech, 1991), although there are no drawings to confirm this.

Project for the Instituciones Provinciales de Instrucción Pública. Barcelona, 1877. Arxiu Històric del COAC.

Barcelona redevelopment. Building in perspective. Barcelona, n.d., Arxiu Històric del COAC.

Hotel Internacional. Journal *Hispania*, 1902.

1888. The Hotel Internacional for the Universal Exhibition

In the middle of the 19th century, the demolition of the city walls made it possible to extend the city to the Barcelona plain and also reclaimed land from the sea, leading to the development of a new boulevard, Passeig de Colom, which connected the Parc de la Ciutadella with the end of La Rambla, where one of the city's major landmarks, the Columbus Monument, was to be located. Building work on the monument began in 1882.

With the 1888 Universal Exhibition on the horizon, there was a pressing concern to build the grand hotel Barcelona needed so badly at the time. The city council launched a competition for city developers to submit a project for the hotel. Most of them chose sites in the old town and their designs had no urban or architectural ambitions. Lluís Domènech, and the developer Ricardo Valentí, took advantage of the event to erect a monumental, albeit temporary, building by the waterfront on Passeig de Colom, the boulevard that led to the exhibition site. The Hotel Internacional was 200 metres long and its palatial façade was in the style of the grand hotels in other European cities. The building was an eye-catching feature along a boulevard that, according to Domènech's original project, would have included other majestic buildings stretching as far as the Columbus Monument. Unfortunately, the city did not take note of his suggestions.

The hotel resembled a city in miniature. It had a central square and its corridors were like streets that led to the communal areas for guests. It was a compact building which had every amenity you would expect of a hotel. The construction process was a monumental task and was widely reported in its day. The hotel was built in

Lobby of the Gran Hotel Internacional. Postcard from the *Barcelona Retrospectiva* collection. Llibreria Millà, Barcelona, 1920. Courtesy of Rossend Casanova.

42 • Lluís Domènech i Montaner

little more than a month, with around a thousand labourers working in shifts, twenty-four hours a day. They worked at night with electric lamps. The epic nature of the building process has detracted somewhat from the role the Hotel Internacional played in the city, and would have gone on to play had it not been demolished shortly after the exhibition ended. (Ramon, 2011)

1896-1901. From the Institut Pere Mata to the Hospital de Sant Pau, "other cities"

On 19th June 1901, Lluís Domènech was commissioned to design the new Hospital de la Santa Creu. The decision was not without controversy. Three architectural projects were presented for the competition. The judging panel of architects named as the winner Josep Domènech i Estapà's project, which opted for a compact hospital. However, the judging panel of doctors rejected all three projects due to hygiene issues. The institution looked for another, bigger site, based on their guidelines, where Lluís Domènech i Montaner's project came to fruition.

The project continued a way of understanding hospital buildings that Domènech had already embarked on in 1896 with his preparatory designs for the Institut Pere Mata in Reus. In this case, maybe because the new hospital was located on the outskirts of the city, or maybe because it was the express desire of the institution, it consisted of separate pavilions that created a city within a city. Instead of a compact building, Domènech proposed a series of pavilions, not just for hygiene reasons – which were certainly important – but for urban planning reasons too. Domènech wanted to create "another city" with his Pere Mata project. It was to be well ordered around a central core with a row of buildings consisting of a church and the administration block.

At Sant Pau, although Domènech's project had to adapt to the area demarcated by the four blocks in Cerdà's Eixample project, he still proposed "another city": a kind of garden one that would provide an alternative to the existing one. An ordered area with its axes and own guidelines, based on medical and scientific criteria. As we have said, modern hygiene resulted in a hospital set out in separate, well-ventilated pavilions, which had the correct orientation and were surrounded by greenery and bathed in sunshine. The pavilions were connected by a network of underground corridors. The Hospital de Sant Pau is a city within a city. When Léon Jaussely won the first competition for projects linking the Eixample and the surrounding area, held in 1905, and revised his initial proposal, he extended the road in front of the hospital, creating one of the city's new avenues, which connected the Hospital de Sant Pau and the church of the Sagrada Família. (Ramon, 2000b)

1905. The Palau de la Música Catalana in the heart of the old town

The Palau de Música Catalana was also conditioned by urban planning, although it may not appear that way. The home of the Orfeó Català is located in the old part of the city, almost certainly because it is where its members lived. The irregular, awkward plot was defined by its location among narrow streets. Lluís Domènech built the Palau with its back to the new avenue, Via Laietana, which was about to be built, as if he wanted to escape its straight, impersonal layout. The architect took advantage of this cramped urban site to create a covered carriage entrance, in order to give back to the city part of the limited plot of land that was available. The two façades do not come together at an angle, but have a tower on the corner. This would become a key feature of Domènech's work. Here the tower plays a functional role, drawing attention to the entrance, and a symbolic one, with its large sculptural grouping and metal pinnacle. (Ramon, 2000a)

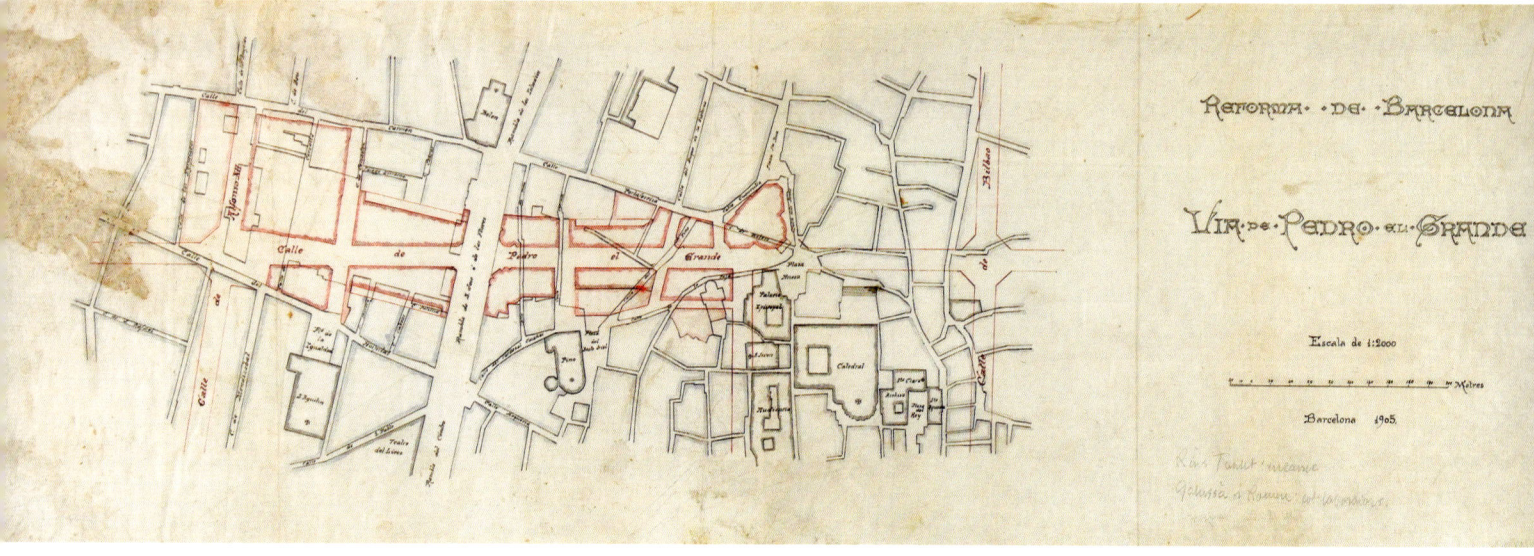

Layout of Vía Pedro el Grande. Barcelona, 1905. Arxiu Històric del Col·legi d'Arquitectes de Catalunya.

1905. The project for Vía Pedro el Grande

Lluís Domènech's unrealised project for the thoroughfare, Vía Pedro el Grande, was developed from a detail in the 1891 *Plano de la reforma interior de la ciudad de Barcelona* and consisted of his redesign of the central strip of the Via C originally set out in the Cerdà Plan. The change of name was not without significance. It had shifted from its abstract nomenclature, defined in 1860, to another based on a heroic past. Domènech remade the image of this part of the city precisely at the time Léon Jaussely had won the competition for the linking plan. His project was in harmony with the other interventions in the historic areas of the great European capitals, such as the boulevards in Paris and the Ring in Vienna and involved the demolition of certain buildings. Domènech intended to preserve only the established historic landmarks, including religious buildings, and regarded the Boqueria Market and the old Hospital de la Santa Creu as unimportant. This formed the basis for the new architectural programmes for the modern city: shopping arcades, shops, a theatre and market built from glass and iron.

In this project, Domènech combined references to his own works – we see this in the Casa Thomas, the metal pinnacle on the top of the café and restaurant in the Parc de la Ciutadella, the corner towers, the new Boqueria Market, built from glass and iron, and a version of the dispensary for the Hospital de Sant Pau project – and references that were more or less true to the spirit of his time, which can be seen, for instance, in a theatre vaguely reminiscent of those designed by Gottfried Semper. However, beyond the architectural references, we should also look at the scale of the redevelopment: Domènech did not design a broad avenue, but a street of a similar width to the current Portaferrissa in the centre of Barcelona.

1903-1908. The monumentalisation of a residential building. The Casa Lleó i Morera and the Casa Fuster

Lluís Domènech i Montaner's projects for residential buildings reveal another way of understanding the role of architecture in the urban environment. They are not merely anonymous buildings, like the first ones in the Eixample district, constructed by master builders, but are steeped in significant monumental values. From the composition of the buildings to their overall look and details, Domènech's residential buildings, like the ones designed by his fellow *modernista* architects,

Project for the gate in the Plaça Nova. Ink and watercolour drawing. Museu Nacional d'Art de Catalunya.

seek to carve out a distinctive place among Cerdà's homogeneous grid layout. One of the true highlights is the Casa Lleó i Morera (1903), which resolved the problem of the corner site by including a plethora of different-shaped windows, galleries, balconies and tempiettos that turn the building around and break up the corner angle.

However, the sadly incomplete Casa Fuster (1908) would have provided the most spectacular solution. Located on a superb plot of land, the architect's project provides a backdrop to the view from Passeig de Gràcia, with a slender tower on the corner. The architect often used this device, which was inherited from the towers of medieval castles that had been revived by European neo-Gothic architecture. If the tower, surmounted by a pointed pinnacle, had been built, it would have been a wonderful sight from the end of Passeig de Gràcia.

1914. The project to link up Via Laietana with the old streets

In 1907, Pere Falqués updated the layout of the Via A in the Cerdà Plan. The project launched in 1909. After demolition work had begun, and due to widespread protests against the redevelopment, the city council commissioned Lluís Domènech i Montaner, Josep Puig i Cadafalch and Ferran Romeu to design a new project that would connect the new thoroughfare with the existing old town. Lluís Domènech was asked to design the first section, which was nearest the port, from Plaça Idrissa Diallo to Plaça de l'Àngel.

Domènech considered that Via Laietana, which was to stretch from the port to the new city, was the perfect location to build a series of civic buildings placed around squares, in addition to housing. With this aim in mind, he proposed a network of passages that would make better use of the land and created three new squares: Plaça de l'Àngel, which stood symmetrically at the junction of Via Laietana, and widened the thoroughfare. The Biblioteca de Catalunya and the Academia de Buenas Letras were to be located in the Square Vilanova, which would provide wider views of the church of Sant Just. The square was to be the site of the landmarks committee museum, the Museo de Comisión de Monumentos, which was to be housed in the Palau Requesens. The third square, at the entrance to Via Laietana by the sea, was to be the site of a series of institutional buildings, including the main post office, the library of the Chamber of Commerce, a brand-new building with a round central courtyard, and the sailing school, the Escola de Nàutica.

Proposal for the redevelopment of the area in front of Santa Maria del Mar. Barcelona, n.d. Arxiu Històric del COAC.

The most spectacular part of the project was to draw attention to the city's most important Gothic landmark: the church of Santa Maria del Mar. To achieve his aim, Domènech proposed an avenue running perpendicular to the façade of the church, which would end with a porticoed square separating the landmark from the historic urban fabric. The section at the beginning of Carrer Joan Massana was the only part of the project to see the light of day.

1915. International Exhibition of Electrical Industries and their Applications

After the 1888 Universal Exhibition, a number of initiatives sought to repeat the experience in the belief that these kinds of events could be engines of growth. In 1913, a series of officials and institutions, including the king of Spain, the Spanish government, Barcelona Provincial Council and Barcelona City Council, launched the proposal to host an International Exhibition of Electrical Industries and their Applications in 1915. A working committee, chaired by Lluís Domènech, and with Josep Puig i Cadafalch as vice-chair, drew up the master plan for the exhibition. The plans for the exhibition palaces and halls were never realised, but we know that the layout of the project was based on the academic guidelines for international exhibitions, which had their origins in the World's Columbian Exposition, held in Chicago in 1893.

The area chosen made use of the 1888 exhibition site and extended it in two directions: one towards the Arc del Triomf, where they planned to build a stadium for celebrations and sporting events, in the style of a Roman circus, and another towards Avinguda Meridiana. A viaduct and a stadium emerged onto a square which would form an articulation point encompassing the geometry of the Eixample and lead to a second site along Carrer Marina, with a central section with an illuminated fountain and a party hall as its centrepiece. A suspension railway, based on the one in the German city of Wuppertal, would transport visitors to different areas of the site. The extension of the project was not only excessive, it was incompatible with the running of the city. However, it was the outbreak of the First World War in 1914 that put paid to the initiative.

1915-1917. International Exhibition of Electrical Industries and their Applications and the General Spanish Exhibition

Nevertheless, the project was not completely shelved, and the organisers planned to host the event at another time on a new site. When Manuel Vega i March suggested holding the exhibition on a kind of belvedere or viewing point, overlooking the Mediterranean, Montjuïc seemed an ideal spot. The advent of the Commonwealth of Catalonia, the Mancomunitat de Catalunya, provided a favourable political framework, and in 1914 a draft bill officially declared that Barcelona would be hosting a dual exhibition in 1917. Josep Puig i Cadafalch was entrusted with the preliminary work for the project, and he oversaw the different sections, along with Puig, Domènech, Amargós, Font, Sagnier, Falqués, Busquets and Vega i March.

Although the opening date was delayed due to the war, the initiative continued. A drawing signed by Lluís Domènech and Manuel Vega i March dated 1917, which depicted the section devoted to the electrical industries, provides proof of the architects' intentions. It is an aerial perspective in colour of white buildings set against the backdrop of the blue Mediterranean horizon. The buildings make up a classical landscape, with a nod to the *noucentista* movement, with domes, colonnades, elliptical squares, artificial lakes inside the abandoned quarries on Montjuïc, and a plethora of fountains and monumental columns. These elements are somewhat surprising if we compare them to Domènech's usual designs.

Or maybe they aren't, particularly if we look at the room where Lluís Domènech's students' projects were exhibited at the Saló d'Arquitectura in 1916. Lluís Domènech i Montaner entered the Barcelona School of Architecture the year it was founded in 1875 and left in 1919. This means that his life and work were inextricably linked to the institution, which he was director of for fifteen years. Successive generations of Domènech's students shifted from *modernisme* to academicism. Was this under his influence?

Canet de Mar, Comillas and Reus. Lluís Domènech i Montaner's creative triangle outside Barcelona

Gemma Martí · Xavier Mas i Gibert · Carles Sàiz i Xiqués

Lluís Domènech i Montaner spent most of his professional career in the city of Barcelona, but he also worked in Canet de Mar, Reus and Comillas, where a considerable number of the architect's works are concentrated. Domènech always had a family connection to Canet de Mar, given that both his mother and his wife were born there. In Reus, his creative activity was mainly through his friendship with the local lawyer and illustrious figure, Pau Font de Rubinat. And his relationship with Comillas could not be understood without the patronage of the Marquis Claudio López Bru. In other words, he was working in one place due to his family origins, in another through personal friendship and in the latter for strictly professional reasons. In the cases of Canet de Mar and Reus, there was a clear, deliberate component of his own will. And in the case of Comillas, his presence there lies in the demand for quality by the most unique patron of his time. Therefore, in all three cases there were obvious elements of generosity and a romantic disposition, which were typical and even a cliché at the time, but are almost incomprehensible and inexplicable today.

Canet de Mar, hometown of both mother and wife

The maternal line of the Domènech i Montaner family, that is, the Montaners, traces its roots back to the 16th century in Canet de Mar. In 1840, Ramon Montaner i Esteve, Lluís Domènech i Montaner's grandfather, was forced to sell his property and the Montaner-Vila family moved to Barcelona, where they experienced hard times. Due to the new situation, all Ramon Montaner Esteve's children had to start working, and Maria Montaner i Vila, the eldest, married Pere Domènech i Saló, owner of a fledgling bookbinding business that eventually became the *Taller de Encuadernaciones de Lujo Pedro Domènech*, one of the top bookbinding establishments in Spain.

The business had become firmly established by the middle of the 19th century, and the Domènech family began spending the summer away from Barcelona. The middle class sought peace and quiet and fresh air far from the city, and Maria Montaner chose Canet de Mar as their summer holiday location. Lluís Domènech i Montaner was born into this middle-class milieu on 27th December 1849 in a first-floor apartment on Carrer Ferran, on the corner of Carrer Avinyó, in downtown Barcelona. The couple had seven children. The first-born was Anaclet; the second, Eulàlia; the third, Clotilde; and the fourth Lluís, followed by the rest of his siblings: Enric, Eduard and Tul·li. Lluís Domènech recalled his childhood experiences in Canet on one occasion, saying that: "on autumn evenings I enjoyed wandering through the streets in the dark, [which was] striped here and there by streaks of light emerging from the shops. The hubbub of work was buzzing everywhere; above it rose, in leaping, high, trilling notes, the distant sound of the anvil struck, the heavy thuds of the roving frame alternating with the crackling cry of the spinning jenny, like that of a gigantic cricket, and the light and cheerful clickety-clack from the handloom." (Domènech, 1914)

The young Domènech must have been completely captivated by those scenes, so unusual in his day-to-day life as a child growing up in a flat in Barcelona, and he also remembered the nascent textile activity of the town, saying "I liked to get close to the silk knitting loom to see the curious things that were made with it,

← Canet de Mar. Casa Roura (1889- 1892). View of the dining room.

of a certain national philosophy; purple bishop's gloves, high, ceremonial white stockings for the royal palace officials, red sashes for generals and strong, solid cloth with double weave for the tight-fitting breeches of the *toreros*..." (Domènech, 1914, p. 4)

During their early years of summering, the Domènech Montaners soon connected with the well-to-do of Canet de Mar, to the extent that Lluís and his brother Anaclet married two sisters from the Roura Carnasoltes family, a wealthy dynasty of landowners from the town. Anaclet Domènech married Caterina Roura and, years later, Lluís Domènech married Maria Roura (Soler, 2014, pp. 186-193). Lluís Domènech i Montaner and Maria Roura Carnasoltes' wedding was held on 11th August 1875 in Barcelona and although the couple established their main residence there, they continued to spend the summers in Canet de Mar as per family tradition.

The arrival of the Domènech i Rouras in Canet, and that of the entire summer community, was always an event. Lluís Domènech would send the maids to ready the house and, days later, the whole family would arrive in town by train. Soon they had acquired two small houses on the chamfered block corner at the confluence of the Riera Buscarons and Riera Gavarra (streets built on dried-out creek beds), and at the turn of the century the architect joined them together through the rear courtyards with Can Rocosa, which became his studio and archive. Francesc Guàrdia, Domènech's son-in-law, recalled "how he loved the house, the town, the sea and the mountains. How many dozens of times, being a deputy for Barcelona in the Spanish parliament, or director of the School of Architecture, or president of the Athenaeum, did he enjoy his greatest pleasure – leaving the corner where he worked to stroll together [with me], he with a scarf around his neck and a cane picked from the roadside, along the sea or through the neighbouring mountains, talking about politics or the monographs he was writing." (Guàrdia, 1924, p. 121)

When he was in Canet, Domènech not only lived there but was also closely involved with its people. The entire Domènech family enjoyed the local festivities and traditions to the full. The Domènechs' simplicity always brought them closer to the townspeople and they played an active role in the events held there, giving them renewed vitality and fresh impetus. Lluís Domènech always put his artistic abilities at the service of the people of Canet and he was often found making sets for plays, such as those for the premiere of Àngel Guimerà's *Judith de Welp* (1881), (Sàiz, 2011, pp. 14-17), or participating in the design of the Santa Florentina Giants (1899) that enlivened the annual celebration of the Festival of the Virgins (1881-1899). His mother, Maria Montaner, was the confratenity leader of the latter. In the summer of 1892, Lluís Domènech designed the banners, lanterns and floats for the festivities commemorating the fourth centenary of the discovery of America held in the town. He also drew ribbons for the region's Red Cross Festival (1898) and, years later, directed the artistic parade for the second centenary celebrations of the Canet Town Vow (*Vot de Vila de Canet*, 1903). (Sàiz, 2008, p. 157 and Mas, 2017, p. 140)

In an absolutely generous, selfless manner, he created the first cross on top of mount Pedracastell. In addition to being its architect, he was also the technical director for the work on its foundations and oversaw the building process. He also coordinated the transfer from Barcelona to Canet of all Alfons Juyol's sculptures, a feat of great complexity due to the poor means of transport available at the time and the difficulties of climbing to the top of Pedracastell. (Mas, 2022, pp. 16-21)

Lluís Domènech also drew emblems and pennants for local entities such as the Canet de Mar Athenaeum (1884), the Brotherhood for Labour Invalids (1892) and even the municipal coat of arms (1915). And Domènech's continuous presence in the town left an architectural legacy that fully represented all his creative stages.

The Canet de Mar Athenaeum (1884) was his first commission. Despite being an eclectic work with a medievalist aesthetic and academic composition, the building lent new meaning to materials such as iron, glass, ceramics and the Italian-style stucco made by Saumell i Vilaró in Barcelona, where several scenes from *L'Atlàntida*, the epic poem by Jacint Verdaguer, are depicted. And Domènech's interest in heraldry and the medieval bestiary as iconographic and symbolic elements is also evident in the decorative treatment of the facades. (Sàiz, 2020, pp. 8-31)

Some years later, Domènech completed two new works: the Casa Roura (1889-1892) and the extension of the fortress, the Casa Forta, in Canet (1896-1916).

The Casa Roura was designed as a summer mansion for his brother- and sister-in-law, Jacint de Capmany and Paquita Roura Carnasoltes. He used a German-style composition, with the sobriety of exposed brick and glazed-tile roofing, while the interior is a decorative explosion, with stained glass by Antoni Rigalt, classical-style flooring attributed to Mario Maragliano, carpentry work and cabinetry by the Viladevall brothers and sculptural reliefs by Eusebi Arnau. The building contains one of the most complete ranges of Domènech's *modernista* decorative programme. (Sàiz and Alcalde, 2018, p. 92)

Domènech's most monumental work in Canet de Mar was, without a doubt, the alteration and extension of the medieval fortress, the Casa Forta, in Canet to turn it into the present-day castle of Santa Florentina. Ramon Montaner, Domènech's uncle, restored the former family home in 1882 and years later commissioned his nephew to extend the building. Domènech proposed a recreation in the purest Viollet-le-Duc style, though not a historically false one, since he wanted to carry out the extension using authentic elements taken from other landmarks in Catalonia, and completed with recreations made by *modernista* craftsmen; sculptural works by Miquel Blay, Dídac Masana, Antoni Samarra and Carles Flotats, leaded stained glass by Josep Pujol, polychromy by painter and designer Tomàs Rovira and ambient interior design by Ricard de Capmany and Lluís Domènech himself.

In the 1910s, when Domènech's sojourns in Canet grew longer, he put his experience at the service of Canet town council with urban improvement projects. He suggested the council draw up its first town plan for reorganising the urban space. He also put on the table the need to make pavements along the streets, open wider roads and scale back the houses that were projecting too far out, as well as putting forward a plan for the town's future expansion. From this last period emerged projects such as the redevelopment of Passeig de la Mare de Déu de la Misericordia (1913) – which never materialised – and other, hygienic proposals such as channelling the waters of the Murtra (1912), which was completed shortly thereafter with the construction of the town's first sewerage system (1914). (Sàiz and Arcas, 2022, p. 89)

Stained-glass in the Ateneu at Canet de Mar (1885).

He was fully at home in Canet de Mar and his love for the place meant that his son Lluís, who was born and died in Canet, was buried in the town's cemetery, where Domènech had already planned various tombs and mausoleums for the family. This deep-seated attachment to the town made Canet the summer gathering point for all his descendants and, as Francesc Guàrdia said, "his greatest pleasure was to see his children and grandchildren enjoy the traditional festivities, bringing them all together at the same table" (Guard, 1924, p. 121). So much so that in 1918, in anticipation of his upcoming retirement from the Barcelona School of Architecture, he did not hesitate to alter his two old fishermen's cottages, redistributing the interiors, building a second floor and linking the facades with a large enclosed balcony at the chamfered corner of the block between the former creeks, or *rieras*, that were now streets. The Casa Domènech was the Domènech i Montaner family home and the architect's last work.

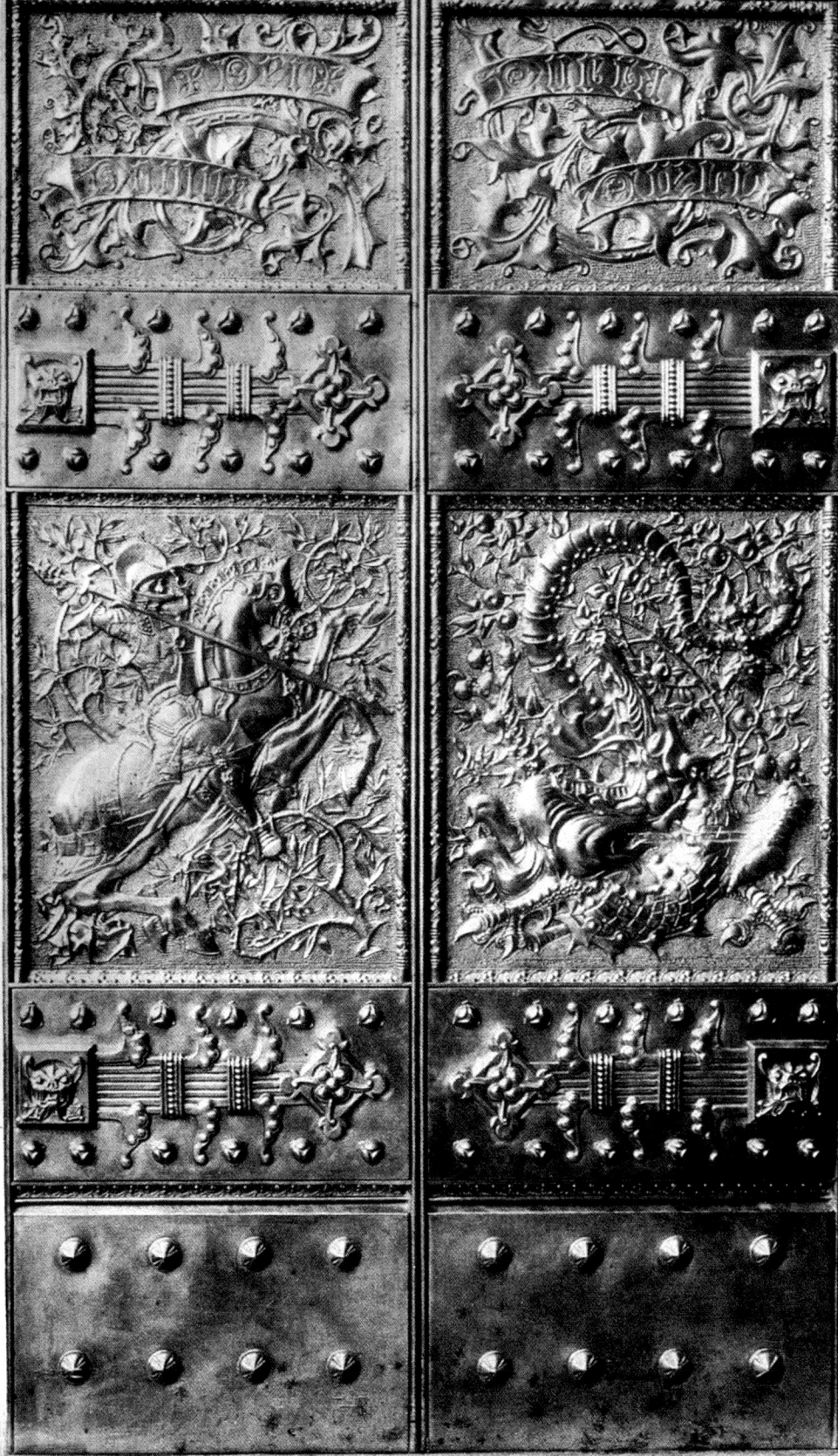

Comillas, the marquis's villa

At the end of the 19th century, the Cantabrian town of Comillas became the place to spend the summer. Indeed, once the *indià* (wealthy returnee from the West Indies) and shipowner Antonio López, Marquis of Comillas, – who hailed from this town but resided in Barcelona –, decided to implement a programme to lend his home town greater dignity, summer houses were progressively built that were frequented by everyone, from the aristocracy to the thriving industrial bourgeoisie of the day. Invited by the marquis, the royal family visited in the summers of 1881 and 1882. (Arnús, 1999, pp. 58-59). As a result, during those years, Comillas experienced momentous urban improvements such as the new ring road around the town, the reform of the port and the installation of public streetlighting, with twelve electric streetlamps powered by a steam engine. Antonio López had a palace built so he could spend the summers there with his family, as well as a pantheon chapel on his Sobrellano estate, following the death of his eldest son Antonio López Bru. Both buildings were designed by Joan Martorell Montells beginning in 1878 in the Central European neo-Gothic style.

Years later, when Father Tomàs Gómez proposed the Jesuits build a seminary for young people without resources, the Marquis of Comillas granted the religious order a significant financial endowment to erect the building. Father Miguel Alcalado was initially commissioned to design the project and he was succeeded by Joan Martorell. The death of the marquis in 1883 did not put a halt to the works. His son, Claudio López Bru, fulfilled his father's wishes and continued with the large-scale project that completed the town's transition from a small fishing village to an aristocratic summering spot.

Martorell designed a neo-Mudejar building based on the classical layout of a building with two porticoed courtyards on either side of the central body of the complex and a church at the back. The works for the seminary began on 20th May 1883 but lasted longer due to various liquidity problems experienced by Claudio López.

← Seminary in Comillas (1883-1896).
Door of Sant Jordi. Journal *Hispania*, 1902.

Upon the death of the architect Cristóbal Cascante, who had directed the works, the Marquis of Comillas commissioned Lluís Domènech i Montaner to continue the project in 1889. Domènech knew the López family and had even illustrated the cover of Mossèn Cinto Verdaguer's epic poem, *L'Atlàntida*, whose publication was entirely funded by Antonio López. However, it was the publisher Ramon Montaner i Vila's friendship with Claudio López Bru that probably brought Domènech into contact with the marquis.

At the seminary, Domènech lent importance to the will of his patron and integrated the constructive elements made by Martorell and Cascante into an unprecedented decorative programme. While the initial Martorell-Cascante phase was renowned for the understated sobriety of its surfaces, the refurbishment of the building, begun by Domènech in 1890, led to a radical change of course, with an aesthetic display in which all the decorative arts of *modernisme* converged. To make this possible, Domènech drew on the projects he had undertaken at the Castle of the Three Dragons in Barcelona, where he had set up different workshops to finish the building's decorative elements (Casanova, 2009, pp. 49-55). And these Barcelona workshops also produced the pieces used to complete the interiors of the Comillas Seminary, the Palau Montaner in Barcelona and the Casa Roura in Canet.

Domènech also drew up a set of structural measures that were used throughout the seminary building. He modified and emphasised the main facade by lending it more volume, framed the corners with small square towers and completed the central access with a bronze element in the flamboyant neo-Gothic style weighing almost three tons: the Door of Virtues (*Puerta de las Virtudes*), designed by Eusebi Arnau. The architect demolished the walls of the lobby designed by Martorell to let in more light, replaced the wooden staircase with a monumental stone one and created theatrical spaces of monumental visual exaltation, with arches, capitals, hanging fleurons, sculptures, and elements of cabinetry, stained glass and mural painting. Eusebi Arnau contributed all the details and sculptural figures that embellish the interior of the seminary and the zoomorphic pieces in the monumental coffered ceiling in the lobby, carved by Alfons Juyol and the Viladevall cabinetmakers; the mural paintings inside the religious premises are

by Eduard Llorens Masdeu, Joan Llimona and Josep Maria Tamburini and all the stained glass is by Antoni Rigalt Blanch.

To solve the constructive problems of the seminary church and eliminate water leaks, Domènech chose to clad the exterior walls with a ceramic design of the four evangelists in ochre tones with a metallic lustre, manufactured at La Ceramo in Valencia and at Pujol i Bausis in Esplugues de Llobregat. The classic flooring of the interior of the church is by Mario Maragliano and fulfils the desire for an ornamental and constructive, highly symbiotic confluence with the restoration of the Door of Saint George (*Puerta de San Jorge*) carried out by Valerio Testos Guimbao.

The works to embellish the seminary lasted until 1896 and overlapped with other commissions from the Marquis in the same town. Domènech created the *Monumento al Marqués* (1889-1892), begun by Cristòfol Cascante; the bronze tombstone in the pantheon chapel (Capilla Panteón, 1892); and some final work on the interior of the Palacio de Sobrellano.

In 1893, Claudio López wanted to promote the expansion and beautification of the town's cemetery and commissioned Domènech to carry out the renovation project. The architect went above and beyond the Marquis' expectations and built a stone wall that adapted to the lay of the land to completely surround the entire new premises, with details such as buttresses, crosses and pinnacles, and crowned the entrance with a large arch and a wrought iron gate, and added a guardian angel by Josep Llimona. Due to its artistic, aesthetic and almost psychological value, this sculpture never fails to impress when you enter the cemetery (Sama, 2013, pp. 107-111). Here, Domènech carried out a major project of scenographic interpretation exalting the historical and symbolic values of the older areas. He integrated the ruins of the former San Cristóbal church and pierced the walls with large arches to allow the seascape to be viewed from within the cemetery. Domènech ended up transforming the funerary space into a romantic, monumental complex, with clear Ruskinian influences and an entirely Wagnerian décor.

← Reus. Casa Rull (1900-1902) and Casa Gasull (1911-1916).

In 1898, Claudio López entrusted Domènech with the Piélago tomb (1898-1901) for the marquis' late brother-in-law, who had been manager of the Compañía Transatlántica. The architect designed a marble tomb shaped like a marine wave whose crest was ridden by an apocalyptic angel sculpted by Josep Llimona, and an ironwork cross inspired by the seven deadly sins wrought at the Masriera i Campins foundry in Barcelona. Domènech also designed the Tres Caños Fountain (1899) in the middle of town in honour of Joaquín de Piélago. It was commissioned by the people of Comillas to pay tribute to him for carrying out different improvement projects over the course of his life, such as the urbanisation of the rural road from Trasvía to Rioturbio, and the pipes and distribution of running water to the centre of Comillas.

Reus, Font de Rubinat's home town

In the late 19th century, Reus was one of the most important towns in Catalonia. The capital of Baix Camp county was second to Barcelona in terms of population and had become an economic powerhouse because of its dryland farming – vineyards, olives, almonds and hazelnuts – and exports. It also excelled in finance. This economic boom was evident in the progress of the city where, at the beginning of the century, old streets were renovated, sewerage systems were built, running water reached homes and a new electrical grid was installed. Reus was being modernised and this was accompanied by a process of urban expansion, with new, wider streets, where buildings intended for the emerging wealthy classes were constructed.

Lluís Domènech i Montaner went to Reus in the late 19th century at the invitation of the lawyer, pro-Catalan politician and bibliophile from Reus, Pau Font de Rubinat, the most prominent businessman of the day in the Baix Camp area. Domènech already knew the city. He been in contact with the Associació Catalanista de Reus since, as a leader of the early pro-Catalan movement, he had been president of the Catalanist Union and had been a driving force behind the first assembly of the organisation held in 1892 in Manresa (Sàiz, 2017, p. 67). He also knew Pau Font de Rubinat through their pro-Catalan activism, to the point that he became one of Domènech's trusted men at the Bases de Manresa Assembly. This rapport led to the second Catalanist Assembly being held in Reus, in the Hall of Justice. (Sàiz, 2019, pp. 89-92)

Thus, when in November of 1896 some people from Reus – among them Pau Font – decided to set up a company by the name of "Manicomio de Reus" to build a psychiatric centre for the town, Font de Rubinat did not hesitate to ask Domènech to do the project.

The architect accepted the commission and some months later, submitted a proposal for a modern psychiatric facility along the lines of the leading hospitals of the time, such as London's Saint Thomas, Hospital and other hospitals with pavilions that were being built in France, Germany and also the United States.

The model construction of the Pere Mata facility was key in Domènech's creative career, given that a large part of the residential works he would design in Reus would be commissioned by shareholders of the Sociedad Manicomio de Reus. Domènech designed projects for some of the psychiatric institution's partners, including the notary Pere Rull, the lawyer Pau Font de Rubinat, the merchant Joaquim Navàs and the doctor Emili Briansó.

Casa Rull (1900-1902), on Carrer Sant Joan, is a singular work by Domènech. Pere Rull i Trilla was born in Falset, Priorat and moved to Reus in 1883, after obtaining a post as notary there. Rull was one of the founders of the Associació Catalanista de Reus, together with Bernat Torroja, Eduard Toda, Pau Font de Rubinat, Ramon Vidiella and others. Domènech designed a home for Rull with an extremely interesting façade in exposed brick ornamented with medievalising elements and touches. (Alcalde, 2014, pp. 11-15)

The Casa Navàs (1901-1908) was another emblematic project. It stands in the town's "nerve centre": the market square, the Mercadal. Domènech was attempting to achieve a total work of architecture, and the project that most approaches this is the Casa Navàs in Reus.

At Casa Navàs, Domènech brought together and deployed his entire ideological, technical and artistic panoply. Joaquim Navàs had amassed a significant fortune and decided to commission the architect with a residential building with a shop and warehouse on the ground floor. Due to the project's complexity, Casa Navàs was a long-running project.

Domènech also worked for his friend, Pau Font de Rubinat, who commissioned works such as the project for irrigation canals for the Mas Misericòrdia gardens as well as his private library (1908-1910) on Carrer Galianes. The Pau Font library was remarkable for the decorative design of the entire interior space, of great height, with wooden shelving on two levels lining several walls, different sculptural elements such as the helical staircases and the fireplace, attributed to Eusebi Arnau. Also interesting were the stained-glass windows and the sculptural frame to the door accessing the library from the inner courtyard.

Domènech also designed the Casa Gasull, on Carrer Sant Joan. In 1910, Fèlix Gasull Roig decided to construct a new building as a warehouse for his olive oil stock and two flats on the upper floor. The works began in 1911, and by 1914 the warehouse was already active but the two flats were not finished until 1916. Casa Gasull, however, is not a very Domenechian work, displaying more of a *noucentista* style than a *modernista* one, with smooth facades and hardly any reliefs, which certainly corresponds more to the style of his son, Pere Domènech i Roura than to his own.

The Margenat mausoleum-chapel (1905) in the Reus Municipal Cemetery is also the work of Domènech i Montaner. It was commissioned by Josep Margenat i Fàbregas following the death of his eldest son, Josep Margenat i Fernández (1882-1905). Inside the funerary building, Domènech designed a reticular vault combining ribbed and lierne vaults. The walls are clad in yellowish marble in an alternately protruding and recessed pattern and a mosaic of Roman-style tesserae and tiles with light blue Maltese crosses. (Alcalde, 2014, pp. 167-170)

At the same time that Lluís Domènech was working on the warehouse project for the Jover i Serra factory in Canet de Mar (1909-1910) – ten years earlier he had designed their production plant (1899-1900) –, he also proposed building the Cinema Kursaal in Reus (1908-1909). The Kursaal was commissioned by Dr Emili Briansó, although the plans ended up being signed by

Pere Domènech i Roura, who also collaborated in the design and directed the works. For the Kursaal, Lluís Domènech designed an imposing brick facade, with elements in common with those of the cooperative winery in Espluga de Francolí.

The Llopis warehouse (1911) in the Raval de Sant Pere district rounds off the typological diversity of Domènech's works in Reus. The architect designed Joan Llopis Fontana's almond and hazelnut warehouse as a high-capacity building with an irregular floor plan and three façades. The building has been greatly altered, but one can still see how the interior was conceived as a wide, open space without dividing walls. Although it was a minor work, Domènech also intervened in the Llopis residence, which was just across from the warehouse.

In Reus, Domènech designed other architectural projects that were not built. In 1900, for instance, the Societat El Círcol de Reus commissioned him to design a noble staircase for the organisation's headquarters on Plaça Prim. Domènech presented a project for a monumental staircase very similar to the one he had built shortly before in the entrance to the Casa Thomas on Carrer Mallorca, in Barcelona. The monumental project for the Teatre Circ (1899), which was also commissioned by the Círcol and likewise failed to materialise, was a project for a large-capacity theatre hall with a circular layout that he designed with a series of Catalan vaults supported by pillars and converging in a large dome crowned with a lantern in the centre. (Alcalde, 2015, p. 152)

By way of conclusion

Domènech brought *modernisme* to the three municipalities, which are an integral part of his creative oeuvre with the common denominator of modernity. And it is thanks to this parallel renovation process, carried out in the late 19th century and the early 20th, that Canet, Comillas and Reus are today towns that are the repositories of Domènech's highly interesting, important and exceptional legacy, both qualitatively and quantitatively; an exploratory body of work in the most explicit sense that reveals all the creative elements of identity that contributed to forming the architectural corpus of the father of Catalan *modernisme*. The three municipalities interact as if they were communicating vessels of Domènech's creativity, which form the vertices of a triangle where the precedents for the most plethoric and authentic Lluís Domènech i Montaner were set. The field of experimentation of Domènech i Montaner's great works in Barcelona, which are now World Heritage Sites, such as the former Hospital de Sant Pau and the Palau de la Música, would not be what they are and, above all, look the way they do, without these peripheral precedents.

And it was also in the towns of Canet, Reus and Comillas where Lluís Domènech projected his genius to a degree in which the artist far surpassed the architect, attaining the creative zenith of the total artist. At the Pere Mata Institute, Domènech placed at the service of the ill what had not yet been fully formulated, not even by the medical establishment of the time. In Reus, Domènech discovered his facet as a sublime architect and at the same time, the psychological function of art. He realised that the supreme balance of beauty can help counteract the disorder of mental imbalance. The terrible darkness of the disease must be countered by the exquisite correction of art taken to its greatest heights, as perceived when entering the distinguished guests' pavilion for the first time. And the same impact is perceived under the fine coffered ceiling of the Comillas Seminary, where the incoming rays of light give the premises an atmosphere that is hard to put into words. Or in the great hall of the castle of Santa Florentina in Canet, whose atmospheric lighting, sifted by the colours of the stained-glass windows, subliminally transports us back in time.

These are the testing grounds that Domènech went on to use as a model for his mature works and major projects carried out afterwards in Barcelona.

Architect of *Modernisme*
The most significant buildings

The Montaner i Simon publishing house (1879-1885)

Café and restaurant for the Universal Exhibition (1887-1892)

Palau Montaner (1889-1897)

Cemetery in Comillas (1893-1899)

Casa Thomas (1895-1912)

Castell de Santa Florentina (1896-1912)

Institut Pere Mata (1897-1912)

Refurbishment of the Fonda España (1900-1903)

Gran Hotel in Palma (1901-1903)

Casa Navàs (1901-1907)

Hospital de la Santa Creu i Sant Pau (1902-1920)

Casa Lleó i Morera (1903-1905)

Palau de la Música Catalana (1905-1909)

Casa Consol Fabra de Fuster (1908-1911)

Can Rocosa (1905-1906) **and Casa Domènech** (1918) **in Canet de Mar**

← Palau de la Música Catalana.
Detail of the central lantern dome.

Montaner i Simon: the publishing house that resembled a bullring

1879-1885

Núria Homs

"Barcelona, 358, Carrer d'Aragó, between Passeig de Gràcia and Rambla de Catalunya: the Dante publishing house. An early example of Catalan art nouveau, or *modernisme*, a milestone on the city's monumental plan, and a landmark that is rigorously referenced in foreign tourist guidebooks, one of which, from England, mistakes it for a bullring, to its eternal shame." (Moncada, n.d.)

These are the words Jesús Moncada (Mequinensa, 1941- Barcelona, 2005) used to describe the headquarters of the publishing house, Montaner i Simon, transformed into the fictional firm Dante, in his unfinished novel that gave an imaginary account of the changes in fortune of the publishers where he once worked, which had been founded more than a hundred years earlier. In the 1860s, Ramon Montaner i Vila (Canet de Mar, 1832-Barcelona, 1921) and Francesc Simon i Font (Barcelona, 1843-1923) founded a publishing house in Barcelona. Montaner i Simon soon became the most important publishers in Spain, in terms of output and the quality of its publications. It was the main exporter of books to America and signed agreements with publishing companies on the continent to become its subsidiaries. The publishing house was a shining example of the way art and industry could coexist harmoniously. It used industrialised printing methods to publish painstakingly crafted, deluxe art editions. Some of its most outstanding works were weighty tomes published in multiple volumes. They included the *Historia general del arte*, the *Biblioteca universal ilustrada*, the *Diccionario enciclopédico hispano-americano de ciencias, artes y literatura*, a book on world geography, *Geografía universal*, and the journals, *La ilustración artística* and *El salón de la moda*. (Castellano, 2008; Llanas, 2004; Llanas, 2005)

During the early years, Montaner i Simon had its headquarters in a number of buildings. In 1879, Ramon Montaner and Francesc Simon purchased a plot of land on Carrer Aragó in Barcelona, between Passeig de Gràcia and Rambla de Catalunya, with the intention of building premises on the site which they could use on a permanent basis. This was the first major period of growth in the new city expansion scheme, or Eixample, after the central government finally acceded to the repeated requests from the municipal council to demolish the ancient city walls in 1854. Ramon Montaner commissioned his nephew, the young architect Lluís Domènech i Montaner (Barcelona, 1849-1923), to design the building. Although Domènech i Montaner had signed the contract for his first professional project, the villa, the Torre Simon (Sàiz, 2013), a year earlier, Montaner i Simon publishing house, which was built between 1879 and 1881 (Homs, 2015), was his first project of note.

Style and structure of the building

The Montaner i Simon publishing house exemplifies the shift from the characteristic eclectic architecture of the 19th century to a new style, known in Catalonia as *modernisme*. Lluís Domènech i Montaner and Antoni Gaudí, who built the Casa Vicens on Carrer Carolines in Barcelona between 1883 and 1885, laid the architectural foundations that would define the two different paths this new movement would follow: Gaudí embodied an expressionistic trend, characterised by exuberant forms, while Domènech i Montaner preferred a rationalist approach in a search for maximum efficiency in spaces and materials.

← The Montaner i Simon publishing house on Carrer Aragó with the railway line running below ground. Unión Postal Universal. Missé Hermanos, Barcelona, c. 1920. Courtesy of Rossend Casanova.

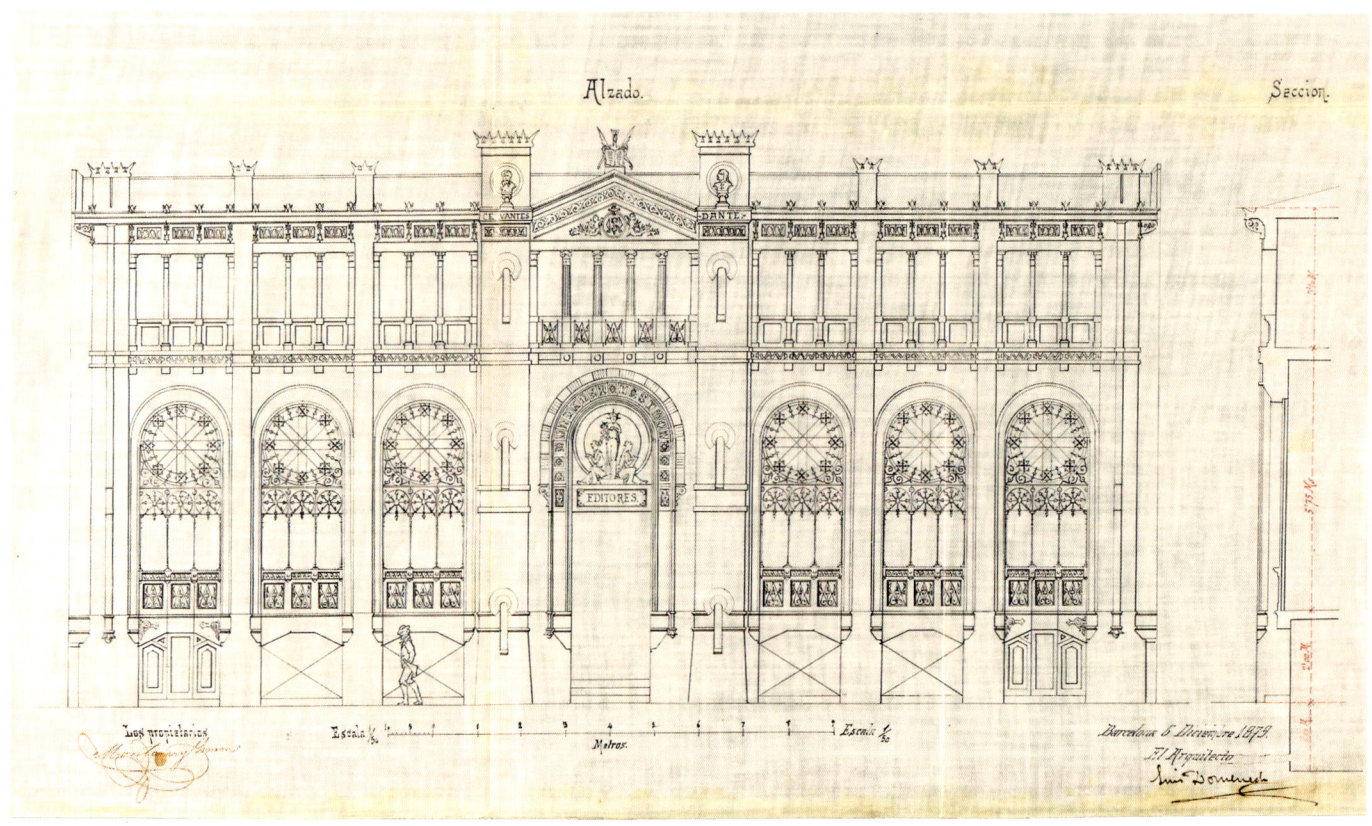

Elevation and section of the main façade (1879).
Arxiu Municipal Contemporani de Barcelona.

Like many buildings from the early years of the Eixample, the Montaner i Simon publishing house is three storeys high. The façade has been designed as a harmonious network of vertical and horizontal elements. It is divided into three distinct sections, one in the centre and a symmetrical section on either side. The main entrance is flanked by two square towers, while the side sections are divided by pilasters that split the façade into seven vertical sections. The façade has three horizontal sections, corresponding to the three levels of the building: the street entrances and the iron grilles on the lower part of the façade, a section with tall round arches and, finally, a row of windows on the top floor, three on either side of the central section.

An aerial view reveals the solid, rather conventional structure of the building overlooking Carrer Aragó, with its flat roof; the adjacent modern industrial unit, which had originally had a skylight to allow natural light into the ground floor and semi-basement; and a third, lower section in the courtyard of the block.

The building was the first one in the city to use exposed brick – a ductile and lightweight material that was widely used in industry – and iron, which could be used to build bigger, open-plan spaces due to its durability and lightness. In addition to these materials, glass was used to fill in spaces. It was the perfect medium to create the different hues of colour that can be seen in the windows on the façade and former warehouse. It also allowed natural light into the building. Despite the use of predominantly industrial materials, the structure of the building resembles a palazzo with a central courtyard.

The decorative elements on the façade

The façade combines classical influences (the central doorway and the two side sections) and Muslim ones (the use of brick, Mozarabic-style elements and geometrical compositions redolent of arabesque decorations).

Domènech i Montaner decided to alter his original 1879 project for the façade after building work had begun. The first important element is the brick frieze below the row of horizontal windows on the top floor that runs along the entire façade, covering the pilasters and the two towers. The frieze, which is decorated with ornamental tiles with a white background, forms a linking thread between the curved rhythm of the picture windows on the ground floor and the square windows on the top floor. These windows take up the original idea of including columns on the façade, placing them subtly between the glass panes: a double metal bar hints at the shape of the column, while a single one marks its divisions. The Ionic volutes are made from wrought iron and, together with the geometrical designs on the upper part of the window, bring to mind Arabic decorative motifs.

The top of the building is inspired by medieval art and architecture: the crenellations, which usually help to reinforce the pilasters, serve a purely decorative purpose here, and the helmet and angel playing the trumpet are a symbolic representation of tradition – the helmet refers to Catalonia's glorious past as a nation – and modernity – the angel announces the publication of a new book. (Casanova, 2000)

There is also another series of symbolic elements on the façade that emphasise the industrial modernity of the publishing house and the quality of its publications: there are three terracotta busts below the helmet and angel playing the trumpet made by Rossend Nobas i Vallbé (Subirachs, 1994). They are standing on classical-style pillars depicting three great literary figures: Dante, Cervantes and Milton, in tribute to the classics Montaner i Simon were publishing at the time (Rogent, 1897). These sculptures are accompanied by four plaques bearing the names of the geographer Malte-Brun, the historian Lafuente and the astronomer Secchi. The name inside the fourth plaque has been missing since the end of the 19th century and we do not know the name of its dedicatee. There are three cogwheel-shaped carvings below the plaques, which hint at the mechanisation of the industrial era. There is an eagle, or phoenix, inside the central wheel symbolising the national resurgence of Catalonia (Sàiz, 2013). It stands on an open book surmounted by a star. The cogwheel is the emblem of the publishing house, and the star crowning the eagle may suggest the success of the company. The name of the publishers, Montaner i Simon, can be read in Gothic letters decorated with plant motifs around the archivolt above the main door. There are a number of decorative elements on the façade made of iron, such as the grilles outside the semi-basement, which are decorated with eagles made from cut-out sheet metal, two intertwined snakes and floral motifs; the balustrades and windows set inside the round arches; the balustrades on the rooftop with their plant motifs; and the Mozarabic-style grilles decorated with floral motifs inside the openings in the towers that flank the main entrance.

The layout of the space

As the façade reveals, the building consists of three superimposed floors: the semi-basement, main floor and first, or top, floor. The first two floors had very high ceilings underpinned by 6-metre-high cast-iron columns and were the main, stand-out spaces inside the building. The top floor is much smaller and was used for in-house purposes. Initially it served as a studio – most probably for photography and producing collotypes (Rogent, 1897) – and, subsequently, as offices. The entrance lobby, which was solely intended for use by the public, had a metal staircase in the centre, which led down to the semi-basement, and staircases on either side that led to the main floor. An octagonal structure made with white glass set inside an iron border rose up to the dome overlooking the rooftop (Marlí, 2010). This dome, which cannot be seen from the street, allowed natural light into the building. The main entrance had two doors: an outer one made of wood, which survives today; and an inner one, containing white panes of glass with an iron border, which was removed when the first refurbishment and redesign of the building was being carried out between 1986 and 1990. The service entrance and the staff entrance were on the left- and right-hand side of the main door and led straight to the lower floor.

There were counters on the main floor landing (Álvarez, 2015) to deal with visitors' enquiries. The landing led to the offices of the company owners and the square space with the warehouse containing the finished publications at the back, and the packing and dispatch room and the accounts and cashier's department on one side. (Fuchshuber, 1992) There was a large opening in the middle of the floor surrounded by an iron balustrade decorated with two points of a star interspersed with wheels featuring a plethora of plant motifs and enclosed by two friezes, one at the top and another at the bottom, with floral designs (this design is repeated on the balustrade of the rooftop overlooking the street and the octagonal opening on the first floor), which connected this floor with the semi-basement. The printing machines were housed in the centre of the semi-basement, as this was the place where there was the greatest amount of light. The typesetting equipment, the bindery and machines where the paper was prepared for printing were placed around the printing machines. The space housing the steam boiler was at the back of the room (Rogent, 1897). The chimney, which was built at the beginning of 1882, was 22 metres high (Arxiu Municipal Administratiu, Barcelona. File no. 345.528). The workspaces on the main floor were divided by wooden structures and partitions, however, the semi-basement had no partitions or dividing walls. (Fuchshuber, 1992)

The publisher's new premises were equipped with powerful industrial machinery, including twelve typesetting machines, six lithographic printing presses, a collotype press, three roll presses, a stereotype printing section and a photography section. Some two hundred and forty workers handled this major infrastructure, along with the draughtsmen and engravers. (Cabana, 2001; Castellano, 2008; Llanas, 2004; Llanas, 2007)

The new owners

Following the deaths of its founders at the beginning of the 1920s, the publishing house was passed on to their heirs, Júlia de Montaner, Ricard de Capmany and Santiago Simon, and, later, Ramon de Capmany i Montaner, who continued in the same editorial line as his predecessors. In the 1940s, Montaner i Simon began outsourcing the printing of its books and used the basement as a warehouse. In 1951, the square opening on the first floor was filled in with glass blocks. (Arxiu Municipal Administratiu, Barcelona. File no. 31.256)

José María González Porto (Torreboredo, 1895-Mexico City, 1975), the former representative for the publishing house in Latin America, took charge of the company towards 1950 (González Porto, 1950). Under his management, Montaner i Simon mostly published dictionaries and encyclopaedias, as well as technical handbooks. A few years after González Porto's death, the heirs sold the company and it went bankrupt in 1981.

The Fundació Antoni Tàpies

Antoni Tàpies first visited the Montaner i Simon publishing house in 1984, and, although the building had been standing empty for three years and its original structure had been damaged, he immediately realised that the extraordinary spatial and structural qualities of the building would make it ideal to house the foundation he had set up that same year, with the help of Barcelona City Council – the owners of the building – the Catalan government and the Ministry of Culture. The Fundació Antoni Tàpies opened in 1990 after a major refurbishment of the building.

The restoration project was undertaken by Roser Amadó and Lluís Domènech Girbau between 1986 and 1990. The building's new use as a museum was superimposed onto the original structure, while respecting the original features. The existing floors were reorganised taking into account the new requirements. The first floor was still used as office space. On the main floor, the shelves from the former warehouse were preserved and are now used for the books in the foundation's library. The opening which connects this floor with the one below was also preserved. The semi-basement became the main public area due to its ease of access and spacious proportions. It was remodelled using fixed, parallel panels that divide the space into continuous sections, and an auditorium was built at the back. A basement was finally dug out in order to provide more warehouse space and galleries. With regards to access, new staircases were designed connecting the different areas. A terrace was built above the auditorium to re-establish the original exit into the courtyard, which had been out of use due to the nearby buildings. In order to ensure the galleries were well lit, the architects decided to replace the central skylight that allowed sunlight in with a new roofing system, a skylight underpinned by columns. (Amadó and Domènech, 1988; Amadó and Domènech, 1989-1990)

The building was hemmed in between the two side walls of the adjacent buildings. Antoni Tàpies made the sculpture entitled *Núvol i cadira* (Cloud and Chair, 1990), which stands on the top of the building, with the technical assistance of Pere Casanovas, with the intention of making the building higher and to underscore its new identity. The sculpture is made from silver anodised aluminium and stainless steel mesh. It represents a chair – a recurrent motif in Tàpies' work – protruding from a vast cloud. Seen in this context, it alludes to a meditative attitude, reflection and aesthetic contemplation (Borja-Villel, 1990). The sculpture does not dominate the façade. Instead, it seems to fly over it in order to avoid taking away its personality. It has become an emblem of the foundation. (Tàpies, 2004)

The foundation closed again in 2008, to embark on a second refurbishment phase to make it fully compliant with current accessibility, safety, evacuation and fire-protection guidelines. This second intervention, carried out by Ábalos-Sentkiewicz Arquitectos, remodelled the exhibition spaces in order to re-establish the building's original industrial appearance, which is particularly apparent in the semi-basement where the vertical panels were removed. The steps leading from the street to the semi-basement were replaced and the museum entrance was redesigned to improve the reception area and bookshop. The refurbishment also reclaimed the second floor of the museum (where the offices were located) for public use. This involved moving the offices to a new site: a brand-new two-storey building, similar in height to the adjacent buildings inside the courtyard, above the auditorium, which has now been converted into a multipurpose space.

The two renovation projects in the building that is now home to the Fundació Antoni Tàpies, which was named a Cultural Asset of National Interest (BCIN) in 1997, have sought to respect the innovative approaches to dealing with the light and the layout of the spaces which the architect Lluís Domènech i Montaner applied to this project and his previous ones.

Stained-glass window and skylight in the lobby.

Name of the publishing house around the archivolt above the main door.

← Façade with Antoni Tàpies' sculpture
Núvol i cadira (Cloud and Chair, 1990) on the top.

Grille on the basement level of the building with the emblem of commerce.

→ Angel playing the trumpet on top of the helmet, the busts of Dante, Cervantes and Milton by the sculptor Rossend Nobas, and the shield of the publishing house set inside a cogwheel, the symbol of industry.

The Montaner i Simon publishing house

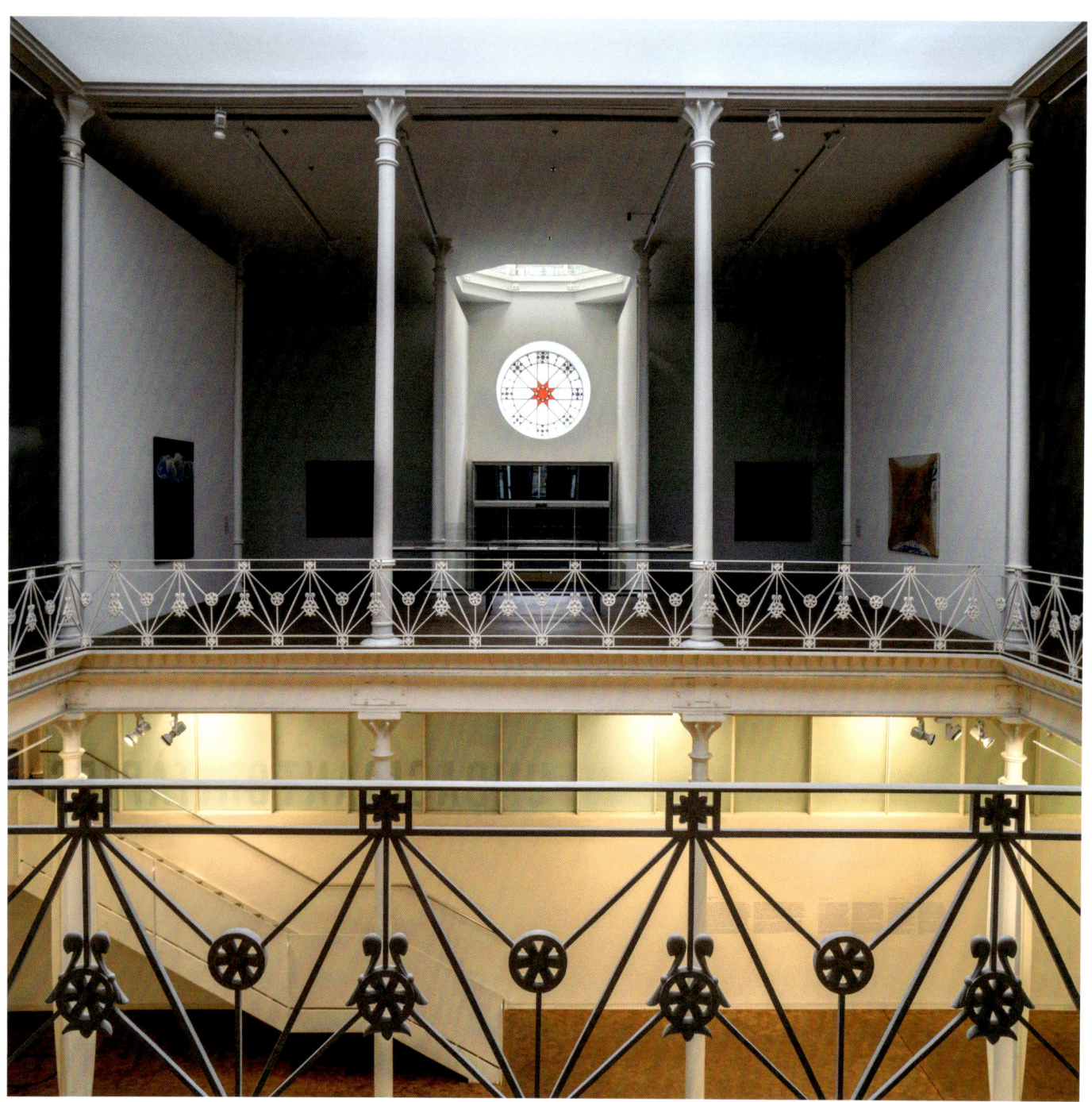
Interior seen from the gallery.

Basement.

Skylight

Library.

Library, the former warehouse at the publishers.

Café and restaurant for the Universal Exhibition

1887-1892

Rossend Casanova

This building, popularly known as the Castell dels Tres Dragons – or Castle of the Three Dragons – after a play of the same name by Frederic Soler, was the café and restaurant for the 1888 Barcelona Universal Exhibition. It was intended to be a permanent building (unlike the exhibition halls which were ephemeral structures) and an exemplary showcase that would reveal to the world, and preserve for future generations, the arts and crafts of the day in Catalonia and the rest of Spain. Lluís Domènech i Montaner's design combines the magnificence of medieval buildings with a schematic neo-Gothic style, which were the defining features of his architecture, and hinted at the Catalan art nouveau, or *modernista*, style he would develop some years later.

The Castell dels Tres Dragons has had a chequered history associated with the complex nature of the structure and the fact that the building has been used for different purposes (Casanova, 2009). It occupies the western corner of the Parc de la Ciutadella and replaced the café designed by Josep Fontserè, who also created the gardens. The project's developers, Barcelona City Council, decided that the new building should continue to serve this purpose – going to cafés was a favourite pastime of well-to-do Barcelonians – and include it as part of the works to improve and finish the park and turn it into a useful space. The building was earmarked for use as a banqueting room, because city hall did not have the necessary amenities to host these kinds of celebrations. The main entrance is inside the park on an avenue of white poplar trees and overlooks Passeig Sant Joan – the new artery on the right-hand side of the Eixample district. One side of the building leads directly onto Carrer de la Princesa, the street that leads to Carrer de Jaume I, via Plaça de l'Àngel, which, in turn, leads to Plaça de Sant Jaume – then known as Plaça de la Constitució – the site of city hall. The building only occupied half the assigned plot and left room for a terrace that looks as if it is both inside and outside the park, thereby establishing a dialogue with the gardens and the urban surroundings.

The building of the café and restaurant was fraught with problems from the very outset. Some of them were caused by chance events – such as the workers' strike of 1887, which had a major impact on building work – and others by financial difficulties, as the cost far exceeded the initial budget. This resulted in frequent arguments between the architect and the executive committee of the exhibition.

A singular architecture

The building has a rectangular ground plan with square towers on the corners. An elevation view of the building reveals that each tower is different at the top, thereby lending the building its singular appearance. The structure of the building is unusual and consists of a double-brick wall. The outer one features exposed brickwork and the inner wall is covered with a painted-stucco render. The double-wall structure includes double columns and double arches in the openings, and was designed to make the walls with the towers on each corner more stable. This creates a parallelepiped-type structure that is covered by a low-pitched roof underpinned by four large arches, joined together in twos. They can be seen from inside the building and rest on sturdy pillars. They remind us of the stone arches in Gothic buildings, such as the grand chamber, the Saló de Cent, inside Barcelona City Hall. Domènech brought them into the modern era by replacing the old, heavy stone with new, lightweight rolled iron, which also lent a new, and evocative, expressivity to the material. The connection between the histo-

← Castell dels Tres Dragons, c. 1930.
Photograph by Josep Brangulí.
Arxiu Fotogràfic de Barcelona.

ry of the past and the modernity of the present is evident in the Gothic style and its modern version, between city hall and the café and restaurant, between solemn events and official banquets.

Domènech took other examples from the architecture of the past and gave them a modern twist in his building. They are mostly contributions to the history of art from the Iberian Peninsula. In the café on the ground floor, the double-wall structure and row of columns is reminiscent of one of the courtyards at the Alhambra in Granada. The columns are surmounted by capitals, which are replicas of the ones in the Santa María la Blanca synagogue in Toledo (clay reproduction by Cosme Maurell and plaster copies by Joan Olibé). Above them, Domènech built a series of pointed arches that resemble the doors of Saint Stephen and the Palms in the mosque in Cordoba. On the ceilings inside the towers, he built replicas of the mihrab and maqsurah from the same mosque.

Domènech built terraces on both sides of the café to extend the space. He constructed a tower on the biggest one, which featured a replica of the crossed-arch dome from the maqsurah. Although it may seem irreverent, the space was used as the café toilets and powder room. A bridge connects the tower to the kitchen, which had a service lift to carry the dishes up to the restaurant. The restaurant was in a separate space on the first floor and was reached by an imperial staircase. The space was as high as the entire building and lit by an impressive stained-glass window. The restaurant had a separate entrance to allow it to hold banquets for the municipal corporation or be hired out for private events.

The interior of the restaurant was originally painted sky blue. The double columns led to the side terraces which were covered by awnings. They were decorated with stained-glass windows on a floral theme. The rooms inside the towers were used as private dining rooms and ventilated by innovative squat windows, instead of the traditional vertical ones. The grand dining room inside the restaurant features a balcony in the form of a gallery that runs around the entire perimeter of the second floor. In addition to breaking the cathedral-like verticality of the space, it connects the different towers and access points leading to the bandstand, where the municipal band would provide musical entertainment.

When viewed from the outside, we can see the building materials, such as iron and exposed brick, were applied directly onto the surface and are devoid of any ornamentation. Domènech does not seek to conceal them and leaves them exposed to view. The composition of the exterior side walls reminds us of the Gothic Doge's Palace in Venice, lightweight and with openings at the base, and opaque and solid at the top. These walls were floodlit at night by electric lamps.

A large team of artisans and artists worked on the Castell dels Tres Dragons, as well as other projects for the exhibition and buildings by Domènech. Particularly noteworthy were the ceramic crenellations by Magí Fita, the outside awnings by Pau Estapé, the stained glass by Antoni Rigalt, and the drawings on the coats of arms on the outer walls by Joan Llimona and Alexandre de Riquer, which were produced in glazed ceramics at the Pujol i Bausis factory in Esplugues de Llobregat (Casanova, 2006, pp. 71-80) based on a pattern also designed by Josep Llimona. Only some of the panels were manufactured. None of the interior panels, representing allegories of arts and trades in different places at different times, came to fruition. They were designed by the painter and interior designer Ferran Xumetra. They were to be sgraffitoed onto the walls by the company Saumell i Vilaró. (Bru, 2019, pp. 18-41)

Delays in building work caused great annoyance among the executive committee. When they saw that Domènech wasn't meeting the deadlines or requirements, they made him leave the building just as it was. This angered him and he resigned. He was replaced by his assistant Josep Forteza, who worked for a month to complete the necessary work to enable the café and restaurant to open to the public on 17th August, four months after the exhibition had opened. Many features were begun but remained unfinished. These included the interior coats of arms that were to be rendered in sgraffito work. Only one of them, representing a sculpture of two clay lions by Josep Llimona and Antoni Vilanova, had been carved and placed on the walls. The large coat of arms intended for the corner of the room, depicting two dragons holding a shield, also by Vilanova, was never put in place. The most notable one was the tower, the Torre de l'Homenatge, which was never completed, and the inexistent exterior ceramic decoration that was to cover the lintels above the balconies and windows. (Casanova, 2002, pp. 155-174)

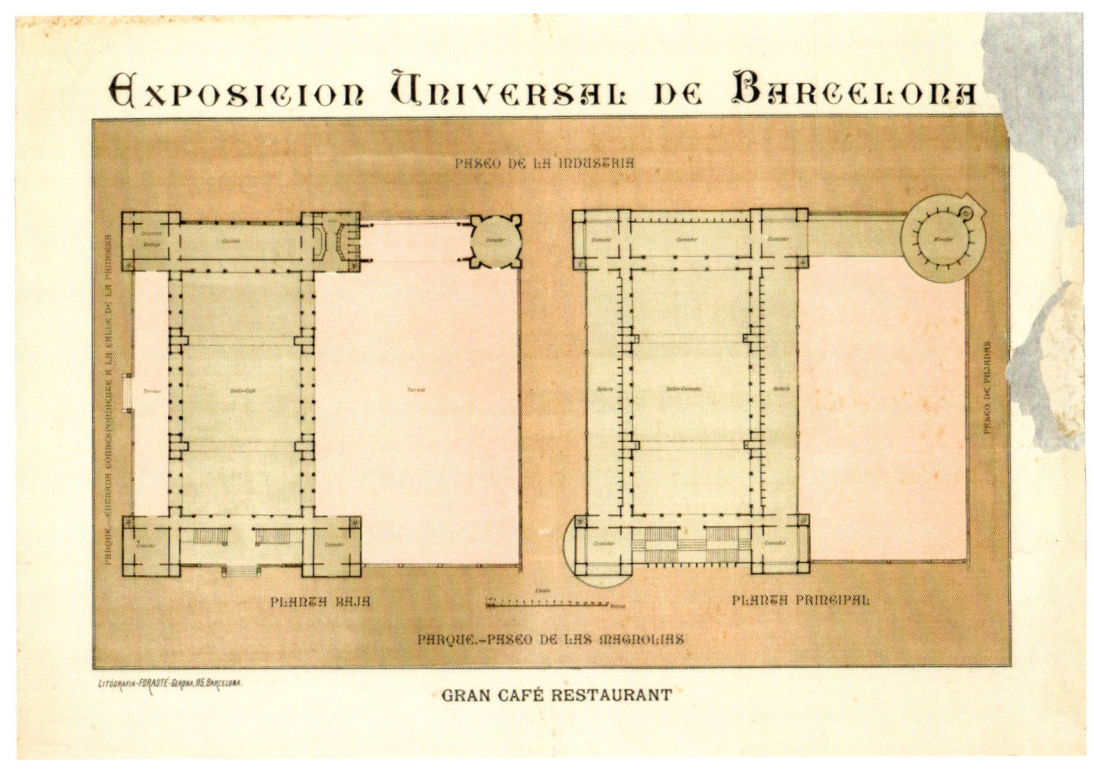

Floor plan of the café and restaurant published in the magazine *La Exposición* (1887). Arxiu Històric de la Ciutat de Barcelona.

Original capital inspired by the ones inside Santa María la Blanca, Toledo.

Period postcard of Santa María la Blanca, Toledo.

From a café to a museum: the myth of the Castell dels Tres Dragons

During the exhibition, the building served its intended purpose. The café served drinks and light meals throughout the day and the restaurant served lunches and dinners. The restaurant was run by the restaurateur Martí Pagès, who enjoyed a great reputation in the city and had a restaurant on La Rambla, in front of the opera house, the Liceu. The prestigious florist, Ramon Oliva, was in charge of the floral decorations on the tables and inside the building, depending on the occasion, and particularly the candelabra on the balustrades of the balcony and gallery and the chandeliers hanging from them.

The restaurant hosted a number of banquets, some of them for four hundred diners. The most noteworthy included the one for the French exhibitors, the one for the king of Portugal and the closing banquet hosted by the royal commission for the people in charge of the exhibition, the consular corps and authorities. When the exhibition was over, the leaseholder packed up the furniture, which included Thonet bentwood chairs, and the other fixtures and fittings. The building remained closed for a time until the city council decided to finish it. The exhibition had given impetus to exhibition culture and brought to light the fact that Barcelona needed a large space to display the historic collections it had amassed over the centuries. Then, quite unexpectedly, the use and function of the building changed when the decision was taken to use it to house the city's history museum, the Museu de la Història. Somehow, Domènech and the developers were reconciled and he was commissioned to finish the building and convert it into a municipal amenity (Domènech, 1892, pp. 1661-1663). Domènech chose the young architect Antoni Maria Gallissà, who had been a student of his at the Barcelona School of Architecture, as his assistant, and entrusted him with creating four studios for the remaining building work: the metalworker's, where the sheet-metal decorations would be completed, directed by the company Batalla y Cía.; the locksmith's, run by Bartolomé Domènech; the workshop responsible for the repoussé work, run by the company Malagrida i Casellas; and the mould-making and modelling studio that produced the decorative elements, set up by the company Oliva i Martí. These companies took care of the building finishes, particularly the top of the Torre de l'Homenatge and the surface ornamentations. Domènech also took advantage of the opportunity and asked them to make pieces for the other projects he was working on at the time in Barcelona, Canet de Mar and Comillas. Domènech was paying for private buildings with public money and this irregular situation led to him being reported by the city council. This resulted in him giving up the project: this time, for good. The companies that had won the tender were submitting invoices for work, covering up the fact that subcontracted collaborators were taking part and had enabled Domènech to conceal the works by the sculptor Eusebi Arnau and the ironsmith Francesc Tiestos, who were working at the time on other buildings, including the Pontifical Seminary in Comillas and the Palau Montaner.

The administrative process prevented this state of affairs from coming to light and it was only mentioned in a few written documents, most notably in the article Domènech wrote years later in *La Renaixensa* paying tribute to Antoni Maria Gallissà, who had died prematurely at the age of 42 (Domènech, 1903). Domènech looked back on his friend and colleague's life, describing their experiences at the Castell dels Tres Dragons: the shared processes, the acquired expertise and the results achieved. After the years of ostracism endured by Catalonia's home-grown art nouveau movement, *modernisme* – of which Domènech was the main exponent – the matter was forgotten until half a century later, when Alexandre Cirici revisited it in his book *El Arte Modernista catalán*. It describes the events as a great feat and compares them with the experiments of William Morris with the impactful title "el Taller del Castell dels Tres Dragons" – the workshop at the Castell dels Tres Dragons – (Casanova, 2019, pp. 8-25). This is how the legend began. Cirici presented the workshop as a unique experiment that was unparalleled in the history of Spanish art and sought to revive the decorative arts of the past to apply them to nascent *modernisme* (Cirici, 1951, pp. 203-204). A doctoral thesis defended in 2002 (Casanova, 2002) demythologises this idea on the grounds that subsequent historiographical studies had overestimated the importance of the workshops because they had not consulted any documents. The workshop studios were only active for eight months and produced very little work, most of it for the Torre de l'Homenatge. Different artists and artisans took part, including the aforementioned Francesc Tiesto, who had been entrusted with the project for the doors of the Palau Montaner, and Eusebi Arnau, who presented his ideas for the sculptures at the Pontifical Seminary in Comillas at the workshop. The controversy surrounding Domènech led him to abandon the project in late 1893.

Torre de l'Homenatge.

Nevertheless, the Museu de la Història was the first cultural amenity in the city where the architect of the building had also been responsible for organising the collection displays.

An overused building

The Museu de la Història was open from 1892 to 1896 and showcased numerous pieces from the municipal collections, which were arranged according to the logic of the time and following existing European models (Casanova, 2001, pp. 231-242). All the collections were grouped together in sections, regardless of their value, and not in chronological order. The collections of smaller pieces, including scientific instruments, prehistoric objects, jewellery, enamelware, clocks, coins, medals and repoussé work, were displayed inside the towers. Stone and marble pieces were placed in the courtyard as they could withstand the elements. Sculptures, furniture and carriages were displayed on the ground floor, in the former café, and furniture, bronzes, ceramics and ironwork were on show in the restaurant on the first floor. A series of weapons and the flags of the city's guilds were displayed on the balcony and gallery in the dining room. Domènech had decorated the ceiling of the dining room with allegorical sculptures of the ancient counts, viscounts and barons of Catalonia, which he interspersed with allegories of Catalonia and Saint George. He placed twenty-four pressed-cardboard shields at the top of the walls, similar to the ceramic ones on the exterior of the building. In this case, the drawings evoked the Catalan

Fitting out the archaeological museum (1896).

The hall on the first floor (1903) with the exhibition dedicated to Norberto Quirno Costa, vice-president of the Argentine Republic.

The hall on the first floor (1907) during the prize-giving ceremony for the trade association, the Centre Comercial Hispano-Marroquí, to students of Arabic. Photography of Fernando Garrigosa. AFB.

regions. The decor was completed with a series of large Flemish tapestries from the 15th century, *The Siege of Rhodes* and *The Asian Migration*. The collections were on display until 1896, when, after a number of projects in other buildings, the site of the former arsenal in the park was refurbished and converted into the city's decorative arts museum, the Museu d'Arts Decoratives, and the collections were moved to their new location. The building is now the home of the Catalan Parliament.

While the transfer of the exhibits from one building to the other was being organised, the Castell dels Tres Dragons was still being used as an impromptu archaeological museum (from 1896 to 1902). All the pieces that had not been moved were crammed into a new display on the first floor. From 1903 to 1916, the former restaurant staged temporary exhibitions and provided a rehearsal room for the Municipal Band. From 1896 onwards, the vacant ground floor was used by the Municipal School of Music. The municipal architect Pere Falqués adapted the space and built classrooms with wooden partitions, which removed Domènech's decorations done years earlier. The music school stayed on the premises until 1928, when its newly built, permanent headquarters opened on Carrer Bruc.

At the same time, the Barcelona Board of Natural Sciences was looking for a new site for its collections, as they had outgrown their current premises, the Museu Martorell. The Castell dels Tres Dragons seemed a natural choice, as it was located nearby and had also preserved and displayed the city's historic collections. In 1912, the building hosted the Exhibition of Fish Farming and Fishing, which was the first of its kind to be held in the city. It was so successful that the city council offered the space for use as a future natural history museum, the Museu de Catalunya d'Història Natural, which would be dedicated to Catalan flora, fauna and geology. The municipal architect, Antoni de Falguera, supervised the work to adapt the building. He painted over the surviving decorations in grey, a colour more suited to the new times. In 1923, the municipal architect in charge of cultural amenities, Josep Goday, designed a project to increase the interior space, which consisted of building a new floor above the balcony and gallery. This was a radical transformation of Domènech's project, and, although it had been approved and budgeted for, it came to nothing following the dictator Primo de Rivera's unexpected power grab: Catalan symbols and culture were supressed and the board members replaced. The new "Dictatorship Board" was set up. It scrapped the expansion of the museum, and changed its name to the Museo de Biología.

The missing ceramic shields were placed on the outside of the building during this period. They referred to examples of flora, fauna and geological features that tied in with the new use of the building, instead of food and drink. The botanical drawings were by the conservator Pius Font i Quer and the zoological and geological drawings were by the museum director, Juan Bautista de Aguilar-Amat. They were manufactured and put in place by the Seville-based ceramics factory, Casa González, under the supervision of the architect Goday. Other work carried out included

Opening of the Municipal Labour Exchange (1934) by the mayor Jaume Aiguader. AFB.

Epiphany (1936). Provisions being shared out among the needy in front of the Municipal Labour Exchange. Carlos Pérez de Rozas. AFB.

The café and restaurant building for the 1888 Barcelona Universal Exhibition. Barcelona, c. 1887. Arxiu Històric del COAC.

the "restoration" of the iron pinnacle on the top of the Torre de l'Homenatge. Domènech's spectacular layer of gilding, that had been there since 1892, was painted black and the damaged stained glass removed. Improvements were made to the entire ground floor, which was standing empty, and it was converted into an exhibition space that was eventually used for the 1929 International Exhibition. Goday designed a grille for the entrance in his own highly distinctive style.

Political changes affected the building again following the establishment of the Second Republic. From 1932 onwards, the ground floor of the building was used as the premises of the Municipal Labour Exchange, which had been set up to help unemployed workers find a job. It shared a space with the Municipal Service for Enrolment in Primary Schools, which also occupied part of the first floor, adjacent to the zoological collections. This led to complaints from the Board of Natural Sciences.

The bombs dropped on the city by the fascist side during the Spanish Civil War caused major damage to the walls of the building, especially the doors and windows, resulting in the loss of almost all the stained glass. However, the structure was not affected. After the war, the nationalist political group, the Falange Española, which was supported by Franco's new government, set up the dining rooms of its social services organisation, the Auxilio Social, on the ground floor. They were intended to feed the people who had lost everything and didn't have enough money for food. The dining rooms remained open from 1941 and 1945, when the space was given to the Museu de Zoologia. The municipal museum is still there today and is dedicated to research and the preservation of the collections. Between 1984 and 1987, the museum space expanded with an underground annex, below the large terrace which cannot be seen from the outside. It was designed by Cristian Cirici, and meant that the building was able to commemorate the centenary of the Universal Exhibition with different improvements and restorations.

All these details about its history, help us understand the many changes in fortune experienced by the Castell dels Tres Dragons: the former café and restaurant, which has been transformed yet, paradoxically, remains unfinished one hundred and thirty-five years later.

Souvenir cigar holder from the Universal Exhibition. When the base is held against the light you can see the café and restaurant. Rossend Casanova private collection.

Café and restaurant for the Universal Exhibition • 87

General view from the Parc de la Ciutadella.

Winged dragon on the Torre de l'Homenatge.

Café and restaurant for the Universal Exhibition

↑ Spiral staircase inside the Torre de l'Homenatge.

← Top of the Torre de l'Homenatge.

Stained-glass windows.

Stairs.

Café and restaurant for the Universal Exhibition

Capital underpinning one of the arches on the first floor.

→ General view of the first floor from the gallery.

Palau Montaner

1889-1897

Gemma Martí

An experimental project that marked the transition to Domènech's *modernisme*

Ramon Montaner Vila (1828-1921) was born in Canet de Mar, the son of Ramon Montaner Esteve and Teresa Vila Misser, who came from families of traders who owned large plots of land and properties in their hometown, including the Casa Forta. (Sàiz, 2008)

Ramon Montaner married Florentina Malató i Surinyach (1835-1900) and they had three children: Joaquim, Carles and Júlia.

After the death of his father, Ramon Montaner went to work at the publishing house run by his brother-in-law, Pere Domènech Saló, who was Lluís Domènech i Montaner's father, where he learnt bookbinding and typesetting. The years he spent at the workshop gave him an in-depth knowledge of printing and led him to set up his own company in 1861 with the Mallorcan entrepreneur, Francesc Simon Font. They gradually built up their business, publishing collections and part-works and eventually started producing encyclopaedias, dictionaries and luxury editions. The publishing house, which had started out with small-scale projects became one of the most important ones in the country.

With the fortune they had made, Ramon Montaner and Francesc Simon commissioned Lluís Domènech i Montaner to design new premises for their company in 1879. Against this prosperous backdrop, the two partners decided to build themselves huge mansions on the right-hand side of the Eixample district, which was home to Barcelona's bourgeoisie. In 1883, Francesc Simon and Ramon Montaner purchased a large plot of land from Pablo Casador, equivalent to the footprint of an entire block, between Carrer Mallorca and Carrer Llúria, which they divided in two to build a mansion for each family. Montaner and Simon commissioned the architect Josep Domènech i Estapà to design both projects, but he only completed the Palau Simon (demolished in 1966). This is because, in 1891, Ramon Montaner asked his nephew, Lluís, to take over the building work on his mansion, which he completed in 1893.

The Palau Montaner was the permanent family home of the Montaner-Malató family until Ramon's death in 1921. His wife Florentina had died in 1900. Their daughter Julia inherited the house.

In 1936, the Palau Montaner, which was still owned by Júlia, was rented out to the Institut Balmes, which remained in the building until 1942. In 1950, Álvaro Muñoz Ramonet bought the building from Júlia Montaner, and sold it to the civil governor, on behalf of the Falangist political party, the Falange Española Tradicionalista y de las Juntas de Ofensiva Nacional Sindicalista. From this time, the Palau Montaner became the Provincial Headquarters of the Falangist Movement and subsequently the Spanish Government Delegation in Catalonia.

The building was later adapted for different purposes, including a school and offices. The part Domènech added to Estapà's structure at the rear of the building was demolished as a result of the extension carried out in 1951.

← Interior view of the hall, *c.* 1895.
Arxiu Històric del COAC.

From Domènech i Estapà's classicism to Domènech i Montaner's *modernisme*

In July 1889, Domènech i Estapà began working on the part of the project that involved building the wall at the side of the building and the outer structure. It was a square, palatial house, with a basement, ground floor and two upper floors. He also designed the bee-shaped railings for the wall crowned by five-pointed stars, which were made by Francisco Jené. The wrought-iron work was placed between pillars made of stone from Montjuïc, carved with plant motifs by Banafet and Deulofeu. The walls dividing both mansions and the wall on the perimeter of the plot were built by Geroni Boltas, using stone from Montjuïc, supplied by the quarryman Miquel Piera. This was the first wall to be built, and the wrought-iron gate leading into the garden was left until last. It was designed by Lluís Domènech i Montaner and made by the ironsmith Francisco Tiestos i Vidal. (Amenós, 2011)

In 1891, work resumed under Lluís Domènech i Montaner's supervision after he had taken over from Domènech i Estapà. His uncle had been so pleased with the work he had done at his publishing house that he gave him creative free rein to bring his future home to fruition, in accordance with his social status, sparing no expense and using the finest-quality materials.

Domènech i Montaner's design had to adapt to the part of the building that had already been completed. The architect added ornamental elements and volumes to the cube-like structure that broke up the straight lines. Although eclectic in style, we can see elements that broke with the historicist style that was prevalent at the time.

Domènech added a narrow volume to Estapà's design that protrudes from the façade on Carrer Llúria and extends as far as the first floor, like en enclosed gallery. It leads into the big garden around the house. The side wall of the building has been altered with regard to the original, which had windows arranged symmetrically on either side of the central gallery, with the addition of a volume on the rear façade where there was once a terrace. This intervention resulted in the addition of three more windows on the left-hand side of the façade where the new rooms were built during the work carried out in 1951.

Domènech's other contributions included the cresting he added to the rear façade of the building and the ornamental motifs on the balustrades of the terrace that overlooked the garden, which were removed when the building was being remodelled.

Domènech also altered the canopy designed by Estapà, making it wider and more prominent. He added wooden cladding with ornamental mouldings and fleurons and applied pieces of red glazed ceramics, which he and Antoni Maria Gallissà had experimented with in the workshop at the Castell dels Tres Dragons, in order to revive the old techniques used in manufacturing ceramics and their finishes. (Figueras, 1994)

The main entrance to the building is on Carrer Mallorca. There are four windows on the ground and first floors arranged symmetrically on either side of the door. The ones on the ground floor line up with the day rooms: the office and library. The windows on the first floor, where the bedrooms were located, are slightly different in style. The two at either end have classical-style stepped lintels and stone openwork balustrades. The three windows in the centre look into the master bedroom. There is a long balcony in front of them made of stone openwork with intertwining plant motifs and two blank coats of arms in the centre.

The third floor is not as high as the lower floors and has three narrower windows on either side of the central section, which Domènech used to create the building's most outstanding decorative elements at the top of the main façade. In this central part, the windows with the segmental arches designed by Estapà were covered with floral motifs made of stone openwork and Domènech carved the same motif into two rectangular forms that were used as air vents. At the top of the central section there are two German-style shields containing a laurel wreath: the one on the left bears the inscription "FOU FETA" (it was made) and the one on the right "ANY 1893" (year 1893). In the centre at the top of the façade there is a sculpture of a phoenix, the symbol of the Montaner i Simon publishing house, which also alludes to the rebirth of Catalonia.

The current façade on the rear of the building is the annex that was added at a later date. It undermines the stylistic unity provided by the architect. When these refurbishments were being carried out, the architects removed part of the canopy and the cornice that was on the rear façade and placed it along the side wall, leaving the former incomplete. In Domènech i Montaner's project, the rear façade was the most profusely decorated and the most faithful to the style of his work. Although he suffered the drawback of having to work with a pre-existing structure, Domènech designed a large terrace which he placed over the dining room, smoking room and sewing room. It was accessed through the rooms on the first floor. He designed a large architrave with stone decorations that framed stained-glass windows that let light into the service staircase, the rooms on the ground floor and the hall.

Domènech put the kitchen, larder and lavatories in the semi-basement. They were accessed via the service staircase that also led to the basement, where there was a large coal-powered boiler that heated the house and provided it with hot water that was distributed through pipes to every room.

The façades of the Palau Montaner have a ceramic frieze running all the way along the top. It features a series of allegorical figures representing the art of printing, showing how it evolved from its beginnings.

On the roof, Domènech used glazed tiles in a burst of ochres and browns, like the ones at the Casa Roura in Canet de Mar, which he was building at the same time.

The first works by Antoni Rigalt, Lluís Bru and Gaspar Homar for Domènech i Montaner

Once inside the main door of the building, a marble staircase leads to the porch which communicates with the office, library and house, protected by a screen for privacy. Antoni Rigalt (Gil, 2013) was commissioned to design the screen, which is surmounted by carved wooden cresting featuring plant motifs and translucent glass painted with leaves and thistle flowers. It is flanked by two winged horses carved in stone by Eusebi Arnau, which are very similar to the ones he designed for the Palau de la Música Catalana.

Domènech i Montaner added a plethora of symbolic elements consisting of fantastic beasts: stone dragons on the staircase balusters, mermaids holding up the lamps on the first floor, winged stone lions on the first landing and winged dragons carved in wood on the lintels above the doors in the rooms on the first floor, which evoke the medieval past. There are also real animals including a dog, an owl, an eagle, a stork and a dove, accompanied by children who are holding them, playing with them or threatening them with tridents and axes.

The porch opens onto a spacious reception area with an imperial staircase that led to the rooms on the first floor. Domènech placed the day rooms on the ground floor. They had anterooms with Roman mosaic flooring made by Lluís Bru. The mosaic floor leading to the staircase features the thistle flower, which Domènech also used, in a similar design, in the entrance to the Casa Lleó i Morera. He covered the walls in the lobby with red marble with gilded incisions that create the effect of damascening. The door frames of the rooms have stone mouldings featuring different types of leaves and have sculptural reliefs above the lintels. The doors with their stained-glass windows in the music room and sitting room, on either side of the staircase, have stone jambs and lintels that form a segmental arch. They are flanked by two fluted columns with Ionic capitals. There are busts on either side of the arch, which Domènech also used in the Casa Roura in Canet de Mar (Martí, 2014), and there are stone benches flanked by lions between the doors.

The red marble treads and the handrail on the imperial staircase contrast with the stone balusters featuring winged dragons repeated in a sequence as far as the first floor. In the wall above the landing, where the staircase branches off, Domènech designed a stained-glass window with the Montaner family crest, flanked by four caryatids made by Eusebi Arnau, which welcome visitors and symbolise hospitality. The male figure on the left is proffering salt and the one on the right bread. The two female figures in the centre are holding water and wine. The stained-glass window in the centre, with the Montaner crest, is set into a rounded arch with fan-shaped ribs above it. They are clad in wood decorated with geometric motifs by Gaspar Homar. A semi-circular wooden panel underpins the vast skylight that lets light into the dual-height hall and stretches as far as the opposite wall, where the door leading into the master

Refurbishment of the Palau Montaner. Barcelona, c. 1891. Arxiu Històric del COAC.

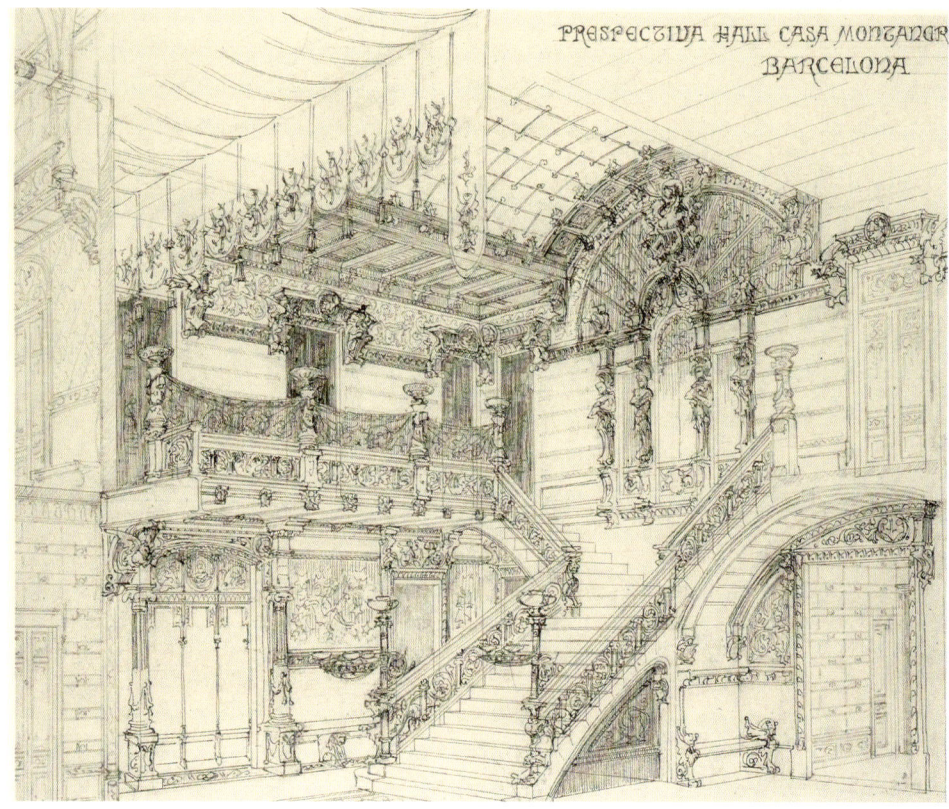

Refurbishment of the Palau Montaner. Hall. Barcelona, c. 1891. Private collection.

bedroom is located. The stained-glass windows, made by Antoni Rigalt's workshop, depict intertwining green and yellow leaves and pink passion-flowers against a blue background resembling the sky.

The service staircase, which connected all the floors, from the boiler room to the servants' quarters on the top floor, is hidden behind the central stained-glass window on the imperial staircase landing. Light entered the service staircase through the central stained glass window on the landing and another stained-glass window on the rear façade, which ran parallel to the central one. When the building was refurbished, this façade was demolished in order to build a new volume adjacent to the original, thus preventing light from entering the landing through the central stained-glass window.

Each one of the stained-glass windows at the Palau Montaner was made using different techniques and different styles. The ones in the windows and doors of the rooms on the ground floor are pre-art nouveau in technique and use silver stain and enamel to draw the motifs. Mosaic glass was used to make the skylight, a medium which the Rigalt workshop would adopt in other completely art nouveau, or *modernista*, works.

The day rooms

Domènech placed the large music room on the right-hand side of the staircase. It had a large wooden harp in the ceiling. This was his way of reviving the symbol of the harp as recognition of the glorious past of Catalonia, its language and the homeland. This was the symbol adopted by the Catalan cultural revival movement, the *Renaixença*, and it was used in poetry and even as a symbol of the poetry competition, the *Jocs Florals* (Pons, 2007). Domènech's large harp consists of a five-pointed star, the symbol of the phoenix and, therefore, rebirth. This room was demolished during the refurbishment to make space for offices.

Domènech put a large sitting room on the left-hand side of the staircase, which had doors leading out onto the gallery. The flooring in the room is different to the rest and consists of yellow marble combined with different types of glazed white and blue ceramic tiles. Two of them bear the Montaner family crest and the others bear the inscriptions ANY (year) and the date of completion in Roman numerals MDCCCXCV (1895). The sitting room has a coffered ceiling made of wood combined with ceramic pieces with a metallic finish. There is a gryphon inside a quadrilobate motif carved inside each panel, a motif Domènech also used in the circular dining room at the Casa Roura in Canet de Mar. The long crossbeams are decorated with a frieze depicting gilded swirling plant motifs and have small ornamental mouldings featuring the Catalan flag at the points where they intersect.

The gallery in the sitting room, which has doors leading into the garden, is made of longleaf pine wood and has leaded stained-glass panels combining transparent and coloured glass. They were made by Antoni Rigalt.

At the back of the hall, there are two reception rooms on either side of the staircase, with neo-Mudéjar-style wainscoting made by the Pujol i Bausis ceramics factory. They have simple coffered ceilings inset with glass panels that let natural light into the only rooms that had no doors or windows directly overlooking the street.

The reception room on the left led into the bathroom, smoking room, large dining room and the service staircase that in turn led to the kitchen in the basement.

The walls and coffered ceiling in the smoking room, where there was probably a billiard table, are clad in wood. The stained-glass windows made by Antoni Rigalt's workshop bring light and colour to the room. The scenes depicting the four seasons were painted with silver stain and are framed by architectural forms. Domènech used this method of framing a central motif in subsequent projects, including the semi-circular stained-glass panels at the Casa Lleó i Morera.

The recreation rooms – the smoking and sewing rooms – led into the dining room that had a door leading into the garden via the terrace, which was removed during subsequent renovations. The main feature of the dining room is the coffered ceiling combined with glazed ceramics around an elongated central dome with a large fleuron in the centre underpinning a big lamp that lights up the table. The vertical walls that raise the dome above ceiling height are inset with stained-glass windows that alternate the Montaner family crest and a rope resembling plant stems with an armband and lions facing each other.

The walls of the room were covered in densely woven fabric with fleurs de lis painted in blue and cream. The floor is made of two shades of oak parquet with a frieze at the side. The centrepiece of the room is Joan Brull's oil painting, *La tonsura del Rei Wamba* (The Tonsure of King Wamba), one of his early works. (Boronat, 1999)

The night rooms

These rooms were arranged around the gallery on the first floor, flanked by winged dragons and zoomorphic figures in high relief. The wooden sculptures on the doors and the mermaids holding up the lamps on the first-floor landing, were made by the cabinetmaker Gaspar Homar. The frieze on the sides of the walls on the first floor depicts a series of scenes on paper that has been painted and gilded with floral and plant motifs. Allegorical figures representing music, sculpture, painting, agriculture and the inventions of the day – the telephone and the telegraph – emerge from these motifs.

Domènech entrusted Gaspar Homar with the interior decoration (Carbonell, 2014). He produced the fabrics and the furniture for the room. This was the starting point of the close relationship and collaboration between Domènech and Homar that lasted throughout their professional careers. Homar featured in every one of Domènech i Montaner's projects, and became one of the most prestigious cabinetmakers and interior designers of the *modernista* period.

Ramon Montaner and Lluís Domènech: passionate about the past

Ramon Montaner was a great aficionado of art and antiques and a major collector of works and pieces from different periods and cultures, which he displayed in cabinets at the Palau Montaner and the castle of Santa Florentina in Canet.

The fabrics, the torches, the velvet pennants with heraldic crests, the damask silks by Gaspar Homar, the marble panels engraved with the Montaner and Vila family crests, and the stone and wood zoomorphic figures on the banisters and the door lintels, designed by Domènech, bring the medieval style that Ramon Montaner wanted for his home and which his nephew knew how to execute with his technical expertise and knowledge of history and symbols.

The Palau Montaner is one of Domènech i Montaner's early works and still denotes a certain eclecticism while revealing a desire to lend continuity and unity to the building as a whole in order to achieve absolute harmony in each of its spaces.

→ Wood and ceramic coffered ceiling and dome in the dining room.

Palau Montaner

General view of the façades on Carrer de Llúria (garden) and Carrer de Mallorca (main entrance).

Façade on Carrer de Llúria. Ceramic detail showing ink being spread with an inking ball: a tool consisting of a piece of leather stuffed with wool with a wooden handle.

Imperial eagle over the main entrance. It is holding an inking ball in its claws. Domènech repeated this motif on different elements at the Casa Thomas.

Façade on Carrer de Llúria. Ceramic decoration showing a rotary printing press of the period.

Façade on Carrer de Llúria. Mosaic with an allegory of painting.

Garden railing.

← → Winged horses on the corbels above the wooden screen.

← → Busts decorating the segmental arches in the lobby that lead to the music room and sitting room.

View of the imperial staircase from the first floor.

→   Skylight with passion-flowers.

Wall on the landing with a stained-glass window flanked by two caryatids by Eusebi Arnau, symbolising hospitality.

→ View of the imperial staircase from the hall.

Roman-style mosaic floor in the hall designed by Lluís Bru.
The one leading to the staircase (right) features a thistle flower.

Allegory of the telephone. Wallpaper in the gallery on the first floor.

Dragons decorating the foot of the imperial staircase.

Allegory of love. Sculptural relief on the ground floor.

Winged zoomorphic figures by Gaspar Homar flanking the doors of the rooms on the first floor.

The marine cemetery: Domènech i Montaner's funerary architecture in Comillas

1893-1899

Antonio Sama

Lluís Domènech i Montaner's intervention at the cemetery in Comillas has become, over time, one of the most representative examples of the romantic side of the great Catalan architect.

Curiously enough, the specialist critics almost completely overlooked the fact that Domènech i Montaner had designed the cemetery, until the last twenty-five years of the 20th century, when documents were published that confirmed he was responsible for this enterprise. Today, we know that the refurbishment and redesign of the burial ground and the building of the Piélago family tomb took place sometime between 1893 and 1900.

A project for the marquisate

The project must be placed in the context of the generous patronage of the marquises of Comillas in their hometown (which became a wonderful showcase for late 19th-century Catalan art) and, more specifically, Domènech i Montaner's role as the architect for the marquisate, following the death of Cristóbal Cascante in July 1889. Indeed, it appears that the developer behind the improvements to the cemetery was the second Marquis of Comillas, Claudio López Bru, rather than the local council or parish.

The Cantabrian aristocrat's proposal aimed to benefit the local community by adapting the burial site to the burial requirements in force, stemming from the growth in the population and the adverse effects of epidemics. In this way, he was able to act as benefactor – a role traditionally played by the wealthy Cantabrians who had made their fortunes in the Indies, who counted his father among their number – and the perfect exemplar who was so widely praised by his supporters. Nevertheless, it seems that the marquis had personal interests in the project, as we will see later on.

There is evidence that Domènech i Montaner visited Comillas several times to plan and supervise the work. This certainly gave him the opportunity to gradually soak up the character and charm of the coastal town. The diary published by Joan Bassegoda reports that the architect began working on his first project while he was staying there in the summer of 1893:

> "24th August (Thursday). I make a sketch of San Cristóbal cemetery from life. …
>
> 28th August (Monday). I go to look inside cemetery with Joan Sánchez. I complete the ground plan and begin working on the elevation. I don't have time to finish it and take the ground plan to Don Claudio. He approves it, in principle, and invites me to lunch the following day. I am unable to go.
>
> 29th August (Tuesday). I complete the sketch of the exterior of the cemetery and outline the location of the burial niches. I have a meeting in the evening, followed by the approval of the design, in principle." (Bassegoda, 1994, p. 72)

The Architects' Association of Catalonia (COAC) holds the sketch of San Cristóbal cemetery and the refurbishment project drawn up by Domènech in August 1893. It is widely known that there are considerable differences between the drawings and the completed project. This suggests that the architect rethought the project

← Photograph of the clay model for Josep Llimona's sculpture of the guardian angel, c. 1895. Arxiu Històric del Col·legi d'Arquitectes de Catalunya.

at a later date and that this may have been influenced by Don Claudio's instructions.

The analysis of the architectural programme underlying the project will give us a better understanding of the complexity of Domènech's intervention and help us appreciate the brilliance of the results. Indeed, we could say that very diverse determining factors come together in its formulation, which we can list as follows: a) to adapt San Cristóbal cemetery to the hygiene principles of the current legislation; b) to extend the capacity of the burial site and improve its appearance so that it can house the mausoleums of illustrious families with sufficient decorum; c) to preserve and integrate the ruins of the former parish church of Comillas into the burial ground; d) to give "modern" architectural expression to an ambitious symbolic programme that will bring together the funerary monuments per se with others that are representative of the site.

In accordance with this set of specifications, Lluís Domènech i Montaner had to think, first and foremost, about ways of addressing functional and regulatory requirements, while using his personal architectural language to strike a balance between them and "moral" and symbolic needs.

The Royal Order of 17th February 1886 was the main regulation about funerary architecture in force at the time. Fortunately, the cemetery in Comillas fully complied with the specifications of the decree with regard to the location of the graves. In his project, the Catalan architect extended the cemetery by building a wall on both sides of the ruins (running south and north). Not only did this enable him to increase its burial capacity, it also allowed the inclusion of forensic services, such as the autopsy room. Part of the cemetery was reserved for burials in recesses, or niches, thereby satisfying the pressing need to increase the burial space. However, the marquis must have considered Domènech's planned expansion inadequate, because the finished project included a west wing, in front of the steps of the old church. This was the area chosen to build the mausoleums of eminent families from the town who were related to the Comillas dynasty (such as the Piélagos and Correas), and this leaves little room for doubt that Claudio López Bru himself made his architect realise further expansion was necessary.

After dealing with these practical and regulatory aspects on his plan, Lluís Domènech i Montaner set about resolving the above-mentioned specifications (b, c, and d) through the architectural composition. He drew inspiration from a series of elements that made the project an aesthetic success: the ruins of a medieval church and a truly picturesque setting, namely, a hillock overlooking the sea.

Archaeological *vanitas* and terrifying funerary architecture

Domènech i Montaner's passion for archaeology, and his erudition about the subject in relation to medieval architecture and industrial arts, are well known. Nevertheless, in the case of the ruins of the church of San Cristóbal, he was interested in their symbolic as well as architectural value: the ruins acted as a *vanitas*, or image of the fleeting nature of earthly things and the fragility of life. It is true that Domènech's supposed Ruskinesque and late-romantic sensibilities also appreciated the picturesque values of the run-down fabric whose "dimming", far from being to its detriment, instead bore witness to its age and, therefore, its glory. According to the author of *The Lamp of Memory*, a building will not attain this glory until it "has been entrusted with the fame, and hallowed by the deeds of men, till its walls have been witnesses of suffering, and its pillars rise out of the shadows of death" and "that deep sense of voicefulness" (Ruskin, 1849, pp. 23-24). As we will see, Domènech endowed this "voicefulness" with a very specific meaning in order to complete his symbolic programme, but, first and foremost, – and in the specific context of this funerary project – the medieval ruins came to play the role of a veritable architectural *memento mori*, proclaiming that mortals were constantly being stalked by death. Llimona's angel would be the high point of this funerary iconography. However, overall, we can say that the entire cemetery in Comillas is redolent of an extremely severe, almost terrifying funerary language.

As we would expect, the funerary iconography at the cemetery is mainly centred around the gate leading into the grounds. It was here that Domènech placed a rounded arch surmounted by a pitched roof, reminiscent of the Romanesque or, even, Byzantine styles. The regular stone blocks were brought from the Carrejo quarry, not far from the municipality of Cabezón de la Sal, and contrast pleasantly with the masonry of the boundary wall, whose reddish tones mean that the twin pillars underpinning the arch remind us of the porphyry columns found in Eastern Roman temples. The neo-Byzantine style provides a matchless framework for the development of an iconic discourse that warns visitors they are stepping inside the kingdom of mourning and grief. On the iron gate, different symbols taken from the Pharaonic religion and Greek mythology conflate timeless mystic ceremonies with Christian eschatology: the image of the *papaver somniferum* – a narcotic used in Egyptian funeral rites – alternates with the lily, the symbol of Mary and the goddess Isis. The gate contains many invocations to the Virgin, as do the decorative elements of the Comillas seminary which Domènech i Montaner worked on between 1890 and 1897. They can be seen in the wrought-iron lilies and salutations carved into the stone ("AVE MARÍA"), as well as the monogram AM sculpted in relief on the side vaults on the roof. These omnipresent Marian advocations may allude to the Spanishness of the dogma of the Immaculate Conception suggested by the ultra-Catholic Marquis of Comillas. However, they all seem to be part of an iconographic programme that aims to represent the cycle of the Incarnation, Passion and Resurrection of Christ.

However, the apparent placidity of this discourse – which is both comforting and consoling due to the hope it expresses in the resurrection and existence of an afterlife – is suddenly dispelled by the presence of an inscription which, together with the fierceness of Llimona's angel, evokes the terrifying side of the funeral narrative we mentioned earlier. We are referring to the Gothic lettering in gilded metal on top of the gate. It reads:
"*MEMO RESTO / JUDITII MEI / HERI MIHI / HODIE TIBI*".
The text can be considered a simplification of a phrase from Ecclesiasticus (38:22) which reads: *"Memor esto juditii mei, sic enim erit et tuum. Mihi heri et tibi hodie"* and can be translated into English as: "Remember my judgment: for thine also shall be so; yesterday for me, and to day for thee."

Similar inscriptions have been found in epitaphs on medieval tombs, as well as those associated with the most terrible expression of secular ascesis: being walled in or almost buried alive. In the deathly silence of the cemetery, the inscription proclaims the fleetingness of life with a deafening roar and the imminent end of every mortal. The rawness of this unquestionable truth – manifested with cruel eloquence by the sentence in the book of Sirach – has its equivalent in the wrathful expression of the angel who, perched atop the ruins, seems to scrutinise, with a penetrating gaze, the person who is about to enter the kingdom of the dead.

Josep Llimona's sculpture has become an iconic monument at the cemetery, although it looks quite different to the way it was depicted in Domènech i Montaner's initial project. Rather than a statue, it was to consist of a sculptural grouping showing angels in conversation. This first idea was rendered in a clay model, as shown by the photos in the COAC collection. There is no clear explanation for this radical change in iconography, but, it is nonetheless true that the celestial being created by Llimona drew people's attention due to its irate expression. It was exhibited in 1895 at the Salón Parés in Barcelona, as part of an exhibition organised by the Cercle Artístic de Sant Lluch, and drew harsh criticism from the influential critic from *La Vanguardia*, Raimon Casellas:

> "José Llimona's "Guardian Angel" does not live up to the great plaudits garnered by the artist at one time, either conceptually or expressively. Moreover, his strange demeanour and angry expression do not represent an angelic being who stands guard with celestial serenity, confident about the effectiveness of his divine mission. Instead he is a sullen and out-of-proportion creature who, instead of standing guard, lies in wait, in a restless, provocative, furious way as if ready to enter into a fight with the first individual bold enough to emerge before his haughty countenance." (Casellas, 1895, p. 4)

However, other influential critics of the time had a very different opinion and considered that the *Guardian Angel* was "the bravest work created by the hands of Joseph Llimona" and fully imbued with the spirit of the "modern French school" (J. C. y R., 1895, p. 237). The satirical writers at *La Esquella de la Torratxa* agreed with Casellas about the angel's threatening violence and commented that "Instead of placing it above a cemetery gate, the Marquis of Comillas would do better to put it on top of his safe." (P. del O., 1895, p. 323)

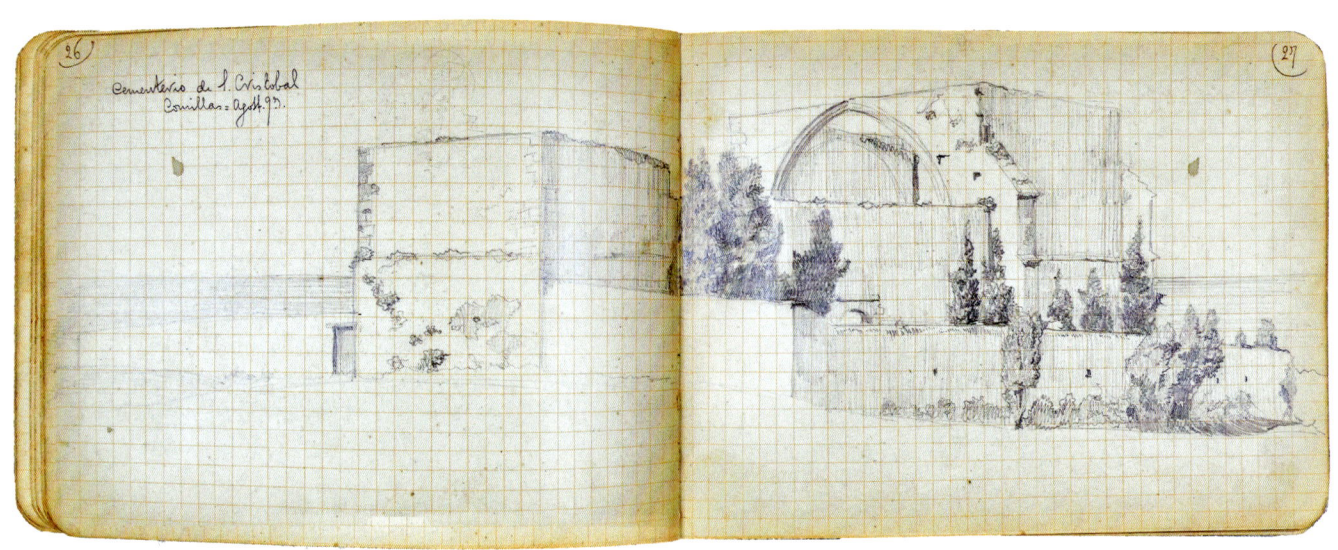

Travel sketchbook. Current state of the cemetery in Comillas. Comillas, 1893. Arxiu Històric del COAC.

Proposal for the refurbishment of the cemetery in Comillas. Comillas, 1893. Private collection.

The critic from *La Vanguardia* concluded by saying "Llimona has committed an error. In any case, his statue could be the angel of doom from the Last Judgement who expels our forebears from paradise. He will never be the guardian of the silent ruins who ensures peace in Christian tombs." Casellas had a point. The angel in the cemetery has often been identified as the exterminating Abaddon rather than the celestial guardian. If we bear in mind that Domènech i Montaner's initial idea was to place an apparently seraphic grouping on top of the ruins, which, when analysed iconographically, more closely resembles the thurifer angel and the book announcing the "end of time" and the beginning of the Last Judgement (*Revelation*, 10:7 and 10:1-6), it prompts us to wonder whether the architect didn't want to incorporate a spirit with apocalyptic hues into his symbolic programme.

This intention to "contaminate" the image of the friendly guardian angel with that of the terrible herald of the apocalypse does not seem unlikely in the context of a dramatic reflection on the closeness of death and the implicit invocation for the Penitential Act. Nevertheless, Domènech may also have been influenced by the "voices" on the site in his deliberate desire to achieve an iconographic heterodoxy.

These voices emerge from the ancient stones of the old parish church and were associated with a bygone legend which the provincial deputy Andrés Lanuza had been responsible for disseminating during the royal visit to Comillas by King Alfonso XII (Lanuza, 1881, pp. 12-14). According to the legend, the ancient settlers in the town had abandoned the church as they refused to recognise the privileges enjoyed by the duke of the Infantado over the church. This "all for one, one for all" spirit was epitomised by Lope de Vega's play *Fuenteovejuna*, and helped create the image of the townsfolk of Comillas as a proud people who would not be cowed. This may explain why Domènech sought to depict the haughty nobility of this whaling town through the fierceness of the angel.

The beat of the ocean

The sea is certainly the linchpin to understanding Domenech's concept of the layout of the cemetery. It is not only the visual determinant of the landscape but also a metaphor for the place and the character of its people. The Cantabrian sea can be glimpsed from the cemetery in a sweeping panorama, and you can hear the roar of the waves as they crash against the nearby cliffs. The sea defines the place as an essential element of the coastline, but it is also populated by "echoes" that speak of the epic voyages of the fishermen and the legendary bravery of the whalers. Not far from here, the locals still refer to the rocky outcrop, where the whales caught by their forbears would be cut up, as the "whale stone".

In the late 19th century, Comillas was still a town inextricably linked to the sea in the collective imagination of the Spanish. Its fishing fleet still went out to sea, but the town had been transformed into a summer holiday resort for the aristocracy due to the opportunities it offered for sea bathing and the generosity of the López family (who had played host to the Spanish royal family in the summers of 1881 and 1882). The marquises of Comillas had built a maritime empire, through the shipping company, the Compañía Trasatlántica, which had steam packets that sailed across the Atlantic and the Pacific.

If we take into account the idiosyncrasy of the humble fishing town and the oceangoing feats of his patron, Lluís Domènech i Montaner set about highlighting the links between the sea and the cemetery. With this aim in mind, he had no hesitation in making holes in the ruins and creating two rows of arches facing north-to-south. With this bold – and to a certain extent sacrilegious – intervention in the ancient church, the architect managed to make the views of the sea an integral part of the funerary setting. By perforating the venerable fabric he made it possible for the beat of the sea – with the sound of the tides and smell of saltpetre – to permeate and take over the sepulchral setting, as if reclaiming the memory of the water.

The cemetery's marine calling was also clearly expressed in one of the tombs built inside its western extension. The marquis must have had it in mind from the very outset when he commissioned the architect to remodel the burial site. It was for the use of the Piélago family, and was specially dedicated to the memory of Joaquín del Piélago y Sánchez de Movellán (1850-1890), who hailed from Comillas and was the administrator and manager of the Compañía Trasatlántica, as well as Claudio López Bru's brother-in-law. It is likely that the marquis commissioned Domènech i Montaner to design the tomb for his relative and friend, in whose honour he had named one of his company's most important ships.

Joaquín del Piélago's links to the sea were not only associated with the fact that he hailed from Comillas and had worked in shipping. His surname had seafaring connotations, and means "open sea" in Spanish. The architect had no hesitation in placing a marble wave at the centre of his funerary composition. An apocalyptic angel child appears, floating above it as if announcing the end of time. Just behind it was a large iron cross, which unfortunately vanished during the Spanish Civil War. It was cast at the Masriera i Campins foundry between 1898 and 1899 and received widespread coverage in the illustrated periodicals of the day. Its was hailed as one of the finest-ever masterpieces of Catalan wrought-ironwork due to its lavish ornamentation and technical perfection.

Once again, Domènech displayed his great erudition and ability to combine different elements to develop a complex iconographic programme in the setting of this monumental yet simple tomb. The petrified wave would become a metaphor for the surname and profession of the deceased, immortalised in a steam packet bearing his name that sailed the oceans. It may also refer to the origin of the apocalyptic beast who emerges from the waters and is eventually vanquished by the white horse. The victory cross with the symbols of the Passion and the subjugated lizards would represent Christianity's final triumph over death and sin, or, the redemption of humanity by the cross.

In a nutshell, the Piélago pantheon confirms the seafaring vocation of a necropolis conceived as an ode to the sea and a marine elegy.

Today, the wind and saltpetre continue with their pitiless erosion and threaten the ruins of the ancient church and Lluís Domènech i Montaner's masterpiece. We hope that awareness of the heritage value of this landmark of art nouveau, or *modernista*, funerary architecture will be reflected in preventive conservation interventions. Only then will we be able to prevent the "evil day" – as Ruskin would say – from coming too early, when we will have to resign ourselves to celebrate it through the "funeral offices of memory".

Comillas. Fuente de los Tres Caños.

Monument to the Marquis of Comillas (1889) designed by Domènech i Montaner from a drawing by Cristóbal Cascante.

Cemetery in Comillas. Guardian angel, Josep Llimona.

→ Cemetery in Comillas. Piélago family tomb.

Casa Thomas

1895-1912

Gemma Martí

The perfect combination of industrial architecture and a family home

Josep Thomas i Bigas was born in Barcelona on 19th February 1852. He had worked as an engraver at a printers' workshop on Carrer Aribau while he was studying architecture, and his interest in the graphic arts led him to found the Sociedad Heliográfica Española, in 1876, with Heribert Mariezcurrena, Joan Serra i Pausas and Miquel Joaritzi. The company was the first to print images in publications using the early photographic technique of heliography. In 1879, the company was dissolved and, shortly afterwards, Josep Thomas founded a photoengraving and phototype company, Tipografia Thomas, on Barcelona's Gran Via.

In addition to publishing, printing and photoengraving, the company produced prints reproducing works of art from museums, architectural landmarks, cards and photographs of places in Spain, as well as a large number of engravings for magazines and publishing companies, including Espasa and Montaner i Simon.

Fifteen years later, the company had become well established and Thomas asked Lluís Domènech i Montaner to design a new building for him. The business premises would be on the ground floor and the family home on the floor above.

The Casa Thomas, an industrial building by Domènech i Montaner

The Casa Thomas is not the only industrial building designed by Domènech. Other projects in this style include the Montaner i Simon publishing house (1879-1881) in Barcelona; the Jover, Serra i Cia. factory (1899-1900) and its warehouse and offices (1909-1910) in Canet de Mar; the Casa Navàs (1901-1908), the Casa Gasull (1911-1916) and the Llopis warehouse (1911) in Reus; the cooperative winery, the Celler Cooperatiu (1912-1913), in L'Espluga de Francolí; and a factory (1905), that was never built, which was going to be part of the redevelopment of Barcelona's old town.

Although these buildings were designed at different times, each one of them shows that the function of the building was of primary importance to Domènech. He created the right structure with practicality, functionality and rationality in mind. His genius enabled him to work on disparate projects that had one thing in common: the unmistakeable Domenechian architectural style that set him apart from his contemporaries.

The functionality of Domènech's designs is reflected in the interiors of these industrial buildings due to the use of iron as a building material. It enabled Domènech to create vast, open-plan spaces that, in the case of the Casa Thomas, could house printing machinery.

← Main façade. Anonymous, c. 1900.
Arxiu Fotogràfic del Centre Excursionista de Catalunya.

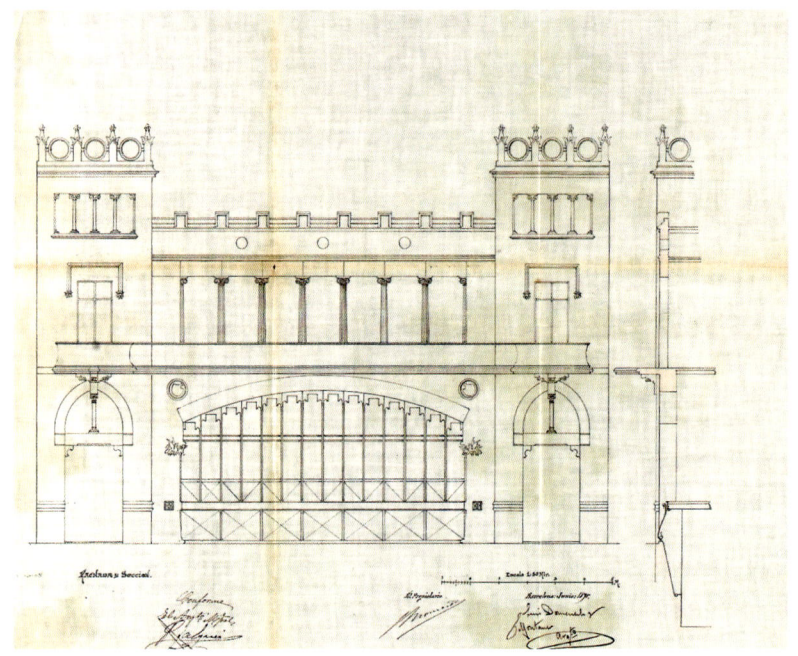

Elevation and section of the façade, initial proposal. Ink drawing, 1895. Arxiu Municipal Contemporani de Barcelona.

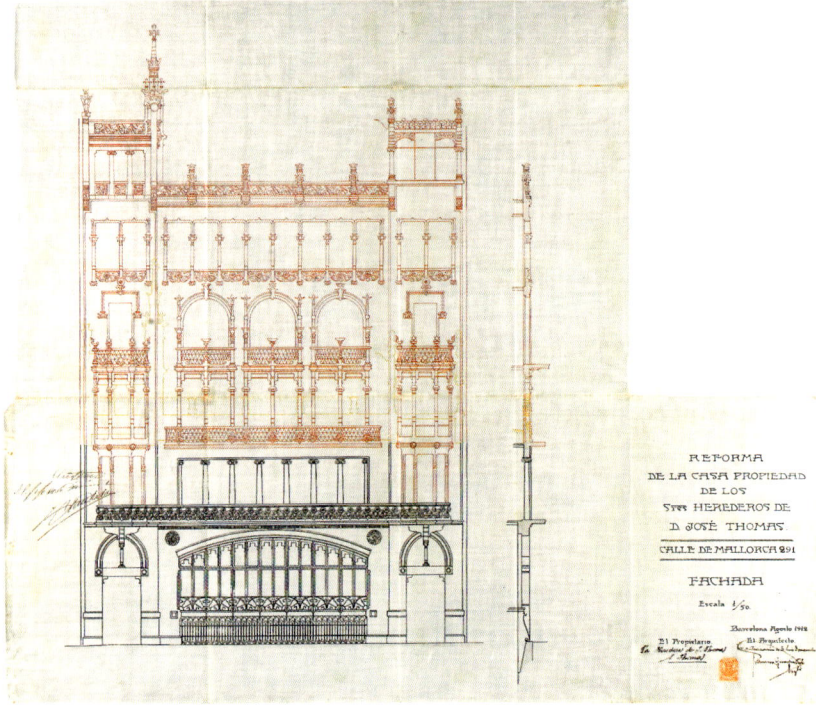

Elevation and section of the façade. Renovation by Francesc Guàrdia i Vial, 1912. Arxiu Municipal Contemporani de Barcelona.

Domènech i Montaner's project for the Casa Thomas

Domènech's original design included a 20-metre-wide façade set between party walls – which stood on empty plots of land at the time – with a semi-basement, ground floor and upper floor. The façade consisted of a central section with a glass frontage surmounted by a segmental arch, protected by wrought-iron railings made by the Flink brothers (Amenós, 2005), a gallery on the upper floor and cresting on the top of the building. The central section was flanked by two taller symmetrical sections, surmounted by stone sculptural details and wrought-iron elements, which broke the symmetry of the building.

Domènech placed two entrances at ground level on either side of the central section. The one on the right led to the family apartments and the one on the left to the workshop. They had wooden doors that were made at the Viladevall brothers' workshop, and were carved with an owl (a symbol of wisdom) and dogs chained together (the protectors of the home).

The symbolic repertoire on the first floor gallery

Domènech designed the loggia on the first floor with classical Ionic columns, with fluted shafts and zoomorphic, plant and floral elements around them that created a wonderful rhythm of light and shadow inside the family apartments. The decorative and symbolic motifs, carved in half-relief, include a lizard, thistle flower, lily, sunflower and chameleon.

None of the decorative motifs was repeated and this means that the six columns in the gallery are all different. Domènech used the same resource in subsequent buildings, including the Palau de la Música Catalana and the Casa Fuster.

Domènech used stone from Montjuïc on the long balustrade in the gallery. The balusters are carved with interlinking sunflowers that convey a feeling of movement and symbolise strength, energy and vitality.

Ceramics with a metallic hue

Domènech combined the stonework with glazed ceramic tiles in shades of blue and yellow on a white background with gilded edges to reflect the light. They featured floral and zoomorphic motifs, including the phoenix: a clear reference to the rebirth of Catalonia which strengthened the Thomas family's pro-Catalan convictions. The birds on the tiles are depicted in a rampant position and there are two coats of arms on their breasts with two Ts in the centre: the acronym of the company, Tipografia Thomas.

The flat ceramic tiles on the wall are combined with a series of convex half spheres, set between the square tiles. They have a lustrous, metallic finish and are very similar to the ones the architect commissioned between 1889 and 1890 for the façade of the church at Comillas (Sama, 2015), which were made by Josep Ros i Furió from the tile manufactures, La Ceramo de Valencia. The half spheres on the façade of the Casa Thomas were made at the Pujol i Bausis ceramics factory in Esplugues de Llobregat. (Subias, 2006)

The cresting on the building

Although Domènech i Montaner's original project included a symmetrical façade flanked by two narrower sections, with cresting in the form of a balustrade, stone circular medallions and small crenellations, it was subsequently altered. Domènech added two different skylights on either side of the rooftop. The one on the left was clad in stone from Montjuïc, as is shown in the original plans dating from June 1895, and the one on the right had a wrought-iron structure, giving it a more industrial look, highlighting his taste for asymmetry.

The architect placed cresting at the top of the façade, which was totally different to the one he had initially designed. It had four medieval-style stone pinnacles, which featured the lozenge-shaped heraldic shield of Barcelona and Catalonia. The pinnacles were underpinned by stone fretwork balustrades with a series of wrought-iron grasshoppers, in a similar design to the poster advertising the company. They were made at the Flink brothers' workshop.

Domènech wanted to make the grasshopper one of the building's most prominent features and placed a sculpture of the insect on the top of the left-hand tower. Christianity associated the grasshopper with the destructive forces of evil, but, in this case, it stands guard, protecting the building.

The architect also designed a tall pinnacle in the flamboyant style, carved from Montjuïc stone and bearing the coats of arms of Barcelona and Catalonia, the seal with the initials of the Thomas family, and, at the top, a timbre consisting of plant motifs.

The periodical *La Frontera* (1897), which was distributed in Camprodon, the town where the Thomas family would spend the summer, reports that the skylight on the left was used as a dovecot, as Thomas's son, Josep Thomas Corrons, was keen pigeon fancier.

The Fototípia Thomas workshop

The entrance to Thomas's phototype workshop was on the left-hand side of the building and led into a reception area decorated with different materials made using different techniques. The walls contained sgraffito-work suns and phoenixes that formed decorative friezes. The lower section, which acted as a wainscot, was decorated with stucco, made with lime, marble power and pigments, featuring floral motifs. The floor was covered in grey hexagonal tiles made by the J. Romeu Escofet factory, and the coffered ceiling was embellished with borders of green and tan-coloured plant motifs, sunflowers and lines ending with a whiplash motif on a white background.

The ground floor was set a metre and a half above street level and accessed by an imperial-style marble staircase, which was not included in the original project. Domènech designed the staircase as a functional and decorative element. It was covered with stucco with floral designs and had wrought-iron banisters. The architect transformed the back of the banisters into the backrest of a waiting bench and added Josep Thomas's monogram in repoussé work. It is flanked by two German-style escutcheons containing a stylised sunflower with a phoenix inside it. These two symbolic icons are repeated throughout the interior and exterior of the building.

This unusual bench was used by clients who were waiting to be seen by the company's managers or owners, who had their offices on the same landing. The offices had wood-panelled walls carved by the Viladevall brothers. The wood was combined with panes of glass, which let in light from the street, thereby avoiding partitions that would make the rooms dark and enclosed. The area where the offices were located was considered the most elegant part of the company's premises, and the architect chose to use the floral encaustic tiles made by Escofet Tejera i Cia and featured in their 1891 catalogue. They were designed by Josep Pascó, and are among his most distinctive works, containing geometric motifs, dragons and fan-palm leaves, in shades of grey, cream and garnet red.

The offices were located at the front of the building and overlooked Carrer Mallorca. They received natural light through the glass frontage with the segmental arch. At the time, the frontage had stained-glass panels by Antoni Rigalt, who was also entrusted with the stained-glass windows on the first floor.

The office area led into the workshop. It was a spacious, open-plan area set out on two levels: the semi-basement that housed the machinery and laboratories, and the ground floor, which was used as a storeroom for their products, including books, magazines, photoengravings, and postcards. Domènech designed a series of large cupboards to store them in, with a sunflower as the ornamental motif.

The ground floor and semi-basement received light from the glass frontage as well as a central skylight above the first floor.

Domènech set aside a space for the chimney at the back of the building, which is still standing today. This chimney was used during the early years of the company to evacuate the smoke from the steam engine that drove the machinery, until electric motors were introduced.

The entrance to the Thomas family apartments

The main door to the family apartments was located on the right-hand side of the building. Domènech wanted to show off the family's status by placing a Roman mosaic carpet by the entrance. It was made by the mosaicist Lluís Bru Salelles, and reproduced, with different tesserae, a series of rampant phoenixes that welcomed visitors. Bru created a mosaic wainscot with floral motifs in shades of red, pink, green, white and black, which contrasted sharply with the tiles on the wall and the marble used on the floor and the columns attached to walls in the hall. On the first-floor landing, almost on the same level as the ground floor of the workshop, we can see the lavish ornamentation achieved through the use of different materials, including stone, marble, tiles with a metallic finish, wood, stained glass and mosaic, which are skilfully combined to make the ensemble elegant and majestic.

The walls of the hall and staircase leading to the apartments are a combination of stone and the tiles used on the façade. Domènech introduces another symbolic animal to this space to accompany the phoenix: a rampant lion.

Domènech also designed different stone sculptural elements, with floral, mythological and heraldic motifs. The eye-catching corbels above the pilasters are carved with blank coats of arms held up by pairs of animals and fantastic beasts associated with cosmogony, or the origin of the universe, and its relationship to the four main elements of nature: water, earth, air and fire.

The iconographic repertoire of these figures is associated with the medieval bestiaries which Domènech sought to revive with the express purpose of conveying moral messages, as well as for purely decorative ends.

When the building was extended in 1912, new corbels were added in the passageway connecting the second staircase and lift. They feature carvings of two primates, the basilisk and anthropomorphic figures with elements associated with printing and photography, which were related to the two sculptural reliefs Domènech included on either side of the segmental arch on Carrer Mallorca, referring to the company's activities.

The stonework in the hall and on the staircase was attributed to Alfons Juyol i Bach (1860-1917), who had already worked with Domènech and Eusebi Arnau on important projects such as the Pontifical Seminary in Comillas.

The stairwell had a wooden coffered ceiling made by the Viladevall brothers. It had rectangular coffers carved with decorative motifs consisting of quatrefoils and fleurons suspended from the intersections of the crossbeams.

The Thomas family home

The mezzanine floor of the building covers an area of 400 metres. The family apartment had three skylights, one in the centre and two at the sides, which had stained-glass panels made by Antoni Rigalt Blanch's workshop.

Once inside the house, the hall or lobby led into the three rooms: Josep Thomas's office, the anteroom that connected the rooms at the front of the building and the passageway leading to the kitchen, dining room and other rooms. The main sitting room had side doors leading out onto the gallery on the main façade and a door in the centre. It had sliding doors communicating with the Viladevall brothers' workshop, Josep Thomas's office and another sitting room.

This room and the two adjacent ones have ornate coffered ceilings, with elongated, rectangular coffers decorated with gilded floral friezes, and square coffers with wooden carvings depicting different elements: the sun, the phoenix, intertwining leaves, lizards arranged in a quatrefoil motif and an olive branch.

Lluís Bru used different tile and mosaic designs on the floors in each room, making each one of them distinct. The coffered ceilings are also individual in style and painted with plant motifs in different shades.

Domènech placed the dining room in the middle of the back wall of the house. It had access to two small rooms that led into the bedrooms, each of which had their own bathroom. The dining room took pride of place in the house and was one of the most elegant rooms with its spectacular coffered ceiling made by the Viladevall brothers. It is a richly decorated piece of work, with crossbeams adorned with plant motifs and friezes in shades of green, red, yellow and gold, and carved fleurons. The square coffers around the edge are painted with the coats of arms of Barcelona and Catalonia. Below them, a dado that marks the transition from the coffered ceiling to the wall is inscribed with the Lord's Prayer in Domènech's trademark Gothic lettering.

There is a mural on a canvas backing on the upper part of the wall. It was painted in oil by Alexandre de Riquer and depicts the four seasons. Alexandre de Riquer's collaboration with Domènech i Montaner should come as no surprise as they had worked together some years earlier when Domènech had taken over the family publishing business, with his brothers Eduard and Enric, following their father's death in 1873. The brothers oversaw the publication of the collection, the *Biblioteca Arte y Letras*, and Lluís Domènech was the art director of the project. They worked with illustrators of the calibre of Apel·les Mestres, Arturo Mélida, Josep Pascó and Alexandre de Riquer.

The group of collaborators who worked on the interiors of the house did not end here. Domènech also worked with the cabinetmaker and interior designer Gaspar Homar, who remained true to his concept of the total work of art. Homar worked on nearly all Domènech's projects, and also designed some of the furniture for the interior of the Thomas family home.

The refurbishment of the Casa Thomas

Josep Thomas Bigas died in 1910 in Berne (Switzerland) where he had travelled to recuperate from an illness.

Two years later, his children, who had taken over the family business, decided to extend the building and add three extra floors. They commissioned the architect Francesc Guàrdia i Vial to carry out the project. Guàrdia built the new floors in the style of Domènech's original design and even transferred the sculptural roof cresting to the top of the new structure. This shows how much Guàrdia respected his associate's original work. Guàrdia hired the same artisans who had worked for Domènech and even used the same materials. This extension project established Francesc Guàrdia's position as the true heir to Domènech i Montaner's designs and showed how much Domènech had influenced him. Domènech entrusted him with such important works as the Palau de la Música Catalana in Barcelona and the Casa Domènech in Canet de Mar.

→ Sculpture of a grasshopper on the top of the building.

Top of the main façade.

Main façade.

Detail of the workshop door.

Detail of the door to the family apartments.

Monogram on the façade.

Monogram on the backrest of the bench in the lobby.

Lobby with the staircase leading to the workshop.

→ Detail of the banister.

Lift and stairs used by the residents.

Corbels in the lobby.

Grand staircase, first flight.

Grand staircase, second flight.

Ceramic decoration on the walls of the grand staircase.

Casa Thomas

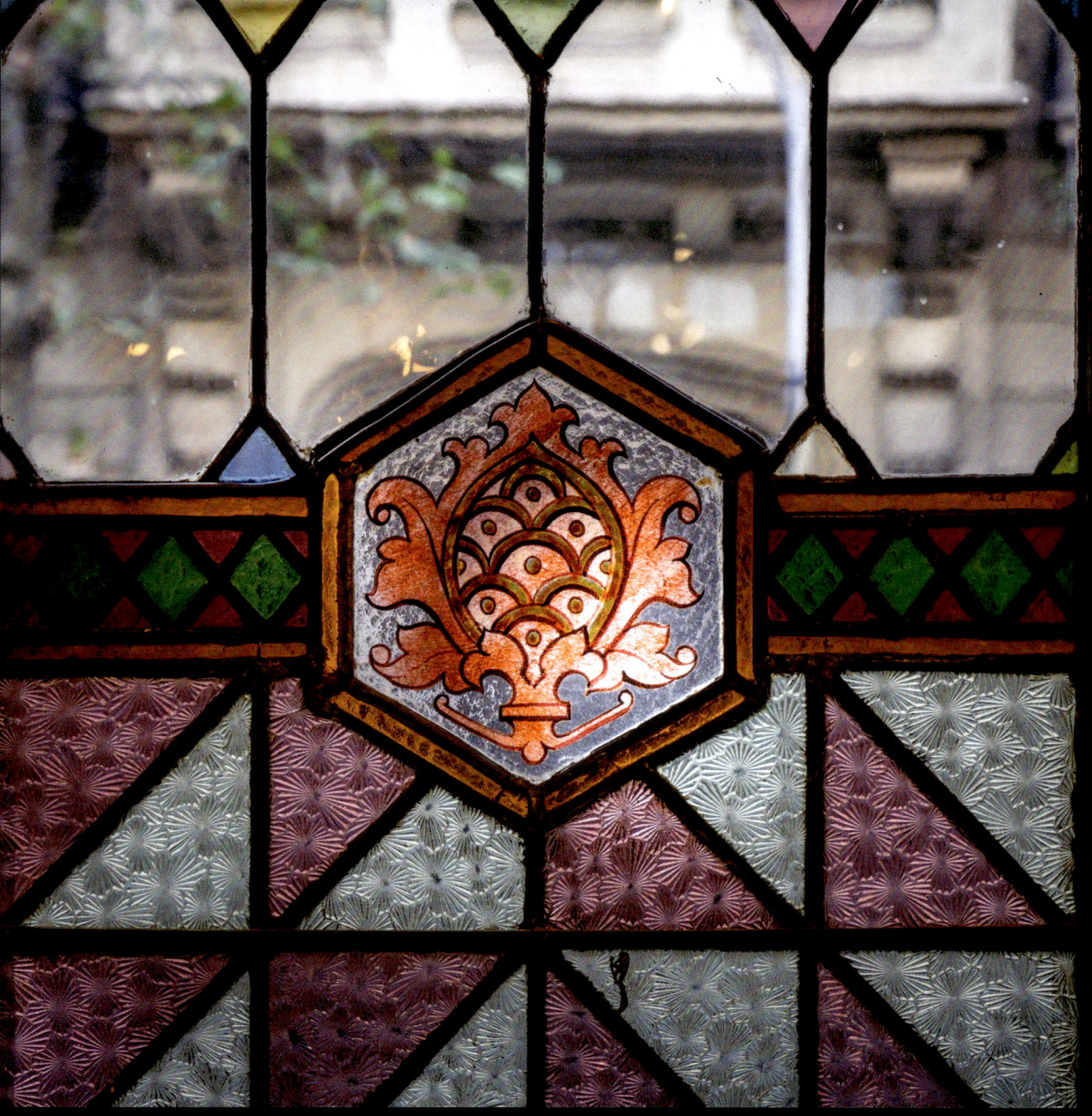
Floral motif in the stained-glass window in the workshop.

Floral motif in the stained-glass in the skylight.

← → The stained glass features a plethora of plant motifs.

← Interior of the lift.

→ Door to the first floor.

Detail of the decorations on the capitals above the columns in the gallery.

← First-floor gallery.

Roman-style mosaic in the passageway on the first floor.

→ Ceramic floor featuring the Catalan saying "Bo es anar, millor a casa s'estar" (There's no place like home).

Wooden carving on the ceiling of one of the rooms on the first floor.

→ Dining room ceiling inscribed with the Lord's Prayer.

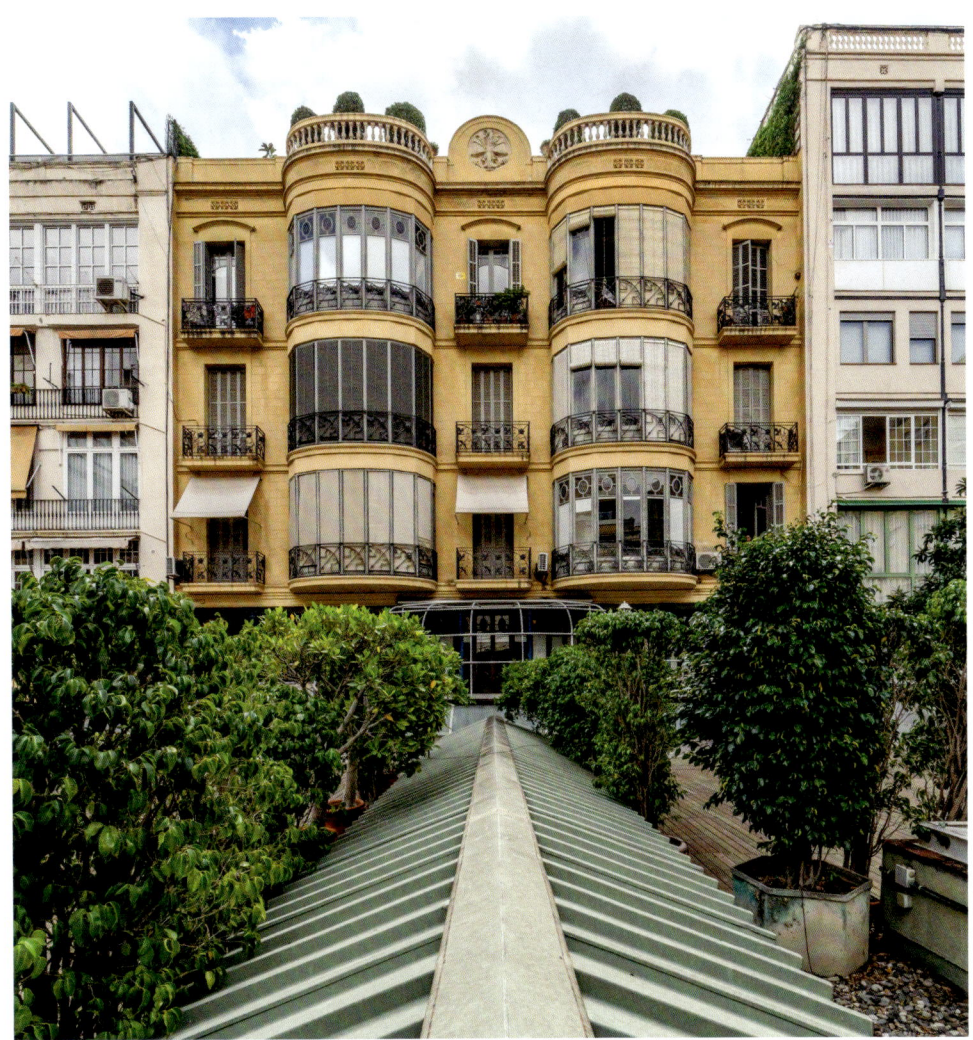

Rear façade of the building.

← Gallery in the dining room overlooking the inner courtyard. The workshop chimney is still standing.

Castell de Santa Florentina 1896-1912

Carles Sàiz i Xiqués

In 1882, Ramon Montaner i Vila, the co-owner of the publishing house Montaner i Simon, expressed a desire to reclaim his ancestral home, the 14th-century fortress, the Casa Forta, on the outskirts of the coastal town of Canet de Mar (Sàiz, 2008, pp. 3-4). After he had purchased the property, he asked his nephew, the architect Lluís Domènech i Montaner, to carry out a complete restoration of the building so that he could use it as his summer home. Domènech rebuilt the roofs that had fallen into disrepair over the centuries, and, to return it to its former state, he started work on refurbishing the interiors. The architect repaired the walls and floors, added new windows and rebuilt the tops of the defence towers that had been damaged. He even restored the former chapel, dedicated to Saint Florentina. (Sadurní, 2008, p. 46)

The "restoration in the style of the original" of the Casa Forta in Canet

However, Ramon de Montaner was not only intent on reclaiming his ancestral home. Over a decade later, in 1896, after completing the decorative work on the Palau Montaner in Barcelona, Lluís Domènech began working on a commission to extend the Casa Forta in Canet. The architect had no hesitation in telling Ramon Montaner that if he wanted to maintain the stylistic unity of the original building, his only option was to create one in the neo-medieval style. With this approach, Domènech echoed the theories of Elies Rogent – the founder of archaeological medievalism in Catalonia – and Eugène Viollet-le-Duc, who invented the concept of modern restoration. Domènech had already read two of Viollet-le-Duc's key works, *Entretiens sur l'architecture* and *Dictionnaire raisonné de l'architecture*, in which he developed the theory of "restoration in the style of the original". Domènech also had in-depth knowledge of the wealth of Catalonia's Romanesque and Gothic heritage and had taken part in several field trips to establish the different typologies of medieval Catalan buildings. As a result of his experiences, in 1879, Domènech gave an interesting lecture entitled "Carácters propis de l'arquitectura catalana á través de diferentas épocas y estils artístichs" (Inherent characteristics of Catalan architecture through different eras and artistic styles), which looked at civil architecture. If we take as an example Domènech's words below, about his proposal for the extension of the Casa Forta, we will see that he had chosen to recreate the structure of a Catalan Gothic palace.

> "An open, central courtyard; main rooms arranged around a gallery with small arches (Romanesque tradition) and on the first floor; a completely open, grand staircase in the courtyard; on the ground floor, auxiliary rooms and the removal of the galleries; large, diminished arches which are extremely wide to allow free circulation. The rooms or buildings let in light from outside. Materials: mainly stone arranged in small, well-worked ashlars [...]. Structure: [...] The arches at the entrance, rounded, with long keystones with small mouldings on the intrados. Decoration: outside, solid forms predominate over the empty spaces: smooth stretches of wall; the decoration is concentrated on the doorways and windows, on the sides, on the balustrades and cornices; predominance of straight, horizontal lines; predominance of square shapes in the cartouches, leaves, fleurons, herringbone motifs, etc.; fine, delicately studied mouldings; the ornamentation is drawn from the human figure, from real and fantastic fauna and the flora of the region [...]. Historical escutcheons and heraldic symbols are frequently used as decoration." (Domènech, 1879, pp. 95-96)

In order to ensure the new building was unique, Domènech wanted to add original Gothic features. Between 1896 and 1899 he purchased elements from

← Castle of Santa Florentina. Anonymous, n.d. Arxiu Històric del COAC.

ancient buildings. He acquired a doorway with a keystone from a mansion on Carrer Ample in Barcelona, another doorway from a house on Carrer Paradís and, at the beginning of the century, when the new thoroughfare, Via Laietana, was being built, he managed to get hold of different elements from the buildings that had been affected by this major urban redevelopment project, which had cut open this part of town. Ramon Montaner also bought 15th-century windows from the counties of Lleida and also wanted to purchase the convent in Bellpuig. However, once the owner realised that Montaner only wanted to strip the building of its most highly prized elements, he soon withdrew from the sale. (Yeguas, 2003, p. 32)

The most important finds – in terms of quantity and quality – date from 1896.

When Domènech was visiting the monastery of Poblet, he decided to visit the old monastery in Tallat and, as Pere Domènech i Roura, who was travelling with his father, recalled, it was:

> "Perfect, carefully crafted 15th-century Gothic architecture, which is more civil in style than religious, consisting of a ground floor, mezzanine and large attic, arranged around a large courtyard, with cloisters on one side [...]. It was all made of stone ashlars, [...] and smooth walls with scarcely any openings outside [...]. You enter through a rounded arch with long keystones and a hallway running lengthways to the courtyard with a 15th-century Gothic ceiling with ribbed vaulting and five keystones. All the splendour of the building is centred on the vast courtyard, with windows, a cloister walk and decorated doors, all of them noteworthy and some of them unique." (Domènech, 1948, p. 1)

The intellectual Pau Font de Rubinat, who hailed from the town of Reus and was a close friend of Lluís Domènech's, owned half of Tallat. He had purchased it to extend his family home, the Mas Misericòrdia in Reus, but the project never came to fruition and, in 1898, Rubinat agreed to sell Ramon Montaner the Gothic windows, the doors in the same style and the monastery gallery. Domènech began working on the Casa Forta a few months later, using the elements purchased from Tallat. (Sàiz, 2014, p. 107)

From the Casa Forta in Canet to the castle of Santa Florentina

Lluís Domènech designed an open-air courtyard at the rear of the old building, and arranged around it the different rooms that were part of the extension project. The ground floor was used for storerooms and cellars, and the grand rooms, sitting rooms, dining rooms, the main bathroom – in the Catalan art nouveau, or *modernista*, style – and guest bedrooms were placed on the first floor. Domènech also designed a second floor in the west wing of the building. It had a gallery of diminished arches, very similar to the ones used in the architraves of Gothic mansions in Barcelona.

The perimeter walls of the new building were already in place by 1904. The roofs had also been completed and the windows and tall cloister from Tallat had been assembled. Pere Domènech, who had just finished his architecture degree, remembered that:

> "We had to design the floor plan in the current trapezoidal shape so that the gallery would fit into the courtyard, which was not the same size as a standard one, and, for this reason, it occurred to us to build an exterior staircase in the courtyard – which is new and did not exist at Tallat – because we were unable to build a monumental interior staircase, due to the small size of the plot." (Domènech, 1948, p. 2)

In order to ensure a supply of natural stone for the extension project, Ramon Montaner purchased a quarry on the slope on the west side of the property. Domènech devised a system of rails with wagons to transport the granite blocks to the Casa Forta.

The architect supervised the extension of the building right down to the last detail. He hired Dídac Masana, Joan Buzzi Gussoni, Antoni Samarra Tugues and Carles Flotats Galtés to create the sculptural elements and to bring his sketches to life. Flotats carved the sixty gargoyles in the new part of the castle of Santa Florentina, while Samarra, who worked at the Masana workshop, made the lions flanking the new entrance to the building with its keystone, the dragon on the outer staircase, as well as the sixty-five corbels with their anthropomorphic and animal motifs that underpin the new wooden beams in the gallery from Tallat. (Sàiz, 2007, pp. 21-33)

The Masana workshop also made the large load-bearing arches and the windows with their pointed arches – one of them with carved fretwork tracery – in the grand hall, the segmental arches in the loggia on the second floor, and the arch leading into the medieval part of the building. The latter was carved by Dídac Masana, and includes in the intrados, three pointed arches made of jasper and capitals depicting maidens, pages and knights who are worshipping Saint Florentina during the festival of the Virgins: an ancient tradition revived by the Montaners in 1882. (Mas, 2017, p. 147)

One of the chroniclers of the day, Pere Pagès, described how building work was progressing in 1908:

> "Beneath a door with broad keystones, taken from an old mansion in Barcelona, you enter the spacious courtyard, which piques the curiosity of the visitor. One of the towers peers out on one corner and, above it, the castle keep rises up boldly. If you look around the courtyard, you will notice architectural details, some of them well known to the hikers who have made a patriotic pilgrimage around our land, visiting what remains of its beautiful ancient monuments.
>
> Exquisite Gothic windows; sumptuous windows with pointed arches, carved with fretwork tracery, supported by slender columns, crowned with artistic capitals; fantastic gargoyles; the typical small chapel; an ancient stone image of the Virgin; a skilfully worked, robust gate preventing access to the chapel of Saint Florentina, a broad and majestic staircase with its typical mounting block. [...]
>
> In the gallery, all the doors are set inside the old door frames from ancient mansions, in the beautiful Gothic style. One of them leads into the grand hall to which Montaner and Campmany have brought a wealth of detail and very good taste. It is an artistically lavish evocation of the medieval style.
>
> It is spacious and well proportioned, with a sumptuous coffered ceiling with sculpted crossbeams. Majestic Gothic windows with delicate fretwork tracery, slender columns and beautiful stained glass stand guard in the courtyard. A monumental and artistic fireplace occupies the length of a wall, with fire irons and other implements from the fireplace of the memorable castle of Casp. We can assume that, around these iron utensils, were arranged images of Saint Vincent Ferrer and the other representatives of the town ruled by the Crown of Aragon. This monumental fireplace has a frieze with figures underpinned by decorative motifs and curious capitals."

The monumental fireplace that is the centrepiece of the grand hall in the castle was also carved by Dídac Masana. It depicts the granting of a municipal charter to the town of Canet by the Marquis of Aitona, Gastó de Moncada i Gralla, in 1599 (Pons, 1999, pp. 12-16). Ramon de Montaner is certain to have wanted to include this scene, as his forbears were witnesses at the ceremony.

The grand hall also has a splendid coffered ceiling and crossbeams, polychromed by Joaquim Rovira Manyé, based on medieval models. The stained-glass windows set inside pointed frames depict the crucifixion of Jesus and the Epiphany. They were drawn by the designer Ricard de Capmany and made by Josep Pujol.

The Montaner crypt

The sudden death of Ramon de Montaner's wife, Florentina Malató i Surinyach, at the end of 1900, brought the extension of the Casa Forta to a temporary standstill. Malató's body was taken to Canet and buried in a niche in the town cemetery. Shortly afterwards, Montaner wrote to the mayor of Canet de Mar requesting him to ask the government minister for permission to build a crypt in the basement of the castle. On 6th March 1901, the newspaper *La Dinastía* published an official announcement that read:

> "The civil government of this province has informed Mr Ramón Montaner y Vila of the authorisation granted by His Majesty's government to build a mausoleum at the castle of Santa Florentina, in the town of Canet de Mar, to bury his wife and other members of his family."

After obtaining permission, Ramon de Montaner asked Lluís Domènech to design a burial crypt, and work began a few months later. The level of the floor in the basement was lowered by 4 metres, and all the foundations in the old part of the castle were reinforced.

Domènech designed a staircase leading down to the crypt and decorated it with different sculptural elements inside quarter-sphere vaults; a Christ Pantocrator with the evangelists, which fully embodies the art nouveau, or *modernista*, style, and, at another end, Domènech depicted the Apocalypse and Last Judgement. Both sculptures were made at Dídac Masana's workshop and are highly interesting.

The architect clad the crypt in marble slabs and underpinned the roof of the funeral chamber with columns made of limestone from Girona with white marble capitals, which feature religious scenes carved by Dídac Masana and Anton Samarra. The festooned arches and ribs with their floral and zoomorphic motifs supporting the vaulted ceiling in the crypt were also made at the Masana's workshop.

Domènech designed a number of burial niches in one of the walls and a series of tombs under the crypt floor. He set aside the central space for Florentina Malató's tomb. It would feature a recumbent effigy of the deceased, with subtle realistic tones of colour on her clothing in the purest French style. The effigy was modelled by Miquel Blay i Fàbregas, who made a special trip from Paris to see its future location, and carved at Frederic Bechini Bagnasco's workshop. (Serra, 2008, p. 455)

The funeral chamber was completed with two small neo-Gothic sarcophagi – made by Dídac Masana to house the remains of Ramon de Montaner's parents – and a highly-prized Venetian-mosaic frieze, around the section of Florentina Malató's tomb in the apse of the crypt. The mosaic was designed by Josep Triadó Mayol, who also drew the festival of the Virgins, featuring maidens dressed in white, wandering through the Casa Forta and in its grounds, holding hortensia flowers, which symbolise spiritual happiness. Triadó also designed the stained-glass windows in the crypt, which were made by Josep Pujol, the one depicting Saint Florentina, and the scene showing Pope Benedict XII handing the relics of the Virgin to Lord Ferrer of Canet. (Sàiz, 2008, pp. 133-136)

The medieval setting of the castle of Santa Florentina

The Madrid newspaper *La Época* (8th November 1908) described work at the castle as follows:

> "The Montaners [...] have restored the old part and extended the living quarters. The throne room is part of the second extension, and is being carried out with such skill, imitating the original building, that nobody would know where it ends and where the modern one begins."

Nuevo Mundo (19th November 1908) also drew attention to the building, and said:

> "Here is the castle of Santa Florentina: the reconstruction of a building in the 20th century, with 15th-century plans and materials, which have been wisely and artistically put to use."

Ramon de Montaner's love of collecting had led him to amass a vast amount of antiques and art objects, which he used to recreate the castle's medieval ambiance. Domènech i Montaner and Ricard de Capmany, who carried out the interior design, decorated it with 15th- and 16th-century chests of drawers; Flemish tapestries; 15th-century imagery from the Castilian school; carvings by the Aragonese school; sculptures by Bartomeu de Robió and Pere Oller; and paintings by Pedro García de Benabarre and Jaume Huguet. Put in a nutshell, it was a complete artistic repertoire, which fully represented Hispanic art of the 15th and 16th centuries. (Sàiz, 2014, pp. 123-124)

The magazine *Agricultura* (20th May 1918) said that the grand hall of the castle had:

> "A large collection of archaeological pieces of inestimable worth due to their age and perfect state of preservation. The collection of tapestries hanging on the walls in the main dining room, the medieval shields, stained-glass windows, chests and coffers; [...] and the beautiful arrangement of the tiniest details, [...] make the castle of Santa Florentina one of the most splendid examples of monumental Catalonia."

Domènech also built coffered ceilings, with geometric motifs, in the bedrooms at the castle. The walls were covered with damask silks, in different tones, made by the textile company, Malvehy. Montaner also purchased a selection of Mallorcan beds with canopies, which he put in the rooms to create a distinctive atmosphere. Domènech also designed a series of carved-stone fireplaces with subtle ornamental elements, which completed the décor in the bedrooms. We have found descriptions of some of the bedrooms. One of them is reported as follows:

> "The bed has a headboard and Solomonic columns. The mattress, the canopy and curtains are deep salmon pink and are embroidered with Empire-style crowns. The walls of the room are covered with the same material. A prie-dieu, in front of a large ivory crucifix. [...]"

Another bedroom has a similar bed: "but the mattress is made of silk and is embroidered with Louis XV-style floral motifs". Others are said to have "a mattress and curtains of rich yellow damask. On one side there is a chest of drawers with marquetry inlays."

We also have a description of Ramon Montaner's study:

> "On the walls, damasks with a blue background blend into silver floral motifs. The table is very ornate, with bone inlays. There is a leather wallet on the table top, a silver smoking tray, and an enamelled inkwell [...]. Opposite, an Italian Renaissance bureau with a curved front. It makes up a set with the table."

With Ramon de Montaner's art and antiques collections, the castle of Santa Florentina soon resembled a museum. From this time on, the Montaners hosted lavish social events at the castle and, in 1908, welcomed King Alfonso XIII who was on a tour of Catalonia. The monarch's visit was a step towards Montaner's ennoblement, and the young king named him count of the Vall de Canet a year later.

Lluís Domènech i Montaner carried out a faithful restoration of the Casa Forta in Canet de Mar between 1882 and 1884. From 1899 onwards, he planned to recreate the building based on the Gothic palace model and Viollet-le-Duc's theory of "restoration in the style of the original". At the time, Le-Duc's solution was the most appropriate to achieve Ramon de Montaner's social aims. Nevertheless, Domènech's rigour and meticulousness, as a scholar of medieval heritage, meant he had to rationalise the excessive neo-medievalism advocated by the French architect. With the recreation of the castle of Santa Florentina, Domènech ended up creating an eclectic building, which established an interesting architectural dialogue between the original Gothic style of the old building, romantic neo-medievalism and the most vibrant art nouveau, or *modernisme*, in the crypt. The balanced stylistic result may be why Josep Puig i Cadafalch had no hesitation in describing Lluís Domènech i Montaner as "the Viollet-le-Duc of Catalonia, but more precise and truthful." (Puig, 1902, p. 546)

← Main entrance.

→ View of the grand hall.

Skylight in the winter dining room
by stained-glass artist Josep Pujol.

→ Fireplace in the grand hall.

Window in the dining room
with a traditional stone settle.

Bath with ceramic floral motifs.

Sculptural relief depicting the Apocalypse made at Dídac Masana's workshop.

General view of the crypt.

Steps leading down to the crypt.

← Crypt. Florentina Malató i Surinyach's tomb.

→ Detail of the sculpture for the tomb modelled by Miquel Blay and carved at the studio of the sculptor Frederic Bechini Bagnasco.

Institut Pere Mata

1897-1912

Jordi March Barberà · Clàudia Sanmartí Martínez

The Institut Pere Mata in Reus is an architectural complex in the garden-city style designed by Domènech i Montaner to house a psychiatric hospital. It was considered a test bed for his subsequent project for the Hospital de la Santa Creu i Sant Pau in Barcelona. When the illustrious administrative board of the Barcelona hospital chose Domènech to plan the new complex, rejecting Domènech i Estapà's project that had been selected in the call for entries, they argued that the architect had "a special knowledge about constructing these kinds of buildings". However, the hospital in Reus took such a long time that some of the buildings were constructed simultaneously in both cities. Building work on the psychiatric hospital was carried out in phases, whenever sufficient funds were available. This was the major difference between this project and the Barcelona hospital. The number of pavilions specified in the original design was reduced and alterations were made based on the needs of the hospital complex and changes in psychiatric treatment.

The building of the Institut Pere Mata also marked the start of Domènech's relationship with the bourgeoisie in Reus, who commissioned him to design a number of important buildings, which had a clear influence on some of the buildings by the municipal architect Pere Caselles, who was responsible for most of the city's *modernista* landmarks.

In the second half of the 19th century, the municipal asylum, known as Ca l'Agulla, was the main psychiatric hospital in the province. It housed mentally ill patients in precarious conditions, with a view to keeping them shut away from society rather than helping them to recover (Poca, 1996). Emili Briansó Planas, who graduated in medicine in 1884, was the municipal forensic physician and one of his tasks was to run the asylum. He realised that there was a need to build new premises that would treat the patients in accordance with the latest breakthroughs in medicine. He was also aware that the local government would not fund these improvements and decided to look for backing from private investors so that the ambitious project could go ahead.

A number of private psychiatric institutions had been founded in Catalonia from the middle of the 19th century onwards: the Torre Llunàtica in Lloret, the Institut Manicomi in Sant Boi de Llobregat, the Nova Betlem in Gràcia (which later moved to Sant Gervasi), the Institut Frenopàtic in Les Corts de Sarrià. In 1875, a royal decree placed charitable services (that encompassed public and private services) under the inspection of the central and regional governments, and regulated the charitable services offered by private psychiatric hospitals, establishing a subsidised payment system (Labad, 2004, p. 211). Dr Briansó obtained the support of thirty-five traders, liberal professionals, proprietors and industrialists who founded the company, the Sociedad Anónima Manicomio de Reus, in 1896, with the purpose of building a new hospital complex, based on the most advanced models of architecture in psychiatric buildings in other countries, while making sure the investment was cost-effective. They commissioned Domènech i Montaner, who was already a prestigious architect, to design the building. Domènech was a fellow activist in the political party, the Unió Catalanista, with the first chairman of the board of trustees of the company, Pau Font de Rubinat. A working commission was also set up comprising Domènech, the municipal architect from Reus, Pere Casellas, and the eminent Barcelona physicians Artur Galceran Granés (a psychiatrist who introduced electrotherapy applied to mental health and was the founder and president of the Societat de Psiquiatria i Neurologia de Barcelona) and Rafael Rodríguez Méndez (hygiene professor at the University of Barcelona, where he was chancellor,

← General services and administration pavilion, c. 1900.
Arxiu Fotogràfic del Centre Excursionista de Catalunya.

and co-director of the psychiatric hospital in Sant Boi, where he introduced music therapy).

By choosing this team, the board sought to define the medical criteria that would guide the architectural project in order to build the best psychiatric institution in the country. Domènech began working on an in-depth study based on the literature available in different languages (continuing with the methodology he had first developed in his project for the Instituciones Provinciales with Josep Vilaseca in 1877) about the most modern hospital typologies in Europe and the United States (Domènech i Montaner, 1900). He used this study shortly afterwards to secure the commission for the Hospital de Sant Pau. Galceran had already studied examples of hospitals in other countries, as reflected in his publication *La medicina mental y los manicomios en Italia. Apuntes de un viaje científico* (1893).

The project brings together the main characteristics that a model psychiatric hospital should have, based on the literature of the time. For instance, in her doctoral thesis, Prudenci Sereñana (Sereñana, 1884, p. 21) points out that it should be located away from urban centres, well ventilated, free of damp and stagnant water and have good views. In November 1896, Domènech, Caselles, Briansó, Rodríguez and Galceran visited potential sites until they came across a plot of land on the outskirts of Reus, on a hilltop in the district of Monterols, near the avenue, the Passeig de la Boca de la Mina. The site met all the criteria specified by Sereñana.

The trust purchased a 4.7 hectare plot that was later extended with the inclusion of adjacent land. In 1897, Domènech presented the general project to build eighteen independent buildings in a pavilion or village-style layout, designed like a small garden city ("Instituto Frenopático Pedro Mata. Reus, Tarragona," 1914). The low density of the buildings was a very important factor along with excellent ventilation, a sunny aspect and a garden setting.

Domènech's ambitious project envisaged dedicated pavilions for different types of patients, not just based on gender but on their financial status (for first-, second- and third-class fee-paying patients and charity-funded patients), a chapel, an administration pavilion, a pavilion providing general services, pavilions for epileptics and people with infectious diseases, who were kept separate from the other patients, an infirmary and a small mortuary ("Instituto Pedro Mata [Manicomio de Reus]," 1915). The residential pavilions had private gardens, separated by fences, which were used by the patients from each building. The other open spaces and the two long avenues that cut through the hospital grounds from north to south and east to west, were to be planted with trees (I. P. M., 1929). Almost all the hospital perimeter was surrounded by solid fencing to guarantee patient safety. It was set into a ditch, so that the patients could still see the surrounding landscape and would not feel they had been shut away.

The different buildings were unified through the use of the same materials and finishes: gable roofs with Arabic tiles, a stone base, exposed brick walls decorated with stone frames and sculptural elements and white and blue ceramic ornamental panels. The façades are replete with symbolic elements. The first buildings feature pansies with the inscription *se refaran* (they will be remade) accompanied by the year *1898*, and the phoenix with the inscription *renascitur* (reborn), a true statement of intent. The rose featured on the Reus coat of arms is a repeated motif, along with the four stripes of the Catalan flag, guardian angels, the monogram IPM and depictions of the theological virtues.

We often encounter different versions of the emblem of the Institut Pere Mata: a female figure holding a torch, and pouring oil onto it with her other hand to keep the flame burning and accompanied by the motto *de nou lluirà* (it will shine anew). The most spectacular example of this emblem is perhaps the one in the ceiling in the distinguished guests' pavilion by the mosaicist Lluís Bru.

The lavish decoration can be understood as part of the therapeutic treatment of the patients. Galceran wrote: "because the aesthetic condition is also a curative condition in such establishments, in view of the influence of beauty on the ethical psyche." (Galceran, 1902)

Work on the general services and administration pavilion and the pavilion for the 3rd-class fee-paying patients, and charity patients, began in March 1898. The first patients were transferred to the hospital from the municipal asylum on 12th March 1900: twenty-four men and sixteen women. Work continued as funding became available but only five of the eighteen pavilions included in Domènech's plan were built according to their original layout. (Poca i Gaya, 1996)

Sketch for the refurbishment project, 1893. Digitised copy of the original image, which is kept at the Institut Pere Mata, published in the magazine *Pragma*.

→ General plan of the buildings according to Domènech i Montaner's project.

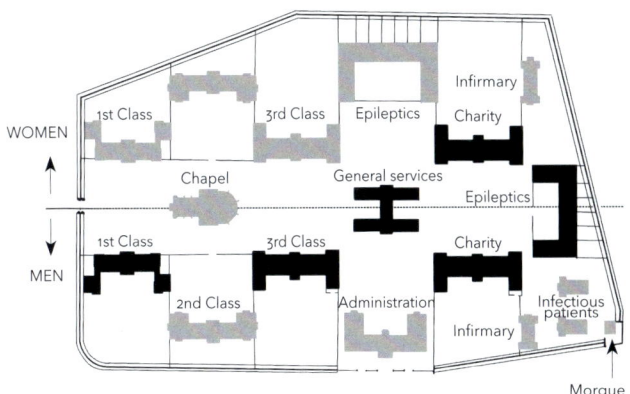

Institut Pere Mata • 187

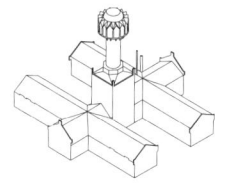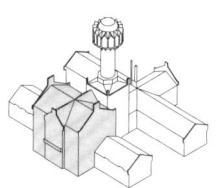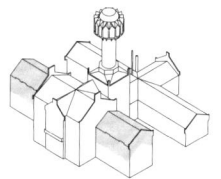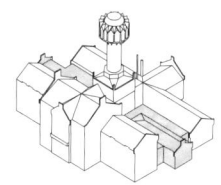

Sketch showing the progress of the general services and administration pavilion. Clàudia Sanmartí.

General services and administration pavilion

The general services pavilion was located where the two main axes of the project converged. The original purpose of the pavilion was to house the services that were essential for the running of the hospital: kitchen, laundry, hydrotherapy and electrotherapy services (which were both truly innovative at the time), the pharmacy and the water tower. However, the project was altered at the start of building work and rooms were added.

Domènech's overall project included a large administration pavilion facing the entrance on Passeig de la Boca de la Mina. The board of trustees rejected the budget as it was too high and asked the architect to redraft a new one at a lower cost. Domènech refused, saying that he was unable to alter the project and suggested postponing the building until a later date and adapting the general services pavilion to house some of the administration offices on a temporary basis. This is what happened and the majestic pavilion that had been planned to mark the main entrance to the hospital was never built.

In November 1897, Domènech presented a new project for the general services building, which now housed some of the administration offices and the rooms of the hospital's medical director and majordomo. Building work began with the drilling of a well to find a water source. The sufficient flow rate was found 60 metres below the ground at a point that did not align with the intended site of the building. This meant that the building had to be shifted a little as the water tower needed to stand above the shaft of the well.

The building had an H-shaped floor plan, with two rectangular sections on the east and west sides with the tall water tower in the centre of the crosswise building that connected them. The eastern section was altered with the addition of two storeys to the central section. They housed the administrative offices and residential rooms. The kitchen, laundry and other services were located in the western section. A guardian angel based on a model by Eusebi Arnau presides over the monumental façade. The three façades of this central section are surmounted by a cross pattée: the medieval emblem of hospitals.

The 28-metre-high water tower rises above the Pere Mata complex and is the representative symbol of the psychiatric hospital. It has a square base with a double wall, repeating Domènech's solution for the café and restaurant built for the 1887 Barcelona Universal Exhibition. He placed the staircase in the space in the middle. On the second floor, the base becomes octagonal with a prismatic shaft and, on the upper levels, the floor plan is circular with a spiral staircase. The staircase finally passes through the ring-shaped tank to the tapered roof which is covered in ceramic scales, with a wrought-iron balustrade and a lightning conductor with a weathervane on the top.

The spaces inside the general services pavilion have been greatly altered. Domènech i Roura refurbished them in 1923 and an extra floor was added to the sides of the building in 1928. Over the years, the open-plan spaces on the ground floor between the different sections have also been occupied by new structures. The pavilion is still used as the administration offices.

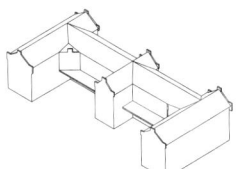 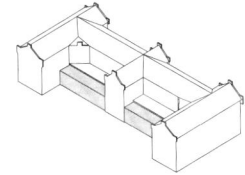

Sketch showing the progress of the charity patients' pavilion. Clàudia Sanmartí.

Third-class and charity pavilions

According to the plans, the pavilions for third-class fee-paying patients and charity patients were to be placed on either side of the lengthwise axis of the complex. The women were to be housed in the northern part and the men in the southern part. The pavilions were built in the same style. The two pavilions for men were the first ones built between 1898 and 1902. Initially they housed all categories of patients. This typology of pavilion was repeated in the second pavilion for women charity patients, built between 1910 and 1912. The third-class pavilion for women was never built and a football pitch for the inmates was built on the site. It is now a car park.

The pavilions have a ground floor, first floor and an attic space under a gable roof. The ground plan consists of a long central block connecting three perpendicular sections, in the manner of a corridor plan hospital, two at the ends and a shorter one in the centre.

The entrance was in the central section through a wooden porch that connected with the vertical staircases. The block running lengthwise had communal dormitories with twelve beds and the sections at the end were used as the day rooms, dining room and for services. There were more communal dormitories on the first floor that slept eight to twelve people. There were surveillance rooms on the corners where the long central block and end sections converge, to keep watch on five different spaces: three rooms and two service areas. These monitoring points also housed the mains switch for the electricity and the stopcocks for the water to prevent the patients from gaining access to them.

The first-floor dormitories had a triple ventilation system: through the window shutters, stone lattices with wooden doors and lattices in the vaults in the ceiling that connected to a series of ceramic pipes leading to the roof through yellow ceramic air vents. Domènech had taught the subject *The applications of the physical natural sciences in architecture* at the Barcelona School of Architecture in 1877, and his projects always used the most advanced techniques of the day: acoustics, natural and artificial light, heating, ventilation, a water supply and wastewater disposal. In order to ensure the spaces were properly ventilated (a subject mentioned in the technical journals of the day), Domènech applied the hygienic principles of the time. He repeated the solution in the pavilions housing the patients at the Hospital de Sant Pau, albeit on a larger scale.

The rear façade looked onto a garden and also had cantilevered sun decks with vaulted ceilings. They were transformed into a porch at the base to provide open-air spaces where the patients could rest and relax.

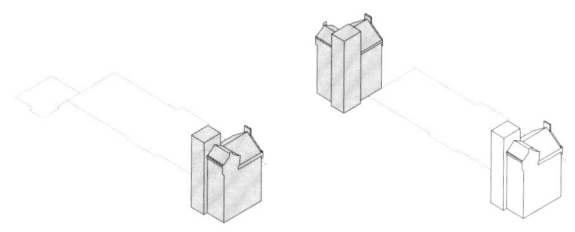 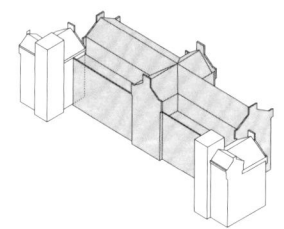

Sketch showing the progress of the distinguished guests' pavilion. Clàudia Sanmartí.

First-class pavilion or distinguished guests' pavilion

The first-class pavilion (known as the distinguished guests' pavilion) was to house the patients who could afford the most expensive fees to stay there and enjoy the best available comforts. This is the pavilion which encapsulates what Sereñana wrote in her thesis: *the true aesthetics of a mental asylum mean that as soon as the inmate crosses the threshold they will not be aware of the reality and will continue to believe, for a time, that the house where they are staying is a holiday home, a health chalet or a summer hotel.* (Sereñana, 1884, p. 21)

Due to high building costs, this pavilion was built in phases. Only the first pavilion for men on the east side was built and the one for women, on the west side, was never completed. We do not have many details about the project for the women's pavilion to enable us to study the difference between them, particularly regarding the spaces where the patients would socialise.

The pavilion was allocated a prime spot on the southeast corner of the complex, at a slight distance from the other pavilions. It had good views of the landscape, received more sunlight and was closer to the monumental entrance, the Portal dels Carros. Building work on one end of the building began in 1900 and it welcomed its first patients in 1902. It was called chalet number 1, as it was a detached building in the middle of the garden. Work began on chalet number 2 in 1903. It stood at the other end of the complex and was completed in 1905. The central section was built between 1905 and 1908 and some of the balconies and windows of the chalets were converted into doors connecting the different areas.

This building is bigger than the other pavilions and has a semi-basement, ground floor and three upper floors. It has load-bearing brick walls and metal girders. Only the dual-height common rooms on the ground floor have richly decorated brick timbrel vaults, which are very similar to the ones at the Hospital de Sant Pau. The attic floor also has a vaulted ceiling, but with no decorations because it was to be used as the servants' quarters. The façades are much more richly decorated than the other buildings and have large ceramic panels, stained glass and applied sculptural elements. The main façade, which is aligned with the avenue, has a representative function. There are large windows in the centre that let light into the elegant interior spaces. The amount of ceramic decorations increases from floor to floor. The rear façade, tying in with its more private use, has fewer decorations and a wide gallery that could be opened and converted into a covered terrace, a porch on the ground floor and an upper terrace.

The distribution and finishes of the interior spaces replicated the bourgeois homes of the day: hall, sitting room, games room, office, dining room, library, bedrooms, bathroom… There was even a dark room for developing photographs. Everything was designed and lavishly decorated in accordance with the tastes of the period and the status of the residents. Domènech's regular collaborators worked on the building: Rigalt i Granell, stained glass; Lluís Bru, mosaics and bespoke ceramic design; and J Paradís, sgraffito. There are also wonderful examples of encaustic mosaic tiles by Escofet & Tejera, and decorative ceramics by Pujol i Bausis and Hipòlit Montseny.

The communal spaces were on the ground floor, the bedrooms were on the two upper floors and the servants' quarters on the top floor. The three communal rooms were the sitting room the dining room and the billiard room, which were all dual height. The central space – the sitting room – had a long interior balcony at first-floor level. It had a balustrade with glass balusters similar to the ones at the Palau de la Música. In this case, they had a base and wooden capitals. Natural light filtered through the stained-glass windows on the two sides of the building, illuminating the space. The marquetry work in the furniture, the mosaic flooring and sgraffito work features chestnuts and chestnut leaves. There is a blindfolded female figure in the vault in the ceiling, pouring oil into a lamp, accompanied by the inscription *de nou lluirà* (it will shine anew). The figure is the emblem of the institution and was based on a design by Lluís Bru.

The sitting room leads into the dining room where the ceramic wainscoting, marquetry work on the furniture, mosaics, sgraffito work and decorative ceramics on the vaulting, depict orange trees laden with fruit. A monumental lamp hangs from the ceiling where we see the emblem of the psychiatric hospital. The billiard room is on the other side, with a billiard table and tables for playing cards and chess. The parquet flooring and wainscoting were made by the Casas i Bardés workshop. The flooring in the sitting room and dining room is a combination of ceramics and Roman mosaic.

The sitting room, games room and gallery lead to the staircase connecting the upper floors. They have ceramic wainscoting with no handrails or stairwell to prevent accidents. On the first and second floors, the individual rooms, some of which had private toilets, are distributed along the central section. The galleries overlooking the garden act as a corridor. The washrooms, toilets and communal bathrooms were at the ends. They were covered with glazed ceramic tiles to guarantee hygiene. The bedrooms are grouped in threes around a visiting room. The supervisor's room was located here. It had spyholes to check on the inmates as well as the mains switches for the electric lighting. The rooms were more luxurious at the two ends of the building, which housed the two chalets: they accommodated one patient per floor, with a bedroom, dining room, bathroom and supervisor's room. There was a small private garden for individual use on the ground floor.

One of the objectives was to make the patients feel they had not been shut away. This is why the architect avoided the use of railings and integrated them into the stained-glass panels in the windows, replacing some of the leaded lines with iron.

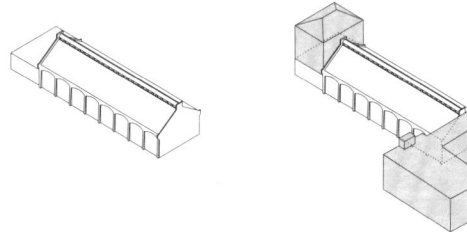
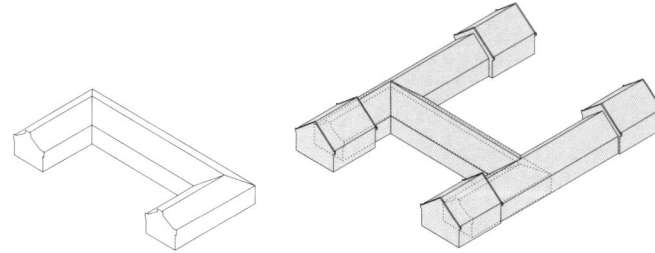

Progress of the laundry pavilion. Clàudia Sanmartí.

Progress of the epileptic patients' pavilion. Clàudia Sanmartí.

Laundry pavilion

The laundry was initially housed in the general services pavilion but had become too small. A new pavilion was built between 1911 and 1912 where the infirmary for men and infectious patients was to be located. Bedding and clothing were washed and disinfected on a special stove, dried, ironed and stored in the laundry.

The laundry pavilion is a large rectangular block, with a completely open-plan interior space. To achieve this purpose, Domènech used diaphragm arches like the ones in the attic spaces in the other pavilions. These structures were typical of Catalan Gothic architecture. In this case, the seven large pointed arches were made of brick fretwork, to make optimum use of the materials, and underpin the gable roof. Pere Domènech i Roura repeated the same structural solution at the cooperative winery, the Celler Cooperatiu, in L'Espluga de Francolí in 1913, and it was widely used in other wineries throughout Catalonia, particularly by Cèsar Martinell. Natural light was guaranteed by the wide windows on both of the longitudinal façades, the windows running along the raised roof, and the large window on the southern façade, which was blocked up by a building erected at a later date.

The building was used as a theatre for a time and a section was converted into a chapel, based on Pere Domènech i Roura's refurbishment project.

Epileptic patients' pavilion

The original project included two pavilions for epileptics: one for men and another for women. They were designed with specific architectural features to aid the treatment of these patients. Eventually, only one was built, which was bigger than had originally been envisaged.

The building has an H-shaped floor plan. The northern section has longer wings and there is a wider section above each wing with a slightly higher roof than the rest of the building. Communal spaces, such as the sitting room and dining room, were to be located here. There were rows of cells inside for the patients with corridors with large windows around the perimeter. All the ceilings had timbrel vaults and the roof had diaphragm arches that underpinned the gable roof and created an attic floor. This is the only pavilion in the hospital complex where coloured tiles were used, creating decorative geometric motifs, similar to those used at the Hospital de Sant Pau.

The pavilion no longer houses patients. One part of the building is used as offices and the other is home to the medical library.

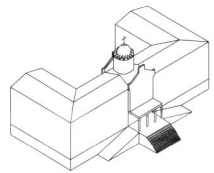

Unbuilt pavilion. Clàudia Sanmartí.

The unbuilt pavilions

The original project included different typologies of pavilion, none of which were built. This was the case with the second-class pavilions, which would have been placed between the first- and second-class ones. From the surviving documents we can deduce that these pavilions – one for each gender – had the same corridor-plan layout as the third-class and charity pavilions, but included a series of drum-shaped sections surmounted by domes on the ends. The patients, who were able to pay higher fees, would have been allocated individual rooms. According to the plans, these rooms would have been placed around a central surveillance space at each end. The pavilions were not as lavishly decorated as the first-class and distinguished guests' pavilions. There were more bedrooms on the ground floor and spaces for general services.

There were other pavilions that remained unbuilt: the large administration pavilion, a chapel, two pavilions for patients with infectious diseases, an infirmary and a small mortuary.

Building work continues

Domènech i Montaner's son, Pere Domènech i Roura, was also involved in building the hospital complex. He qualified as an architect in 1904 and from 1906 onwards visited the site from time to time and also dealt with the developers. After his father's death in 1923, he built the room for the deputy medical director and the priest, worked on the second extension of the general services pavilion and hospital extension plan in 1930.

The complex is still used as a hospital and admits long-stay and day patients. It is also a teaching and research hospital. The hospital also runs cultural tours that include the distinguished guests' pavilion. Many of the pavilions have fallen into disuse as a result of the advances in psychiatric medicine. However, despite the alterations made over the years, Domènech i Montaner's project, which dates back to 1897, still retains a spatial and architectural quality meaning that the buildings could easily be repurposed and their heritage value clearly shown.

Main entrance to the complex.

General services and administration pavilion.

Rear façade of the distinguished guests' pavilion.

Side wall of the general services pavilion.

Ceramic monogram featuring
the initials of the institution.

→ Side wall of the distinguished guests' pavilion.

Ceramic frieze decorating the walls of the pavilions for third-class fee-paying and charity patients. It features a phoenix with the motto "Renascitur" and vases of pansies with the inscription "Se refaran", with the date building work started (Reus, 1898).

← Rear façade of the distinguished guests' pavilion.

Ceramic panel designed by Josep Triadó outside the charity patients' pavilion, depicting the theological virtue of charity.

Ceramic panel outside the distinguished guests' pavilion designed by Lluís Bru.

Dining room in the distinguished guests' pavilion.

← Main room in the distinguished guests' pavilion.

Distinguished guests' pavilion. Main room.

Distinguished guests' pavilion. Billiard room.

← Distinguished guests' pavilion. Vaulted ceiling in the main room.

→ Stained-glass window.

Stained-glass window with the emblem of the institute in the first-floor gallery of the distinguished guests' pavilion.

Detail of the vaulted ceiling in the main room of the distinguished guests' pavilion Ceramics by Lluís Bru featuring the emblem of the institute: a female figure holding a torch and pouring oil onto it with her other hand to keep the flame burning, accompanied by the phrase "De nou lluirà".

Distinguished guests' pavilion.
Ceramic wainscoting in the dining room.

Distinguished guests' pavilion.
Detail of the vaulted ceiling
in the dining room.

Distinguished guests' pavilion.
Patients' rooms on the first floor.

Distinguished guests' pavilion.
Musicians' gallery on the first floor.

Distinguished guests' pavilion. First-floor gallery.

Refurbishment of the Fonda España

1900-1903

Maria Manadé Palau

Hotel España: a brief urban chronicle

The Hotel España was born in what could be considered Barcelona's first "eixample" or expansion district. In the 1800s, the city was structured on both sides of La Rambla, where residential buildings were erected according to the municipal laws that determined the height of the buildings and their respective decoration, and alternated with large palaces and mansions. There were also dwellings, commercial establishments, public service and leisure buildings, such as hotels and theatres, and small factories.

It was also an important period of change in the urban fabric as a result of space being freed up in the city that was still hemmed in by its walls, the development of former convent sites and the expansion towards the gardens outside the walls towards Montjuïc. It was an era of social and urban progress that would later be consolidated through Ildefons Cerdà's Eixample Plan.

The first new streets were laid out in the Gothic Quarter and the Raval as a result of this initial urban expansion and transformation. They cut across Barcelona's main thoroughfare, La Rambla, and became the true core of the city. Canuda, Santa Anna, Portaferrissa, Boqueria and Ferran VII were among the streets in the Gothic Quarter, and Tallers, Bonsuccés, Carme, Hospital Sant Pau, Unió and Nou de la Rambla were among the ones in the Raval. They were an essential part of Barcelona's urban fabric at a time when the city was a hive of industry with a growing population and about to make the leap to becoming a great, modern, cosmopolitan city.

Both sides of La Rambla were lined with hotels, dwellings, shops, cafés, and the 19th-century mansions and palaces where the nobility and the bourgeoisie with their new-found wealth lived. The area was a showcase for the booming city until it gravitated to the grand boulevard that was part of Cerdà's Eixample: Passeig de Gràcia.

It is in this context that the Fonda España opened in 1859 on Carrer de Sant Pau just off La Rambla, in a building designed in 1850 by the neoclassical architect Josep Buixareu i Gallart (1804-1871). The establishment was described as a "*Fonda*" (Inn), not a Hotel, in the company directory of the time, the *Anuari Riera*, which was one of the most reliable sources for finding businesses and personal addresses in Catalonia and the rest of Spain. After it was remodelled at the turn of the century, the name changed and we find it listed in French, as the Grand Hotel d'Espagne (Cabañas Moreno, 2013, p. 386), although the city's press would continue to call it an inn for a time.

According to documents held at the Barcelona Historical Archive (File #1030 from 4th January 1898), Don Miquel Salvadó Llorens applied for permission to make alterations to numbers 9 and 11, Carrer de Sant Pau. The file clearly specifies the work to be carried out, both inside, where the iron grilles were replaced with panes of glass, and outside, where alterations were made to the window sills on the ground floor. It also states the work would be done under the supervision of the architect Lluís Domènech i Montaner.

← Entrance hall. *La Ilustració Catalana*, 1905.

Salvadó was a friend and political colleague of Domènech's (Sàiz and Xiqués, 2013, p. 11). Municipal architect Pere Falqués was in favour and signed the authorisation on 15th January 1898. The refurbishment, which was completed in 1903, won the first prize awarded by the city council for commercial establishments and a complete photographic report was published in 1907 in the *Anuario de la Asociación de Arquitectos de Catalunya para el año 1907* (Yearbook of the Architects' Association of Catalonia for the Year 1907). In 1903, however, some details of the decoration were yet to be completed including the sgraffito mural, *Les Sirenes* (The Mermaids), in the guest dining room.

An ornamental language based on line and form

The commission came at a good time for the architect, who had already completed or was building works as significant as the Institut Pere Mata and the Casa Navàs in Reus; he had already begun the Gran Hotel de Palma in Mallorca and the Casa Lleó i Morera in Barcelona; and was drafting the project for the Hospital de la Santa Creu i Sant Pau, also in Barcelona. This important architectural and artistic baggage was an ideal framework allowing him to act with absolute creative freedom, displaying at all times great mastery and conviction in creating his own architectural style complemented by a broad decorative programme and language.

The contents of Domènech's aesthetic and ornamental repertoire centred on different concepts and sources of information and influences, such as Greek philosophy, the basis of medieval aesthetics; Mediterranean civilisation as an expression of proportion and balance; Nordic and Germanic thought, bearers of vitality and progress; and the English aesthetic concept, an example of renewal of the line and rediscovery of the "natural" and the "oriental". Domènech generated the "form" and always considered it an essential element of all ornamental sequences, as the subject of the composition that emanates from the concept itself.

To design the decorative programme, he divided the space into equal or proportional parts in order to develop in each an ornamental unit, a dominant figure, a characteristic element that predominates over the rest of the motifs, which act as complements. He created an ornamental rhythm that produced sensations and beauty while displaying his technical knowledge and mastery of space. To a first, purely conceptual treatment originating in ideas, the senses and sentiments, he added the application of decorative techniques as creative instruments and imbued the form with textures, colours, lines and surfaces.

Regarding the treatment of the line, Domènech used the geometric concept of the axes of symmetry to create associated ornamental series. They are always minutely related to the space they occupy, based on an aesthetic norm that implies a coherent and defined "ornamental rhythm" formed by images treated in a natural way and others derived from what could be defined as a sort of "analogue film frame".

The other relevant feature of "form" and "line" in Domènech i Montaner's ornamental programme is the use of materials and their decorative implications, not only with regard to their natural conditions and arrangement in order to offer the desired overall effect, but also in terms of their use, duration and qualities of resistance or impermeability.

The decoration of the Fonda España represents a clear exercise in each of the linear and formal concepts and applications discussed thus far. Due to its monumental nature, he organised "backgrounds" on which one or more ornamental units were developed, which could be superimposed, creating an interdependence between them, as can be seen in the great mural of *Les Sirenes* (The Mermaids).

Remodelling the interior of the Hotel España: a magnificent showcase for the applied and decorative arts

The ornamental programme applied to the Hotel España makes use of a studied, meticulous decorative repertoire that brings together a unified formal, symbolic and artistic discourse unfolding from the entrance in three parallel spaces perpendicular to Carrer de Sant Pau, that end in a transversal room in the back parallel to Carrer de Sant Pau presided over by the *Mermaids* mural.

The project is characterised by the overall treatment of the space, both from a technical and volumetric point of view, as well as the exterior-interior relationship. The first thing Domènech does is facilitate the entrance of natural light by removing the mezzanine floor and increasing transparency through the windows and doors on the ground floor facing the street. This solution allows him to create much brighter interior environments and an improved connection to the outside. From the exterior, the façade is much more diaphanous and creates a smooth transition to the interior.

The group of collaborators (mosaicists, sculptors, cabinetmakers...) in Domènech's work maintains a line of continuity in terms of assigning responsibilities, always respecting the architect's ultimate role. These craftsmen and artists are an integral part of the ornamental programme of the architect, the true creator of the linear and formal units that comprise the decorative language.

The lobby and interior staircase

There are eight arches along the front of the hotel on Carrer Sant Pau and the central one is the main entrance. The distribution of the lobby space is defined by the original structure of the building, since it connects directly to an inner courtyard whose large windows provide light for the corridors leading to some of the rooms. The removal of the mezzanine floor facilitates access and lighting, creating an integrated sequence with a continuous rhythm. From the lobby entrance there is a view or transparency all the way through to the back end of the floor, despite the presence of separate spaces.

The decoration of the lobby is light and flat to the benefit of its architectural structure. In the foreground is a freestanding column of smooth, polished marble at the base, clad in rectangular pieces up to the height where the lamp structure is located, which fully embraces the column and branches off, with a lion rampant on each side holding a supporting arm with a glass lantern. The metallic structure is topped off with an element encircling the column by way of a crown, from which the column, now fluted, continues to rise.

The original flooring was made of hexagonal encaustic tiles, complemented by rectangular panels of tessellated mosaic around the columns and a mosaic border trim along the entire perimeter of the lobby and courtyard. The lobby is clad in wooden wainscotting ornamented with stylised floral motifs. A marble frieze between two mouldings displays phrases addressing travellers: *A reveure, Bon viatge, Bon descans, Bon Dalit, Bona anada, Bon profit...* (Farewell, Have a good trip, Have a restful time, Enjoy, Arrive safely, Bon appétit...).

At the back of the lobby on the left are the stairwell and lift. The ornamental programme consists of the staircase balustrade in wrought iron with a floral design. Sgraffito covers part of the walls with alternating heraldic motifs. As for the staircase, each landing has a tessellated mosaic floor with different decorative patterns: flowers, heraldic animals, such as a lion passant, an eagle with its wings spread, etc., and they hold a shield bearing the word "Salve".

The courtyard displays sgraffito decorations in the purest *modernista* aesthetic language. At the top are female figures bearing messages for the hotel guests. These compositions are facing one another on the facades that are oriented east-west, so the messages they send are contextualised: "Good Morning" (*Bon dia*) and "Good Night" (*Bona nit*), respectively. Below the female figures is the representation of the corresponding animal iconography in the form of a sgrafitto-work peacock.

The grand dining room

To the right of the main entrance, the grand dining room can be accessed from the lobby, its width taking up two of the arches along the street. It is a large room noteworthy for the mosaic decorations on the walls. The ornamental programme consists of large panels from the ground up in a longitudinal scheme with independent units of heraldic shields, emblematic of the former kingdoms of Spain, and plant decorations depicting the flowers and fruit of the orange tree. They are all made with glazed mosaic tiles from the Mario Maragliano workshop (Saliné, 2015). The central section of this space is covered by a skylight. Information published in *La Vanguardia* shows that the grand dining room opened on 26th May 1900. (Sàiz i Xiqués, 2016, p. 24)

The reading or *"tertúlia"* room

Also accessible from the lobby but to the left and taking up the width of four of the arches along the street, there are two more rooms intended for guests to relax: an anteroom, behind which is the stairwell, and the reading room, also known as the "informal discussion" or *"tertúlia"* room. Although much altered, it retains the double column, coffered ceiling, chandeliers and wall lamps, and a splendid alabaster fireplace occupying the entire height of the wall facing the arches on the street. The sculptor Eusebi Arnau was commissioned to create the fireplace (Marín, 1993), in collaboration with Alfons Juyol. It evokes the passage of time in humans, with a woman holding a child on the left, and an old man on the right. Between these allegories, infants dance in a circle under the coat of arms of Spain held up by a double-headed eagle, with a floral crown above it. In contrast to the sumptuous finishes near the ceiling, more mundane domestic life is represented at ground level by a cat on the left and a series of mice on the right. Old photographs show that the fireplace was framed by two doors, which still exist, but once led to a courtyard that is no longer there. This has deprived the room of its original visual transparency.

The guest dining room or Mermaid room (*Sala de les Sirenes*)

Parallel to the three areas described above, there is an elongated room at the back running from side to side of the ground floor. A large central skylight floods the room with natural light. It is accessed from the main lobby and the grand dining room (originally also from the reading room).

Domènech creates an illusory architecture with clear Mediterranean roots – an allegory of the canonical models – by making four columns the centrepiece, accompanied by a decorative mural representing the seabed with its flora and fauna. It is a space with different connotations to the grand dining room: the distribution has an ornamental and functional unity but at the same time, allows independent discourse. Part of the shaft of the four fluted columns, with their stylised trapezoidal capitals, is clad in pink marble slabs, which provide a note of colour and a greater variety of materials. At the same time, these columns define four spaces: a central one, under the skylight, two on the sides, running crosswise, and a frontal one looking out towards the courtyard and lobby.

A wainscot made of criss-crossed strips of polished wood with circular, convex ceramic "buttons" at their intersections lends a continuity and unity to the ensemble. The "buttons" bear painted coats of arms representing the cities and former kingdoms of Spain, a theme taken up from the dining room decoration. The wainscot is 1.70 m high and the upper rim has pieces protruding from the linear plane that serve as coat hangers.

The central area with its skylight is the most outstanding part of the room. At the architect's request, there is sgraffito-work all along the walls (Martí, 2016). This decoration simulates the bottom of the sea and lends the space its name, the Mermaid room, or *Sala de les Sirenes*. On the ceiling, the coffering features a sequence of repeated marine elements: fish, octopi, crabs, clams, sea snails, frogs, jellyfish, starfish and plants as well as dragonflies. On the front wall, the room's four eponymous mermaids swim alongside Mediterranean fish, crustaceans and cephalopods. The coffered ceiling is bordered by the continuous rhythm of the waves breaking along the walls above the mermaids, waves that confirm the oriental influence on *modernisme*, as they closely resemble Katsushika Hokusai's *The Great Wave off Kanagawa*. As a result of research by Isabel Coll, based on an article published in *La Veu de Catalunya* on 29th May 1905, we are able to attribute the design of the mermaids to the painter Ramon Casas. The article also describes the opening of the restaurant and shows us that the work was done gradually. The ensemble also reveals a clear Japanese influence (Cabañas Moreno, 2013), which, according to Ricard Bru (2019), was directly inspired by books found in Domènech's library.

Reading room. *La Ilustració Catalana*, 1905.

Coat hooks over the wainscoting in the grand dining room (above) and the Mermaid dining room.

Lamps in the hall.

Grand dining room.

Mermaid dining room.

Mermaid dining room. Sgraffito-work marine motifs designed by the painter Ramon Casas.

Refurbishment of the Fonda España

Sgraffito jellyfish in the Mermaid dining room.

Mermaid dining room. Wooden wainscoting and ceramic elements featuring the coats of arms of the kingdoms of Spain.

Mermaid dining room. Sgraffito-work on the ceiling featuring nature motifs.

Refurbishment of the Fonda España

Details of the sculptures around the fireplace: allegory of motherhood and infants playing.

→ Fireplace with sculptures by Eusebi Arnau in collaboration with the sculptor Alfons Juyol.

The Gran Hotel in Palma   1901-1903

Mireia Freixa

In 1900, the Mallorcan shoe magnate, Joan Palmer, who had made his fortune in Uruguay commissioned Domènech i Montaner to design a hotel in Palma. It was the first truly modern hotel on the island and became a magnet for visitors that played a role in Mallorca's transformation into a popular tourist destination decades later. It was a very ambitious – maybe too ambitious – project if we consider how many travellers were drawn to the island and its capital at the beginning of the 20th century. The hotel stood in the centre of Palma, in Plaça Weyler, on the corner of Carrer de Can Puey.

After the Spanish Civil War, Franco's government converted the building into the headquarters of the Spanish social security department, the Instituto Nacional de Previsión, which drastically altered the building without taking into consideration its value as a heritage landmark. The stepped gable above the glass-fronted galleries on the main entrance in Plaça Weyler and the tops of the attic windows were removed. The upper section of the circular galleries on the corner of the building were substantially altered and the large doors on the main façade were hidden behind new ones. The interiors were completely altered. A few of the original elements, like the staircase, were retained, but almost all the ornamental details were lost.

In 1993, the banking foundation, the Fundació "la Caixa", purchased the building and commissioned Jaime J. Martínez Juan, Pere Nicolau Bover and Frederic Subirats to restore it (Maestro Quetglas, 2006, pp. 129-131). Following its restoration, the building reopened as CaixaForum Palma, which, in addition to hosting cultural activities and temporary exhibitions, houses the permanent collection of paintings by Hermen Anglada Camarasa, which his family had preserved at his house in Pollença.

The Mallorcan intellectual Miquel dels Sants Oliver i Tolrà (1864-1920) is a key figure in helping us understand how such an important project came to fruition on the island. He held a law degree and was a writer, historian and, first and foremost, a great journalist. Since the end of the 19th century, he had defended the need to promote tourism as a way of boosting Mallorca's economy. He gave the inaugural speech at the hotel opening ceremony which was transcribed in full in the newspaper *La Almudaina* (Seguí Aznar, 2001, p. 17). As we will see later, Oliver may have put Domènech i Montaner in touch with the hotel developers.

Miquel dels Sants Oliver and the growth of tourism in Mallorca

Miquel dels Sants Oliver was steeped in the principles of the Catalan revivalist movement, the *Renaixença*, in Mallorca. His father, Joan Lluís Oliver i Sabrafín, was a journalist who was closely involved with liberal movements, and paved the way for his son's career in the profession. He was still very young when he worked on publications such as *La Roqueta* and, most importantly, *La Almudaina*. Since 1881, he had combined these jobs with his law studies in Barcelona.

Oliver had settled in Barcelona in 1904, and was a member of the so-called "Mallorcan School", which had a strong influence on Catalonia's home-grown art nouveau movement, *modernisme*. He had close links to the group who worked for the cultural journal *L'Avenç*. The other intellectuals in their orbit included Miquel Costa i Llovera, Joan Alcover and Ramon

← Postcard of the façade. Unión Postal Universal, Madrid, 1903. Courtesy of Rossend Casanova.

Picó i Campamar, Eusebi Güell's right-hand man who introduced Oliver to pro-Catalan circles. The lawyer, Bartomeu Amengual Andreu, divided his time between Mallorca and Barcelona, and was closely associated with the burgeoning tourism industry. As soon as Miquel dels Sants Oliver arrived in Barcelona he was hired as the chief clerk at the library and secretariat of the Barcelona cultural centre, the Ateneu Barcelonès. Domènech may have had an influence on his appointment to this post, which he held from 1904 and 1916. Oliver was president of the Ateneu in 1917 and 1918. (Pons i Pons, 2014)

While *modernisme* was gaining momentum in Mallorca, Oliver became one of the staunch proponents of attracting international visitors – who until then had holidayed on the Côte d'Azur – in summer and winter. He published a section in *La Almudaina* entitled "Desde la terraza, páginas veraniegas" (From the terrace, summer pages), which later appeared in his book *Cosecha periodística* (Seguí Aznar, 2001, p. 16), where he insisted on the need to have a grand hotel that would attract this type of visitor, as well as providing decent accommodation for business travellers, complemented by improvements to sea transport, the port and local services.

The Gran Hotel in Palma was the first of the city's luxury hotels, but it was soon followed by the Hotel Príncipe Alfonso (1906) in Cala Major, the Hotel Alhambra (1920, in Palma – both designed by the Mallorcan architect Gaspar Bennàssar – and many more (Seguí Aznar, 2001, pp. 32-33). The Gran Hotel also had a maritime "branch", which is of particular interest: the Hotel Villa-Victoria (1910), in Son Sabater, in the bay of Palma. It was demolished in 1963 to make way for the Hotel Melià Victoria. (Horrach Estarellas, 2015)

Oliver was not alone in promoting Mallorca as a tourist destination. Enric Alzamora was the driving force behind the creation of the tourist board, the Foment del Turisme Balear (1903), and Bartolomé Amengual Andreu published a book about the foreign tourism industry entitled *La Industria de los forasteros* (Palma, 1903), which was a compilation of articles that had appeared in *La Almudaina*. It had a preface by Joan Alcover. Amengual, who had already settled in Barcelona, was one of the promoters of the Societat d'Atracció de Forasters de Barcelona, which had been set up to attract visitors from abroad to the Catalan capital (1908).

The commission: an architect and a hotelier with great associates

As we have already said, Oliver had been studying law in Barcelona since 1881 and made contact with young pro-Catalan activists, including Narcís Oller, Josep Yxart, Joan Sardà and Francesc Matheu. He probably attended the cultural gatherings at the Café Pelayo at the top of La Rambla, on the corner of Carrer Pelai. The café opened in 1875 and hosted many of the intellectuals of the day. (Villar, 2013)

Lluís Domènech i Montaner describes one of the gatherings at the café in an article published in *La Ilustració Catalana* in 1905, in which he pays tribute to the writer Emili Vilanova i March, who had died a few months earlier. It bore the emotive title "Records" (Memories) (Domènech, 1905, pp. 489-502). The architect highlights the café's literary discussions, which Vilanova took part in along with Jacint Verdaguer, Jaume Collell, Frederic Soler "Pitarra", Àngel Guimerà – who was one of its key figures –, Josep Yxart, the sculptor Agustí Querol, Eduard Toda, Ramon Picó i Campamar, Antoni Aulèstia i Pijoan and Antoni Gaudí, who he describes as "the future architect of the Sagrada Família" (Domènech i Montaner, 1905, p. 499). One of the prestigious architects from the Bassegoda family, Bonaventura Bassegoda i Amigó (1862-1940), also mentions the group in an article about Gaudí in *La Vanguardia*, in March 1929 (Bassegoda, 1929, p. 7). Miquel dels Sants Oliver moved in these circles and this suggests that he must have met Domènech in his student days.

The hotel developers were Joan Palmer and Ferran Trullols, the Marquis of Torre del Fangar. Trullols was an aristocrat who was also a driving force behind the Societat del Foment del Turisme in Palma. They asked the prestigious hotelier, Antoni Albareda i Canals, to work with them on the project. Albareda ran the Hotel Cuatro Naciones at the end of La Rambla in Barcelona, and the Hotel Ambos Mundos on Ronda de Sant Pere, which stood on the corner of Carrer Bailén and Carrer Ali Bei, near the railway station, the Estació del Nord. Albareda signed a fifteen-year operating agreement for the Grand Hotel. However, his involvement went way beyond deciding the facilities it needed. He was also in charge of the interior design. (Farré Sanpera, 1993, pp. 10-11)

Domènech worked with two architects, Joan Alsina i Arús (1872-1911), who hailed from Barcelona, and Jaume Aleñà Guinart (1870-1945), who was from Palma. Guinart had studied in Madrid, and was a municipal architect in Palma. He was more closely involved with managing the project than the actual building process. The plans were presented on 1st January 1901 and the city council granted planning permission on 17th March. The hotel took a relatively short time to build – although the developers complained of delays – and it opened on 10th February 1903. (Farré Sanpera, 1993, pp. 10-11)

It is worth reemphasising the fact that it was Albareda, not Domènech, who worked on the hotel interiors. This means that Domènech was involved in the more essential elements, probably the wrought-ironwork on the steps and maybe the choice of flooring. However, he did not work on the entire project, as was the case with the Institut Pere Mata, the Palau de la Música Catalana and the Hospital de Sant Pau. Nevertheless, the articles in the press and information from other sources reveal that Joan Puigdengolas worked on the project as the furniture-maker and interior decorator; the Barcelona-based Andorrà workshops and Cererols in Mallorca produced the iron and metalwork; and Vilaró painted the decorative finishes (Farré Sanpera, 1993, pp. 10-11). The sculptor Eusebi Arnau worked on the hotel exterior, with his regular collaborator Alfons Juyol (Farré Sanpera, 1993, p. 14), and the applied ceramic elements have been attributed to the Pujol i Bausis factory (Esplugues de Llobregat) but may have been manufactured by the Mallorcan firm La Roqueta. (Seguí Aznar, 2001, p. 30)

However, the large paintings that decorated the dining room were the true highlights. They were commissioned from two Catalan painters who had strong connections with Mallorca: Santiago Rusiñol (1861-1931) and Joaquim Mir (1873-1940). We will look at them in greater detail later.

A totally *modernista* building

Domènech was at the height of his success as an architect and public figure when he designed the Gran Hotel. We must also remember that he had a reputation as a hotel architect, as he had built the sumptuous Hotel Internacional for the 1888 Barcelona Universal Exhibition at an unprecedented speed. Everybody hailed the originality and uniqueness of the building. Domènech also worked on the refurbishment of the Fonda España (1898-1903). At the Grand Hotel, he achieved the same harmony between the structure and function of the building and its decorative elements as he had done at the other two hotels. (Seguí Aznar, 1975, p. 38)

The hotel had a basement, ground floor, three upper floors and a penthouse as well as a central space with a staircase. It overlooked Plaça Weyler and a side street, Carrer de Can Puey. Domènech created a flow between the corners of the two façades by adding circular galleries with stained-glass windows surmounted by a sculptural pinnacle designed by Eusebi Arnau (1863-1933) and made by Alfons Juyol. It depicts a boy and a girl, dressed in medieval clothing and holding the flag of Palma – the four stripes of the royal standard and the castle of La Almudaina. Below it is the inscription "Gran Hotel" in Gothic lettering.

There is a vertical row of galleries with stained-glass windows that cover the three upper floors. They have a stepped gable which has been completely rebuilt. At the top, inside a pointed arch, there is a ceramic panel depicting the phoenix, the bird that is reborn from its ashes. It is very similar to the one Domènech had designed for the masthead of the newspaper *La Renaixensa* and which had become the symbol of the new Catalonia. It is protected by two winged lions below it. The same motif, which has been resized, can be found on the other ceramic panels placed between the penthouse windows. The balustrade in the first-floor gallery is particularly outstanding. It is carved with two pairs of children holding plaques which once bore an inscription that is now missing.

You enter the hotel in Plaça Weyler through a large door. The irregular L-shaped floor plan is the result of the awkward characteristics of the plot. It has an area that is slotted between buildings which had a small

Living-cum-dining room with paintings by Rusiñol and Mir.
Photograph by Carles Fargas i Borrell. Arxiu Fotogràfic del Centre Excursionista de Catalunya, c. 1920.

garden to let in more light. It centres around a courtyard which has a staircase leading to the upper floors. On the ground floor, the load-bearing walls have been replaced with cast-iron columns, which provide further proof of Domènech's in-depth knowledge of new materials.

Miquel Seguí quotes an advertising brochure of the time about the opening of the hotel, which includes interesting aspects, such as the number of guest rooms and their layout. On the right of the main door, there was a piano room designed for the ladies, while, on the left, there was the café and reading room. An old photograph of this room survives and we can see that it had games tables with armchairs and large sofas: comfortable yet eclectic furniture that was a far cry from the *modernista* fashions of the day. There was a large fireplace at the back of the room with cornucopias on either side. The room led into the first dining room that could seat fifty guests. It overlooked Carrer de Can Puey. There was a small butler's pantry communicating with the main dining room, which ran perpendicular to the lobby and staircase. It overlooked the garden at the rear of the hotel and seated two hundred diners.

The bedrooms were all street facing. They were single or double rooms and ten of them had fully fitted bathrooms. There was even a suite with a private dining room. The hotel had all modern amenities, including running water, heating, gas, electricity and a lift.
(Seguí Aznar, 2000, pp. 104-106)

The main dining room and paintings by Santiago Rusiñol and Joaquim Mir

According to Domènech's original floor plans held in the Municipal Archive in Palma, the main dining room was the centrepiece of the hotel. Period photographs show us what the interior was like. Light entered the room through a large skylight. The picture windows were fitted with decorative stained-glass panels and the ceilings had art nouveau-style mouldings. The two ceiling lamps and the wall lights are the most representative of Domènech's designs.

The large paintings that decorated the walls of the dining room were the most important elements. Fortunately, they have survived, albeit in different collections. Santiago Rusiñol and Joaquim Mir, two "modern" Catalan artists with strong links to Mallorca, were commissioned to produce the works. Rusiñol had discovered the island in 1893 and visited regularly until 1929, and Mir lived on the island between 1899 and 1904. Rusiñol, who was already a highly prestigious painter, made copies of his other paintings, seemingly "in excess", with the help of the Mallorcan painter Antoni Gelabert i Massó (1877-1932) (*Santiago Rusiñol*, exhibition 1998, p. 258). Nevertheless, Mir's paintings are key works in his artistic career.

The paintings are listed below. They are all oils on canvas and have large, ornate frames. Many of them have survived. (Laplana i Palau-Ribes, 2004; *Joaquim Mir* exhibition, 2009)

Rusiñol painted:

Garden at Can Blanes II, 1902 (280 × 190 cm), private collection; first version, in a private collection.

Springtime. The Genoa Valley II, 1902 (280 × 400 cm), private collection; first version, Museo de Bellas Artes de Cuba.

The King's Castle II, 1902 (290 × 400 cm), Banco de Sabadell; first version, private collection.

The Castle at Dusk II, 1902 (290 × 400 cm), Banco de Sabadell; first version, Museo Provincial de Bellas Artes E. Caraffa (Argentina).

Mir painted:

Sunset, c. 1903 (280 × 190 cm.), Es Baluard collection, Museu d'Art Modern i Contemporani de Palma.

Cala Sant Vicenç, 1902 (280 × 400 cm), Museo de Montserrat, donated by J. Sala Ardiz

Enchanted Cove, c. 1903 (271 × 502 cm.), AENA contemporary art collection (there is a smaller version at the MNAC in Barcelona, dated *c.* 1901).

Four of the paintings were the same size (280 × 400 cm) but, for unknown reasons, *The King's Castle II* and *The Castle at Dusk II* were 10 cm higher than the other ones. If we try to arrange them according to Seguí's plan (Seguí Aznar, 1975, p. 88), we can deduce that they were hung on the front wall of the dining room. Photographs taken at the time show that the paintings were displayed as follows: *The King's Castle II* and *Springtime. The Genoa Valley II* outside the butler's pantry and *The Castle at Dusk II* and *Cala Sant Vicenç* (we are not certain in which order) near the picture window. We can tell from the photographs that the largest of the paintings, *Enchanted Cove* (271 × 502 cm), was hung opposite the others, on the side of the room nearest the garden. *Garden at Can Blanes II* and *Sunset*, both measuring 280 × 190 cm, were also hung on the wall outside the butler's pantry. As we can see, Joaquim Mir's *Enchanted Cove*, was the centrepiece of the room.

And one last literary reference

We have already mentioned the role of Miquel dels Sants Oliver in promoting quality tourism on the Balearic Islands. His novella, *La ciutat de Mallorques* (1906), was published by the *modernista* Catalan-language publishing house L'Avenç. It was intended to be part of a larger work entitled *Illa Daurada*, or golden isle, the nickname for Mallorca coined by the author. *La ciutat de Mallorques* was the only text to see the light of day. It was subtitled *Viatge a Mallorca segons les notes d'en Lluís Vidal, mallorquí de professió* (Journey to Mallorca according to the notes by Lluís Vidal, a Mallorcan by trade). Ironically, Oliver became the publisher of his manuscript in which the supposed author apologised for "his lack of familiarity with writing in a language he always spoke" and described his guide to the island as a Catalan snob who was a lover of "art nouveau and an antiquarian". The story begins with a meeting between travellers in the dining room of the Gran Hotel (Oliver, 1906, pp. 8-9). It reads: "There, inside the grandiose room, suffused with electric light, nearly all the tables were occupied. It was easy to tell apart those travelling out of necessity and those travelling for pleasure. There were the ones wearing tuxedos and the ones wearing jackets. Some members of the first group – Germans, English or French – were accompanied by their wives or children. The others dined alone, rereading telegrams or notes between courses." This is a carefully observed and ironic description of the travellers who passed through the Gran Hotel in the early 20th century. The conversation in the main dining room takes up the first twenty-four pages of the novella, and the way it describes Mir's painting and reflects on the directions taken by art is particularly revealing.

Elevation of the façade of the Gran Hotel in Palma.
Photograph by Lluís Marià Vidal, *c.* 1888-1896. Arxiu Fotogràfic del Centre Excursionista de Catalunya.

Façade.

← Pediment on the top of the two façades designed by Eusebi Arnau and carved by Alfons Juyol.

→ Foot of the grand staircase.

→ Gallery.

← Detail of the stained glass inside the gallery.

Wrought-iron dragon that is part of the streetlamp on the façade.

← Ceramic decoration at the top of the main façade.

Casa Navàs

Jordi March Barberà

1901-1907

A shop-plus-dwelling commission in Plaça del Mercadal in Reus

By the latter half of the 19th century, Reus had become the second city in Catalonia, mainly due to the alcohol trade. The city has always been a commercial hub, attracting people from the nearby counties while being different from Tarragona, the administrative and ecclesiastical capital of the El Camp area. It is no surprise that the shop-plus-dwelling commissioned by Joaquim Navàs and Josepa Blasco – a married couple who were shopkeepers – is the city's finest example of *modernista* architecture and one of Lluís Domènech i Montaner's key buildings. Joaquim and Josepa were the children of two families that owned important fabric shops in the centre of Reus: the Navàs' was on Carrer de la Galera and the Blasco's in Plaça del Mercadal. When they got married in 1876, they opened their own business in a rented ground-floor space in the square and set up their home there.

After years of success in the retail and wholesale textile trade, and importing products to Spain and distributing them throughout the country, the childless couple decided to invest a significant part of their fortune in building a shop and a home under one roof. Perhaps they were looking for a way to perpetuate their legacy. In 1898, they bought the Simó-Cardenyes house – a 17th-century mansion on the corner of Plaça del Mercadal and Carrer Jesus – for 42,500 pesetas. It occupied a prominent place in the city centre across from the town hall, where the market was held, along with the city's festivities and the *Tronada* (a massive, thundering firecracker display); and it was just next to their shop, which had grown with the addition of adjacent premises.

In 1901, Lluís Domènech was commissioned with the project. The architect had come into contact with Reus society in 1897 through his work in the construction of the Institut Pere Mata, of which Joaquim Navàs was a founding partner. In 1900 he had already received his first commission to design a private house in the city, for the notary Pere Rull, who was also a partner in the asylum concern.

The commission had a double architectural programme, the shop and the house; with an important premise: the entire ground floor was to be dedicated to commercial use, with a small area at the side for the foyer and staircase leading to the residential part of the building; the shop was the core and the raison d'être of the house. That very same year, 1901, the limited partnership *Sucesores de Joaquín Navás* was created with the shop-workers and the Navàs-Blascos had a majority share. When Josepa "Pepa" Blasco was widowed, she filed a lawsuit to try to dissolve the company, but she lost. From then on, the shop began leasing the space.

In October 1901, the building permit was processed. In March 1902, the contract was signed with the builder Pere Munné, for 21,181.64 pesetas, and the works began. The shop opened in 1905, but the residential part was lagging behind. In the last semester of that year, Alfons Juyol produced the applied sculpture-work in the foyer, staircase and lobby. Work continued until 1908, when – after Tomàs Bergadà completed the mural paintings and the last stained-glass roof and windows by Rigalt i Granell were installed – the house was ready for habitation.

← Postcard. Anonymous, c. 1901.
Arxiu Casa Navàs.

The 1938 bomb attack

That the Navàs house is the best-preserved example of private *modernista* architecture (Sala, 2006, p. 121) is even more extraordinary if you consider that on the morning of March 26th 1938, the Italian air force dropped a bomb from an S79 aircraft, destroying the tower, the crowning element on the facade and a large part of the second floor, including the stained-glass roof over the staircase and lobby, but luckily the first floor was not affected. The owners preserved pieces of the damaged structures with future restorations in mind. In 1940, Antoni Sardà planned the reconstruction of the house, but this was ultimately limited to ensuring its conservation and habitability, and he ruled out rebuilding the tower and the central crowning element on the facade. To reduce costs, artificial stone was used to reconstruct the windows on the second floor and the balcony balustrades.

Stone, light and space

On the facades we find a characteristic solution used by Domènech for corner buildings: he would highlight the corner to act as a sort of hinge linking the facades, in this case with a robust column on the ground floor, and a winding balcony on the first floor bearing a column on which rested a slender corner tower. The tower was made of thin stone columns and stained-glass windows, through which one could glimpse the spiral staircase that led to the upper vantage point. The remaining photographs of the tower, pierced by sunlight, reveal its nearly translucent nature. The curved balustrade on the corner balcony, the chamfered arrangement of its three doors, which are interlinked behind the column, and their decoration help connect the two facades. The sense of verticality of the facade is enhanced by the stepped, gable-like crowning element located above the central enclosed balcony and the large rounded window, marking the central axis from the porch column to the roof.

For the first time, Domènech built the facades entirely of stone, in this case, Vinaixa stone on the residential floors, Montblanc (stronger) on the ground floor and reddish marble in the column shafts of the ground-floor arcade and the first-floor corner balcony. The ground floor is characterised by the porticoes which, despite following the classic layout of the plaza, represent a turning point and modernisation of this architectural typology, with the addition of lobed lintels and foliate capitals. Joaquim Navàs' building permit application to the city council clearly specified that the house would not exceed the height of the pre-existing porticoes, and to enhance it aesthetically, the pillar shared with the neighbouring house would be replaced, which the municipal architect Pere Caselles had shifted so that it would coincide with the median axis of the party wall. The same shapes of the columns and lintels could be found around the doors on the ground floor and the windows under the porticoes, but now they are only visible in the entrance to the residential part. The refurbishment carried out by Francesc Mitjans in the 1940s hid the columns under modern decorations and also dismantled the metal enclosures and stained glass that comprised the shop windows and entrance. The differentiation between the ground floor and the rest of the facade is emphasised by a moulding running horizontally along the two façades, from which the bases of the corner balcony and enclosed balcony emerge. On the ground floor on Carrer Jesús, diamond-shaped ashlars lend the wall rhythm and create a play of light with the sun and their shadows. This decorative resource of a rhythmic wall was used in previous works, such as the Casa Thomas or the Comillas Seminary, but done in ceramics in a hemispherical shape.

It is also the first work in which Domènech used decorative plant motifs everywhere, on the capitals, facade openings and filling the entire interior, embarking on a path he would develop in later works. (Garcia-Ventosa, 1993, p. 63)

To improve lighting and ventilation, Domènech added a third facade to the house, creating a terrace at first-floor level at the west end of the property. This also allowed him to fit skylights on the terrace floor to improve the lighting in the shop. The Cardenyas house had already had a garden at the main-floor level (i.e. the first floor), which Güell i Mercader described as "a garden in the air", built on high vaults supported by massive pillars: "there were eight to ten spans of arable land in which trees and plants took root" (Güell i Mercader, 1902). It seems that the new terrace was a memory of that garden.

With his characteristic mastery of light, he pierced the house vertically, creating a large courtyard adjacent to the party wall, where he placed the staircase and the foyer-lobby, separated by a large stained-glass window. This covered courtyard allowed light to flood the central rooms of the house, while creating triple- and double-level heights of great wealth. It recalls, on a different scale, his creation of a side courtyard at the Palau de la Música that separated the concert hall from the party wall, letting light in from that side. Perhaps the most outstanding space in the house is the stairwell, which draws the eye from the ground floor foyer to the second floor, creating a spectacular stage set to welcome visitors. For the two courtyard terrace roofs, Domènech employed a solution he had used in other buildings, such as the Barcelona café and restaurant or the castle of Santa Florentina: two arches resting on columns support the roof, dividing it into three sectors.

Another interesting resource is the use of decoration to create an illusion of greater space, through both the mural mosaics of the stairwell, where a landscape and a sky full of birds and clouds make the party wall with the neighbouring house disappear, and the commissioned ceramic wall panels on the terrace, where the foreshortened perspective of their representations virtually expands the space. In a *trompe-l'oeil* effect, the panels seem to be scenes visible beyond a structure of brickwork arches, which act as "windows". The panels and arches aesthetically unify the party walls while concealing the service staircase and the laundry room. The representation of Jaume I's fleet departing for Mallorca from the port of Salou in one of the panels seems to be related to the wrought iron weathervane that crowned the corner tower, made in the workshops of Manuel Ballarín, as testified by a photograph preserved in the architect's archive (March, 2006, p. 87): a ship with the heraldic emblem of the four stripes and the cross of Sant George, with a figurehead that recalls the winged dragon from the crest of the Catalan royal coat of arms, and a banner with the Catalan flag on a stylised crown. The two ships, in wrought iron and ceramic, seem to be a kind of tribute to the Royal House of King James (the 700th anniversary of his birth was being celebrated in 1908). The terrace roof was enclosed behind an arcade designed in 1904, lending privacy to the space, which was completed with stained-glass windows that were destroyed in 1938, with only the structure and the supports to hold an awning remaining.

Interiors for commerce and living

The shop is a large, open space, measuring 13 × 35 metres, punctuated by six slender columns produced in the Martí foundry in Reus (with a seventh column in the basement as well), with a semi-industrial aesthetic, allowing the metal structure to be seen, where the latticework covers a large area at a height of 4.25 m, leaving the surface area almost free. Along the walls of the shop, shelving takes full advantage of the height for storing fabric rolls. A light wood and iron gallery allows access to the upper shelves. The light composition of the shelving and the static balance of the walkway integrated into it are remarkable (Lapeyra, 2018, p. 51). At the back of the shop is an office space closed off in acid-etched glass that lends the administrative area privacy. A small corridor connects the shop with the stockroom, one of the most interesting spaces in the building, with a nearly square plan, with triple height (6.60 m), lit from above, and with the walls completely covered with shelves, just as in the shop. At the corners, spiral staircases connect the three levels of galleries. The fabric shop maintained its original use, continuing to function without interruption until it closed in 2018.

We will not linger on the interiors of the house as they are extensively studied in the monograph published in 2006. We will only look at its distribution and original uses. The interior design of the house is the result of collaboration between the architect and Gaspar Homar, who acted as general decorator or *ensemblier*. He was responsible for the furniture, the lamps, the marquetry in the wainscots and ceilings, the parquet floors, the wall and ceiling mosaics, the ceramic panels in the tympani over the doors, the tapestries, carpets, etc. (Sala, 2006, p. 121)

The stone sculpture-work applied to architecture was done by Alfons Juyol and his workshop (Molet, 2006, p. 193). According to documents, certain details followed models executed by another sculptor. The high quality of the capitals in the living and dining rooms suggest it was almost certainly Eusebi Arnau. This is further supported by the similarity of the young girls depicted on the capitals in the sitting room – who seem to be keeping an eye on the people in the square – to the one in Arnau's sculpture *A la Llotja*

(In the Loggia). In fact, his name is cited as the author of the designs and of certain stone sculptures in Juyol's budget for the staircase and lobby.

Along the main facade are the dining room, the drawing room and the owners' bedroom, divided into a living space and an alcove. The dining room is conceived as a private space, with a fireplace with seats on either side, and the decoration, based on vegetarian and meat or fish-based foods, ties in with the function of the space. The drawing room is the main reception area, aligned with the longitudinal axis of the storey, which connects the enclosed balcony overlooking Plaça Mercadal with the access to the terrace through the lobby. The bedroom ceiling consists of Catalan vaulting or flat-brick vaulting lined with patterned ceramic tiling, possibly designed to be seen from the street as well as from the drawing room. At the western end is the study, with parquet flooring and a wooden wainscot, the sewing room or women's room, with a colourful Pujol i Bausis ceramic tile wainscotting, a secondary room and a wardrobe room. These spaces, of smaller dimensions, were intended for more domestic use.

The Navàs Blascos sought a modern house, as indicated by its electric lighting, complemented by gas lighting in the kitchen and bathroom, the warm air heating system, hygienic amenities and the telephone (Freixa, Sala, 2006, p. 105). Two spaces that are given a discreet look in other buildings attract attention here: the kitchen and the bathroom are both fully tiled, including the flat-brick vaulted ceiling. The kitchen's large proportions are due to the fact that not only were the meals for the Navàs family and servants prepared there, but also those of the shop workers. A freight elevator connected the kitchen with the shop, making it easier to take the meals down to the employees and bring groceries up directly from the street. The bathroom retains all the original furniture and fixtures, including the system of taps by the firm Verdaguer i Companyia, which makes it exceptional. Also remarkable is the fact that two of its walls are stained glass opening onto the public area of the house: the staircase and the lobby.

The choice of the different types of flooring was made in accordance with the uses of the different spaces. A rich, marble-tessellated mosaic was chosen for the reception areas and parts of the building that were most on view to visitors (foyer, staircase and lobby); in areas where luxury was combined with the idea of comfort, parquet floors were chosen (drawing room, dining room, master bedroom and study), in areas that were required to be particularly hardwearing we find ceramic stoneware tiles (kitchen and bathrooms), when necessary in rich Nolla models (terrace and women's room or sewing room, which doubled as the access area for the terrace), and finally, there was hydraulic tiling in the shop and on the second floor.

A narrow staircase connects all the floors of the house, from the basement, where the boiler was and where a cooler room has been preserved – a grotto according to documentation –, to the second floor where we find finishes with materials of inferior quality to the ones on the main floor. The parquet and tessellated mosaic are replaced by several models of encaustic flooring by Escofet and monochrome stoneware flooring. Different models of serially-produced ceramics by Pujol and Bausis are used to clad the walls, but in a small room there is a surprising ceramic mosaic fireplace by Lluís Bru. The rooms in the gallery along the square were destroyed by the bomb in 1938. The marks on the walls help us to imagine the original layout: two bedrooms with alcoves, following the distribution model of the main floor, and a bathroom. In the corner of this space, what used to be the access to the tower can still be seen. We do not know the original use of the spaces on this floor, but the narrowness of the staircase and the materials used would suggest it was designed for the domestic servants or the shopworkers, but the rooms with an alcove could indicate a possible modification of the project during its construction, adapting them to rooms for relatives or guests. Later, in the 1930s, the room opening onto the roof was adapted by the Blasco-Font de Rubinats as a playroom for their four children, and in the 1980s, when Maria Font de Rubinat returned to live in the house, it was transformed into the current music room, with the pianola and the sheet music cabinets.

Documents about the house and its inhabitants

The Casa Navàs is an exceptional case for two reasons: the excellent state of preservation of its original decorations, and the records that survive about the building. The Blasco family has preserved a great many documents about the construction process, including invoices from suppliers and estimates, which attest to the participation of some of the masters of the applied arts: Gaspar Homar, Alfons Juyol, Pujol i Bausis, Escofet, Nolla, Hipòlit Montseny, Queraltó i Planas, Tomàs Bergadà, Rigalt i Granell. They also enable us to date each stage of the works. Conversely, there are no surviving plans of the building in the Lluís Domènech i Montaner collection at the Historical Archive of the Architects' Association of Catalonia (COAC). It only includes a photograph of the weathervane on the top of the tower, from which we can ascertain that it was made by Manuel Ballarín, and a sketch of the decoration for one of the ceramic panels on the terrace. The plans submitted for the building permit can be found at the Reus Municipal Archives. The Esplugues de Llobregat Municipal Archive holds documents showing the involvement of the draughtsman and mosaicist Lluís Bru (Saliné, 2006, p. 171), and information about the serial tiles supplied by Pujol i Bausis. (Subias, 2006, p. 157)

Paradoxically, Joaquim Navàs hardly enjoyed the house. In 1907, after emerging unscathed from a bomb attack on the chalet he had had built years earlier on Passeig de la Boca de la Mina, he decided to move to Barcelona, where he died in 1915 (Arnavat, 2006, p. 38), with only intermittent stays at his new house on Plaça Mercadal. The house was inhabited by his widow until her death in 1928. It was inherited by her godson, Joaquim Blasco, who moved there with his family until the bomb hit in 1938. From 1945 to 1980, it was leased to Dr Nolla, who set up his home and medical practice there. Maria Font de Rubinat, Joaquim Blasco's widow, moved back to the house, opened it up to visitors and lived there until her death in 1998. She and her children continued the work of preserving and restoring the building, rebuilding

Elevation and section of the façade, 1901. Arxiu Municipal de Reus.

the two stained-glass roofs, among other things. The continuity of the building's original use together with the conservationist interest of the owners have allowed the house's comprehensive preservation, as if time had stopped in 1908. In 2017, a majority share of the property went to the Reus businessman, Xavier Martínez, and the building began to be widely publicised while significant restoration work was undertaken, such as the reconstruction of the stepped crowning element on the main façade in 2020.

Main façade without the tower that stood on the corner.

Portico along the main façade.

Detail of the front door.

Foot of the grand staircase.

Section of the grand staircase leading to the first floor.

Entrance hall with the terrace in the background.

First-floor kitchen.

Bathroom with stained-glass windows overlooking the stairwell.

← First-floor dining room.

→ Area of the dining room with a fireplace and benches.

← Corbel in the dining room.

→ View of the first-floor sitting room.

First-floor bedroom.

Stained-glass windows on the first floor.

Room once used as Joaquim Navàs' office.

Small sitting room with fireplace on the second floor.

View of the stairwell from the second floor.

Stairwell on the second floor.

Bench in the entrance hall.

Stained-glass window separating the hall from the staircase.

Casa Navàs

Ceramic murals on the terrace depicting Catalan maritime expansion throughout the Mediterranean.

Hospital de la Santa Creu i Sant Pau

1902-1920

Clàudia Sanmartí Martínez

A new hospital, Pau Gil's bequest and the controversial call for entries

In the late 19th century, Santa Creu was Barcelona's most important hospital. It was housed in a medieval building that had been constructed for this purpose in the Raval district in 1401, and was kept running with charitable donations and funding from the local authorities (Figueras, 2001). We should remember that, at the time, the only patients at the hospital were the poor, as people who could afford medical treatment received home visits from their doctor. The mortality rate among the patients was very high, mostly due to infections and contagious diseases.

The medieval hospital had been designed for a population of 50,000 people, and although it had been extended over the centuries, by the late 19th century it had become too small to cater to Barcelona's 600,000 inhabitants (*Un aficionat*, 1900). In spite of its financial difficulties, the hospital purchased land in the area of Guinardó, 2 km from Barcelona's old town, so that it would be able to build a new hospital when it had sufficient funds.

However, after many twists and turns, one event turned the situation around and guaranteed the future of the new hospital: the bequest Pau Gil had made in his will.

Pau Gil i Serra was a Barcelona-born banker who had settled in Paris. When he died in 1896, at the age of 79, he bequeathed part of his fortune to build a hospital in his home town. He had made his will in Paris in 1892, and it contained an addendum that specified it was to be opened by the Spanish consul (García-Martín, 1990). The document stated that he had left a large amount of money (half the assets after his banking company had been wound up) to build a hospital in Barcelona that would bear his name. Pau Gil left precise instructions for his appointed executors about the way they should handle the entire process: they would appoint a commission comprising an architect, a physician and another person qualified for this purpose. There was to be a call for entries to choose the best project, which was to be built on a site chosen for its hygienic conditions and cleanliness. Gil specified that the hospital complex and its facilities should conform to *the improvements made to hospitals in Paris*, and that the capacity and importance of the building should reflect the amount of money he had left in his will. After completion, the hospital would be given to Barcelona City Council or to the corporation Gil's executors deemed appropriate, and they would be entrusted with its running and maintenance.

The executors started the necessary procedures to administer the will, and two and a half years later they had purchased land for the new hospital in the village of Sarrià and issued a call for entries for the building. However, the project ended in controversy.

Three projects were submitted (they have not been preserved) under pseudonyms. They were entitled: *Higiene ante todo* (Hygiene above all), *Santa Cruz* and *Salud* (Health). The competition was to be judged by two panels, as Pau Gil had requested: one of them made up of architects and another made up of doctors. In 1900, the architects' panel declared the project *Salud* the winner, with some reservations. It turned out to be the work of the architect Josep Domènech i Estapà (who had been a member of the technical committee that had advised the executors). Domènech i Estapà (1858-1917) was already a prestigious architect at the

← Façade under construction. José de Olalde, 1910. Arxiu de l'Hospital (AHSCP).

Cartoons in the satirical press lampooning the building of the hospital.

La Esquella de la Torratxa, 1902.

La Esquella de la Torratxa, 1902.

time, with monumental buildings under construction, including the Palau de Justícia (with Enric Sagnier 1858-1931), the Model prison (with Salvador Vinyals 1847-1926) and, most importantly, the Hospital Clínic.

After the verdict, a series of articles were published in the *Diari de Catalunya* (the temporary new name given to the newspaper *La Veu de Catalunya* after it had been banned from publication and which Domènech had drawn the masthead for) in August and October 1900: an exchange of letters between Domènech i Estapà and an anonymous correspondent who signs himself *"Un aficionat"*, or "A fan", about the conditions modern hospitals should meet, and which were not envisaged in the project for the Hospital Clínic. These articles had a knock-on effect and affected the future hospital specified in Pau Gil's bequest. There is no doubt that this *aficionat* was Domènech i Montaner (González Moreno-Navarro, 2015), who had been commissioned to build the Pere Mata psychiatric hospital in Reus in December 1896. In each of his letters, the *aficionat* referred to many foreign hospitals and the characteristics, clearly showing how erudite he was on the subject. Basically, the controversy centred on the fact that the Hospital Clínic was based on the compact hospital model, the French corridor-pavilion type (the Lariboisière hospital, 1839-1854 and the new Hôtel-Dieu in Paris, 1866-1878; St Thomas' in London, 1866-1871; the Stuivenberg hospital in Antwerp, 1878-1885, among others). But there was another model of hospital that was more suitable for preventing disease from spreading: the separate pavilion model (Friedrichshain in Berlin, 1870-74; Wiesbaden, 1876-78; Blegdam in Copenhagen, 1889; Newcastle, 1884; Eppendorf in Hamburg, 1884-90; Sankt Jacob in Leipzig, 1892; Urban in Berlin 1890; Bernburg, 1892, among others), which had been used since the 1870s.

> "Since then, a popular German handbook I have in front of me has said that no large hospital has been built, whose layout does not differ from that of the quarantine hospital shacks, which is today fundamentally inseparable from a system of pavilions". (*Un aficionat*, 1900)

After months of deliberation and eight months after the verdict of the architects' panel, the doctors' panel rejected the proposal on 16th December 1900 and concluded:

> "Nevertheless, it would be unjust to fail to mention that, given the insufficient proportions of the land that has been offered, we believe that it would be impossible for anyone to build a hospital on this site that would meet the conditions required today. [...] We must be permitted to advise and beg

La Campana de Gràcia, 1902.   *La Esquella de la Torratxa*, 1902 above and 1903 right.

the gentlemen executors who have been entrusted with carrying out the last wishes of the generous benefactor Don Pablo Gil: Dispense with the projects we have just examined, extend the plot of land you have purchased to the dimensions indicated as necessary and issue a new call for entries or commission a person who will be the ideal candidate, to draw up a new project that will adhere to the principles of hospital hygiene we have set out and which are accepted everywhere." (García-Martín, 1990)

It is worth mentioning that Dr Robert, who was mayor of Barcelona until October 1899, was a member of the doctors' panel. He went on to be an associate of Domènech i Montaner's in the pro-Catalan political party, the Lliga Regionalista, which they founded in 1901.

At a general meeting held on 19th April 1901, the Santa Creu board of trustees agreed to commission Lluís Domènech i Montaner to design the project for two hospitals: a new Hospital de la Santa Creu, and a hospital built by Pau Gil's executors. They would be governed by a general administrative and management plan (Domènech i Montaner, 2013). Domènech did not have to undergo a selection process and no call for entries was issued. His project had to adhere to the panel's specifications and would be built on a new site in Guinardó owned by the Santa Creu trustees, not on the land the executors had purchased in Sarrià.

Domènech i Estapà had been paid in cash for his winning project by the architects' panel a year earlier, and would protest the new decision, but to no avail. Once again, the situation led to countless articles and lampoons in the press.

The press that was favourable to Domènech i Montaner nicknamed Domènech i Estapà "Domènech the baddie":

> "Domènech i Estapà is the sort of architect we suffer in Barcelona who always has to build a public building subsidised by the State, and has flown into a rage because Don Pau Gil's executors – to the benefit of the poor and architectural good taste – have not made him the director of the new hospital project, depriving him of rights he has invented."

> "Calm down, Mr Domènech the baddie, calm down; if God grants you years of life, and a little influence, you will have time to build other eyesores..."
> (*Cu-Cut!*, 1902, January 23)

Domènech i Montaner was also lampooned in the press.

Once the project and the site had been decided on, and the doctors' technical commission set up to advise the architect (Dr Robert, Dr Roig and Dr Duran), Dòmenech i Montaner began drawing up the ambitious project for 1,000 patients, using the most modern hospitals of the day as his reference point.

Hospital references

In his project report, Domènech reveals that he has made an in-depth study of a wide range of hospitals (as reflected in the articles he signed as an *aficionat*, during the polemic with Domènech i Estapà about the Hospital Clínic):

> "The layout of the new Hospital de la Santa Cruz in Barcelona and the adjacent Hospital de San Pablo has been based on a study of the general principles, altered by factors such as climate, location and special problems, the study of examples that have already been executed, some of them old but built in exceptional circumstances, and the most modern ones to which new scientific principles have been applied, and we have examined the effect on the buildings shown in the plans or details of the following buildings:"

He goes on to list 240 hospitals from around the world, mostly in Europe, ordered alphabetically by cities and quoting the bibliography he has consulted for his study. They included F. Ruppel's *Anlage und Bau der Krankenhäuser* (1896), E. Epalza's *Reseña de una visita. Algunos hospitales españoles y extranjeros* (1899), J. Billings' *Description of the John Hopkins Hospital* (1890), Oswald Kuhn's *Gebäude fur heil* (1897), Cloquet's *Traité d'architecture: éléments de l'architecture, types d'édifices,esthétique, composition et pratique de l'architecture* (1898).

The archives of the Barcelona Architects' Association contain a series of handwritten files about these hospitals and the bibliographical references Domènech used in his study. He did not only look at the different types of layout, such as the separate pavilions. He also investigated the different aspects that had an impact on the quality of hospital spaces: natural and artificial ventilation, lighting and sunshine, hygiene, circulation, medical instruments and equipment, heating, administrative services, transport, sanitation, etc.

Domènech created a compendium of all the proposals, including the arrangement of separate pavilions (above the ground) and interconnecting underground galleries, while maintaining the spacious rooms with high ceilings originally used in the Middle Ages. These were more suited to the Mediterranean climate than the rooms with lower ceilings that were prevalent in Central Europe. Domènech brought a wealth of ornamental detail to the buildings.

Domènech i Montaner's original project

As we have seen in the first section about the controversy surrounding the initial project, the site chosen for the hospital complex was some distance from the built-up city centre, but was within easy access. It was located in the Guinardó district, on the far edge of Cerdà's Eixample, the city expansion project begun in 1860. The site was slightly rectangular, meaning that the project would not be totally symmetrical. It was bounded by four streets which had few buildings when building work on the new hospital began. The site was steeply sloping (35 m high at the most elevated point, the equivalent of twelve storeys) and covered a surface area similar to nine blocks in the Eixample.

The project followed the hygienic requirements and medical criteria of the day (Thompson & Goldin, 1975) and consisted of a series of pavilions, rather than a single, compact building, to favour ventilation and let in sunlight. They were set in spacious, landscaped grounds. The project set aside 145,500 m^2 for 1,000 patients: a ratio of 150 m^2 per patient, which was a much larger area than the 130 m^2 recommended by the doctors' committee.

The hospital complex did not align with the layout of the Eixample, but was rotated 45°×, to achieve the perfect orientation of the longitudinal façades of the pavilions (north-south).

Domènech's initial scheme comprised forty-eight buildings for different uses, but fewer than a quarter of these were actually built.

General perspective. Coloured ink on paper.
Barcelona, c. 1902. Arxiu Històric del COAC.

The site was divided by two main avenues that were 50 m wide and cut diagonally across it, creating four quadrants. The slightly rectangular shape of the site meant that the diagonals did not coincide exactly with the four corners. There were twenty-one pavilions used as infirmaries in the central area of the complex, on either side of the wide central avenue. Each pavilion was used to treat different illnesses. Domènech divided the pavilions in the same way he had done at the Pere Mata hospital. The east side was for men and the west side for women. The northern area was used to treat infectious diseases (consumption, typhus, smallpox, syphilis) and the southern area for non-infectious diseases (keeping patients under observation) as well as surgery and medical consultations. The pavilions used for different services (dispensary, church, boiler room, laundry, workshops, children's hospital, water distribution tower, mortuary chapel) were placed on the perimeter of the site and had separate entrances, meaning that people did not have to walk through the site to access them. These unique buildings interlocked with the stretch of the Eixample, which was rotated 45° to the north-south axis of the ensemble. Domènech also built a guest house on the perimeter for patients who could pay for their stay, and isolation pavilions for patients with highly infectious diseases. The majestic administration block with its clock tower stands on the southern corner, forming a gateway to the entire complex. It was used for patient admissions, the offices, the library and museum, accounts department, the general archive, the secretary's office and the large conference hall. The central pavilion was located at the point where the two main axes converge. It contained the convent (to provide accommodation for the nuns who ran the hospital), the large kitchens and the pharmacy. The pavilion used for operations stood opposite.

The spacious area between the buildings was used for the inner circulation routes and gardens. The main axes were 50 m wide and 500 m long, set at a 45° angle to the grid layout of the Eixample, facing north-south and east-west. The minor routes separating the pavilions were 30 m wide. The landscaped areas resolved the variations in the topography of the site in an east-west direction. The pavilions on the east side had step-free access to the middle of the semi-basement, while the pavilions on the west side were accessed from the ground floor. These variations in the ground level resulted in a series of small paths winding diagonally between the pavilions, leaving a cool summer garden on the north side and a very sunny winter garden on the south side.

The different pavilions were connected by a network of underground tunnels running throughout the complex. One network connected the area for patients with non-infectious diseases with the general services, and another separate network connected the infectious disease pavilions (with the exception of the isolation pavilion). These underground galleries were to be naturally lit and ventilated from above and had pipework and wiring that connected each of the pavilions.

There was a sewage system below this network of galleries that served the entire hospital, providing it with the most advanced hygiene conditions of the day (it was later connected to the city's main public sewage and drainage systems, which had not been built at the time).

The hospital complex was separated from its urban setting by a wall of opaque ceramic brick that encompassed the entire perimeter, except for the southern corner where the main entrance was located. At this point, there was a lavishly decorated gate through which the administration pavilion and the square in front could be seen. The latter provided a transitional space between the hospital and the urban fabric. The porch at the entrance to the building accentuated the transparency that provided views of the interior from this privileged spot.

All the buildings were designed to achieve a coherent whole and Domènech used the same repertoire of materials: façades with a stone pediment and exposed-brick walls, stone frames around the inset windows, ornamental stone elements (imposts, cornices, capitals, rose windows, air vents, pinnacles, the bases of the chimneys), roofs made of tiles of ceramic scales in a rich variety of colours and, above all, a profusion of decorative glazed ceramics on the inner and outer walls.

If there is one thing that sets Domènech's project apart from the hospitals he used as a reference, it is precisely this wealth of decorative elements. But it also has rationalist undertones that he wrote about in his report:

"The structure, construction and decoration of all the rooms at the Hospital are so inextricably linked that they form a single concept; after a room has been built, it will be decorated with its own materials both outside and in, with only the tile wainscoting, rendering or stucco finishes that are necessary to keep it clean completing its decoration".

Structurally speaking, all the buildings used the same system. Brick load-bearing or partition walls combined with embedded metal structures and a special type of system to make the ceilings: flat-brick vaulting. This technique, which is also known as Catalan vaulting, or timbrel vaulting, consists of building the structural elements (vaults, spans, steps) using thin ceramic tiles and quick-setting cement or plaster. The structure is highly resistant, lightweight and economical. The origins of this kind of vaulting are unknown, but they were first documented in Catalonia, and in Valencia in particular, in medieval times. However, the technique began to be used systematically in Catalonia from the middle of the 19th to the beginning of the 20th centuries. Domènech i Montaner was one of the leading exponents of the method that combined flat tiles with metal structures. Each of the ceilings in Domènech's buildings at Sant Pau were made using this technique.

Building the hospital: 1902-1930

The Hospital de Sant Pau archives contain a highly valuable documentary heritage about building work on the complex, including the report, tender documents, measurements, budgets, plans, details of the building and certifications. These documents allow us to follow precisely the building process, which spanned a period of twenty-eight years. (Salmerón & Terreu Gascón, 2014; Terreu Gascón, 2015; Terreu Gascón, 2022)

On 15th February 1902, the first stone was laid during a solemn ceremony and work began to clear the site in Guinardó. Although the project was officially underway, and the site manager's office had been built (Terreu Gascon & Salmeron, 2018), Domènech was still drawing up his definitive project. The land on the edge of the site of the Hospital de la Santa Creu had yet to be purchased (the current plot would have been too small to accommodate the hospital) and decisions taken regarding the plots affected by the development. Barcelona City Council did not receive the application for the building licence until 1905.

Domènech submitted his project for the Hospital de Sant Pau and embarked on the necessary procedures, including the invitations to tender. Gil's executors began work on the Hospital de Sant Pau, which was to be the first to be built and would allow the patients to be transferred from the old hospital in the Raval immediately. But the project was beset by endless problems. In 1903, discrepancies arose about the way the executors were administering the estate, and Pau Gil's funds, which had been deposited with the Banco de España, were withheld, making it impossible to pay for the work that had already been carried out and bringing the project to a standstill. The situation reminded Domènech of his failed project for the Instituciones Provinciales, which he had designed with his colleague Josep Vilaseca (Domènech i Montaner, 2013). In 1904, work on the hospital continued. The remaining documents were drawn up, the copies of the budgets were sent out to the different contractors, and the necessary steps were taken to ensure payments were honoured and the site prepared for building. However, another conflict arose: there were disagreements with the Santa Creu board of trustees, which deemed Domènech's project too lavish and asked him to make changes: the magnificent administration pavilion would be cancelled and, with the money saved, they would be able to build the central pavilion with Gil's legacy to house the convent and general services (Domènech i Montaner, 2013). Domènech had encountered exactly the same problem with his project for the Pere Mata hospital (March et al., 2004). In this case, he agreed to reduce the number of buildings initially envisaged in the project as he thought this would just be a temporary measure, although, in fact, it turned out to be definitive. However, with the hospital in Barcelona, he fought to maintain the original configuration of his project. The Santa Creu board of trustees broke off negotiations with Pau Gil's executors as a result, and they did not resume until almost ten years later, when the money from Gil's legacy had run out and the hospital complex was only half built. This allows us to divide the building of the hospital into two distinct phases: 1905-1912, when part of the Hospital de Sant Pau was built using money from Pau Gil's bequest, and 1914-1930, when the Santa

Creu board of trustees continued with the problematic building process.

In 1905 (Domènech i Montaner, 1905) the builder, Francesc Vilagut, was awarded the construction tender and work began on the first pavilions for the Hospital de Sant Pau. He adhered to Domènech i Montaner's project, which was of the highest artistic calibre, and worked with the finest artisans and builders of the day: the sculptors Pau Gargallo and Eusebi Arnau; the mosaicist Mario Maragliano, who followed Francesc Labarta's drawings; the glazed tiles by the Pujol i Bausis ceramics factory and Guillamont and Peris; the artificial stone elements by Fradera and Butsems; the metal structure made by the Sociedad Material para Ferrocarriles y Construcciones; carpentry by the Viladevall brothers; landscaping by Badia i Ferrer; floor tiles by Escofet, Nolla, Llevat and Toda; paintwork by Vilaró, Inglada and Fraxanet; and stained glass by Rigalt, Granell i Cia, Espinagosa and Vilella. There is a slight imbalance between the amount of stained glass and carpentry work and the other elements when we compare the building with some of Domènech's other projects. This may be because funding had run out before the project was completed and the buildings became operational.

Domènech worked with a large team of collaborators. They included the assistant architects, Enric Catà (1878-1937), Francesc Guàrdia Vial (1880-1940), Pere Domènech i Roura (1881-1962) and Francesc Julià; assistant builders, Alfons Vicente, Francesc Labarta (1883-1963), Joan Labarta and Amadeu Llopart (1888-1970); the clerks, Josep Pellicer, Rossend Carrera, Nicolás Aguilera and Francisco Casals; and the draughtsmen, Gabriel Vinyas, Miguel Curet and Miquel Salines. (Terreu Gascon & Salmeron, 2018)

The pavilions included in this first phase were: the administration pavilion, the two observation pavilions, six nursing pavilions and the operations pavilion.

The administration pavilion marks the main entrance to the hospital complex. It has a monumental façade with a taller central section surmounted by a clock tower, which makes it a recognisable landmark on the urban landscape. The importance of the building is further highlighted by the rich ornamental and decorative programme created by the fine quality materials, particularly the multiple varieties of ceramics applied to the architectural elements. A spectacular mosaic frieze along the outer walls of the side sections of the pavilion, illustrates the history of the hospital institution from its origins to the building of its new premises. Also worthy of note is the rationalist approach to the building process, as set out in the project report, with the use of exposed brick on the inner walls combined with a grey block (of unfired-lime mortar) with no plaster finish.

There are two observation pavilions behind the administration pavilion: Sant Jordi and Santa Apol·lònia, which were used to examine patients who had just been admitted. They were not connected to the network of underground galleries in order to prevent the spread of diseases.

The infirmary pavilions were built on either side of the central avenue. Six of them were built during the initial building phase and two more during the second one. They all had the same layout: a spacious ward for patients with a rectangular floor plan. It was reached through a lobby with a day room and services on either side, with the administration offices and healthcare facilities at the back. The underground floor was initially used as a service area and connected with the underground galleries. The vast interior spaces, including the brick timbrel vaults, were completely covered in richly ornamented glazed or enamelled ceramic tiles, creating a wide variety of textures and colours while guaranteeing hygienic conditions. Natural ventilation and light were studied in depth and described in detail in the project report, and a network of pipes and chimneys was fitted throughout the complex. Domènech had also made provisions for artificial ventilation and heating systems in his project, adapting the specifications of the hospital architecture of the day to the requirements of the Mediterranean climate. Domènech had taught the subject *The applications of the physical natural sciences in architecture* at the Barcelona School of Architecture, and was a great expert on the subject.

The last pavilion to be built during the initial phase contained the operating theatres. These too followed the examples of the time with the spacious operating room with its north-facing façades, which were glazed floor to ceiling to maximise the amount of natural light throughout the building.

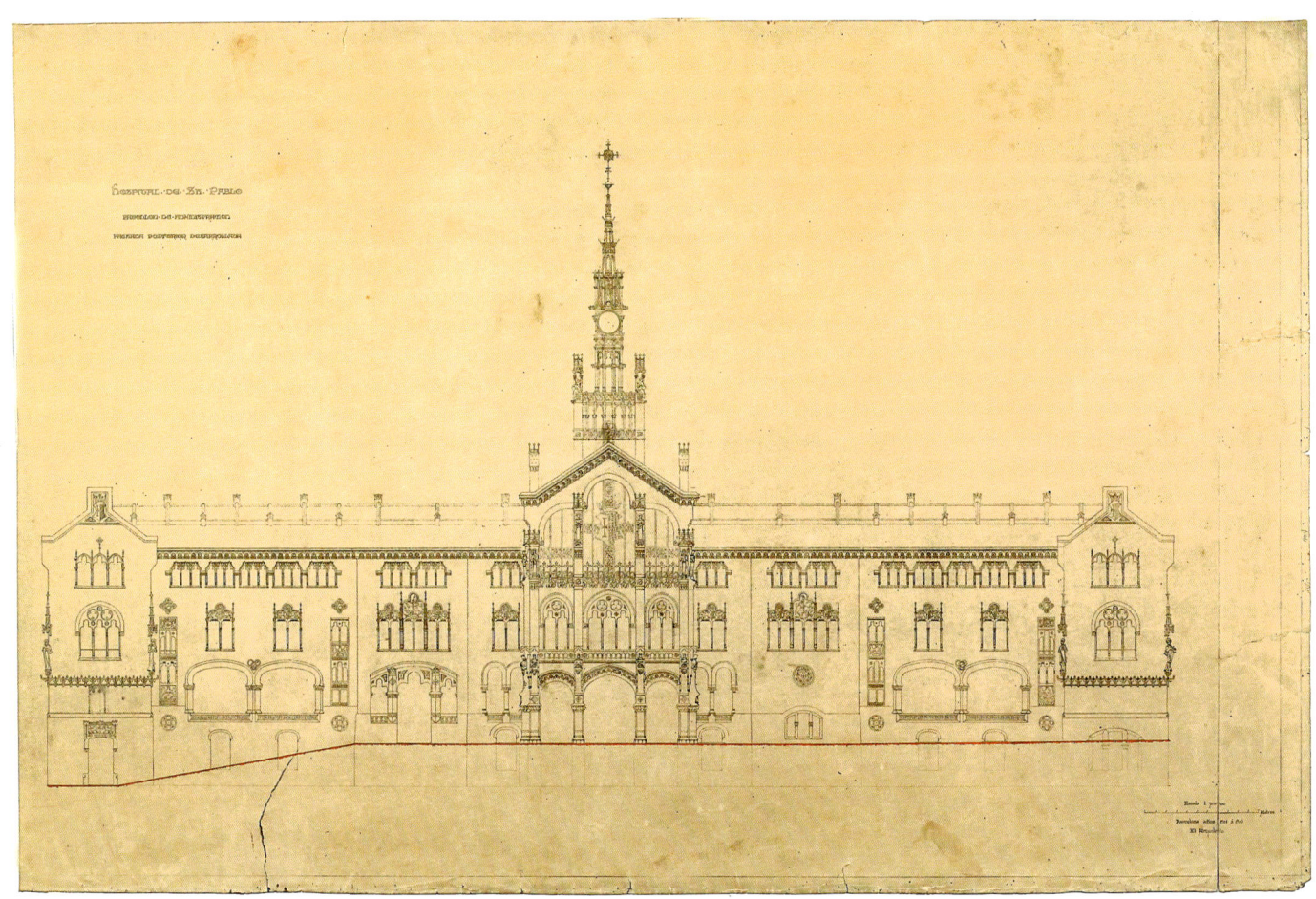

Administration pavilion. Elevation of the main façade.
Barcelona, c. 1902. Arxiu Històric del COAC.

Portrait of Lluís Domènech i Montaner in the lobby of the Hospital de Sant Pau. Francesc Serra Dimas, n.d. Arxiu Fotogràfic de Barcelona.

The landscaping was restricted to the part of the hospital complex that had already been built. It included plant and tree species, some of them with medicinal and therapeutic properties, which made the grounds a beautiful, relaxing place to be.

The iconographic and ornamental repertoire of the buildings systematically repeats the symbols of the two promotors of the hospital: Pau Gil (P and G) and the Santa Creu board of trustees, as well other donors who funded the last pavilions. There are countless sculpted figures, including guardian angels and the tetramorph depicting the evangelists, which have been part of the history of the hospital foundation.

In 1912, the funds from Pau Gil's bequest had been used up and his executors prepared to transfer the pavilions (which remained unfinished and were not ready to admit patients) to the trustees of the Hospital de la Santa Creu, whom they had been trying to resume negotiations with. Building work was halted while they looked for other sources of funding, leaving a half-finished building, of outstanding architectural value, that could not be put to use. The complex won the prize in the annual best building competition in 1912.

> "...from its detailed examination of the Hospital de San Pablo, based on the background information herein set out, the Jury deduced that this magnum opus is of superior and unquestionable importance, and is, in its own right, an ensemble of buildings of monumental scale, that harmonises the idea of charity and exquisite art, united gloriously by the altruistic and generous memory of the illustrious donor, whose idea, the wise architect Don Luis Doménech y Montaner has been able to fulfil, with readiness and excellent good taste..., an ensemble of buildings, each of which could, in its own right, be part of a grand project, which has been, and continues to be admired by all technical and artistic entities, not only in Spain, but by the most important ones abroad..."
> (*Concurso Anual de Edificios y Establecimientos Urbanos Terminados Durante El Año 1912*, 1914).

Work on the hospital resumed in 1914 with the contractor Joan Ors. The project had to contend with financial difficulties and building work continued for another sixteen years based on the funds available to the Santa Creu board of trustees donated by several benefactors (whom the new pavilions they helped to build would be named after). During this second phase, Domènech's son, Pere Domènech i Roura, began to play a more prominent role in overseeing the work. The buildings were more austere as a result of the funding issues and the projects were adapted accordingly. Their monumentality was watered down and there were fewer ornamental elements. Lower-quality building materials were also used. Domènech i Montaner died on 27th December 1923, without seeing his project completed or put to use. His son continued to supervise the building work.

From this moment on, the ambitious initial project was abandoned and the new pavilions were a different type of building altogether. This was not only due to the availability of funding, but was also based on the functional requirements of hospital buildings resulting from the way medical science had evolved in the twenty years since the original project had been drawn up.

The pavilions that were part of this second phase were: the central pavilion, the pavilions of Sant Manel and Sant Rafel, the church and the annexes, the pavilion of the resurrection, the laundry pavilion, the boiler room, the extension of the on-site kiln room, and the pavilions of Sant Carles and Santa Francesca. Many of the pavilions envisaged in the original project were never built. One of Domènech i Roura's final tasks was to ensure the pavilions were ready for use and provide them with the necessary furnishings and equipment.

King Alfonso XIII officially opened the hospital on 16th January 1930, twenty years and eight days after the first stone was laid. Six months earlier, the medical staff and patients had been moved to the new premises, although work on some of the pavilions continued for a number of months.

The life and use of the hospital: 1930-2009

Building work continued after the hospital had opened and become fully operational. It was expanded, new pavilions were built and alterations made to adapt the complex to the new functional requirements. More often than not, these interventions were made with a lack of care, in terms of layout and finishes, compared with Domènech's original concept. Patient capacity needed to be expanded and the facilities adapted to deal with the rapid changes taking place in the field of medicine that the old buildings were not always able to cater to.

Domènech i Roura continued as chief architect and was succeeded by Manuel Puig Janer and, later, his son Manuel Puig Ribot.

Countless alterations were made to the patients' pavilions that had already been built according to Domènech i Montaner's project, which diluted their initial characteristics. The vast spaces where the day rooms and wards were located were divided horizontally to increase the surface area: instead of having a spacious ward with a ceiling height of 9 m, there were now two with a ceiling height of 4 m each. Patients were no longer treated in a large communal space but in rooms for one or two people, meaning that the spaces were subdivided by vertical partitions creating small cubicles. These changes affected the shutters and windows on the façade, which were divided in two and even blocked up. New coverings were placed over the flooring and interior walls.

The natural heating and cooling systems, including harnessing the sunlight, envisaged in Domènech's original project were no longer used, and the new amenities that were required engulfed the building: pipes, cables and air-conditioning units appeared.

The monumental façade of the administration block was preserved, but the interior suffered many alterations. The spacious wards at the ends were split horizontally to increase their useful surface, and the entire east wing was compartmentalised to house a college.

The Fundació Puigvert was built in 1960, and small extensions attached to the art nouveau, or *modernista*, buildings. Prefabricated units were erected around the site.

The hospital was named a historic and artistic landmark in 1978. This designation included the eleven pavilions designed by Domènech i Montaner and nine designed by Domènech i Roura. (Martín, 1979)

It was awarded UNESCO World Heritage status in 1997 (together with the Palau de la Música Catalana).

Despite this recognition of its value as an architectural site, the pressure resulting from its use as a hospital continued to have a serious impact on the complex. Its architectural and functional decline increased and the need to transfer the hospital to a new building became increasingly apparent. Fortunately, nobody was injured when one of the domes in the pavilion of La Mercè collapsed in 2004, but the event probably acted as a trigger that expedited the project for the building of a new, compact hospital. Pavilion hospitals had been outmoded for many years and were no longer being built.

A new Hospital de Sant Pau was built on the northern edge of the site. It had more than five hundred beds, in accordance with the requirements of a 21st-century hospital facility. A number of Domènech i Roura's original buildings – which did not follow the orginal project – were demolished: the pavilions of Sant Carles, Santa Francesca, Santa Faustina, the pavilion of the resurrection, laundry and kiln room.

The new hospital opened in 2009. Domènech i Montaner's original buildings now stood empty meaning that restoration work could begin and their architectural value be fully revealed.

Views of the Sagrada Família from the lobby of the administration pavilion. Jaume Ribera Llopis, 1923. Arxiu de l'Hospital (AHSCP).

Ward inside the pavilion of the Assumption. Jaume Ribera Llopis, 1929. Arxiu de l'Hospital (AHSCP).

The restoration of the site

The decorations of the magnificent *modernista* site had been damaged through its use as a hospital for almost eighty years. A master plan was drawn up in 2008 to analyse the state of preservation of the entire complex, carry out historical research, diagnose critical points and set out the guidelines and criteria for a coherent intervention (Guitart and Tarrés, 2008). Elevations were made of the original plans, historic reports were studied, photographic documents were researched, materials analysed, ornamental elements catalogued and structural studies made. Using these plans as a guide, restoration work commenced on the different pavilions and they were repurposed. However, it proved impossible to restore all the buildings simultaneously. Once again, due to financial restraints, and the new uses of the buildings, they were restored in phases, and some of the contracts for the restoration of the buildings had to be rescinded.

The first restoration phase was completed in 2014, and the Sant Pau art nouveau Site opened to the public. This cultural asset highlights the value of the architectural ensemble and, in addition to being a visitor attraction, is also home to a number of institutions involved in healthcare and sustainability.

Basically, the interventions focused on returning the spatial configuration of the pavilions to its original state, removing any additions, unsuitable partitions and recovering the lavish ornamental details that had been damaged. The open-air spaces were also restored and the original landscaped areas and gardens reclaimed. The inclusion of all the amenities required by the current use of the buildings has been carried out according to sustainable energy criteria while respecting the heritage value of the site at all times. It is a wonderful example of the integration of both elements.

The Sant Pau Art Nouveau Site is currently a magnificently preserved example of an early 20th-century pavilion hospital complex. Many of the hospitals Domènech i Montaner used as references no longer exist or have been badly damaged. Only just under a quarter of his original project was built as the lavish decorative elements drove up the building costs. It was harshly criticised as the time because it was considered unsuitable for use as a charitable hospital. (Domènech i Montaner, 2013)

However, we can conclude that the spectacular ornamental, spatial and functional richness of Domènech i Montaner's complex, which cannot be compared with any other hospital building of the time, is more than worthy of its World Heritage status.

→ Aerial view of the Hospital de Sant Pau.

Pavilion of Our Lady of Montserrat.

← Façade of the administration pavilion.

Ceramic decorations on the pavilion roofs.

Clock tower on top of the administration pavilion.

Panoramic view of the roofs from the clock tower.

Coat of arms on the top
of the main façade.

← Administration pavilion.
Angel perched above the main façade.

Hospital de la Santa Creu i Sant Pau

Administration pavilion.
Angels on the façade by Pau Gargallo.

→ Administration pavilion.
Main entrance with the sculptural grouping dedicated to Pau Gil.

← Administration pavilion.

→ Gallery of the administration pavilion.

Administration pavilion. Basement.

Administration pavilion. Vaults in the lobby.

Administration pavilion. Grand hall.

Administration pavilion. Grand hall.

→ Vaults above the grand hall in the administration pavilion.

Administration pavilion. One of the vaults in the former secretary's office at the hospital.

Administration pavilion.
One of the vaults inside the Cambó library.

View of the rear façade of the administration pavilion from the portico of the church.

← Façade of the church and replica of the cross from the old hospital in the Raval district.

Hospital de la Santa Creu i Sant Pau

Underground network of corridors connecting the different pavilions.

Pavilion of the Assumption.

The Casa Lleó i Morera: the integration of the arts

1903-1905

Pilar Vélez

The Casa Lleó i Morera (1903-1905) is one of Lluís Domènech i Montaner's most outstanding and unique Barcelona buildings. It posed a real challenge to the architect as he had to work with an existing building that only occupied half a corner at the junction of Passeig de Gràcia and Carrer del Consell de Cent. Before we enter into the description of the house, let me introduce you to its owners.

In 1902, Francesca Morera Ortiz, who came from a well-to-do family of overseas merchants, commissioned Lluís Domènech to renovate a building at 35 Passeig de Gràcia, which she had inherited from her uncle Antoni Morera. It was known as the Casa Rocamora and had been erected in 1864 by the master builder Joaquim Sitjas. When Francesca died suddenly in 1904, her only son, Albert Lleó i Morera, a specialist in microbiology at the Hospital de la Santa Creu i Sant Pau, oversaw the completion of the project. He was married to Olinta Puiguriguer Palmarola and they had three children, a girl and two boys. One of the boys died when he was a baby and this event explains the poem, carved by Eusebi Arnau, inside the first-floor apartment, where the family lived. Their other son, Albert Lleó Puiguriguer, managed the family estate until he sold the property to an insurance company, the Sociedad Mercantil Bilbao, in 1943. He removed the furniture and decorative objects from the family home and stored them elsewhere.

As we said at the beginning, the Casa Lleó i Morera is not a new building, but a large-scale renovation of an existing one. The original façade was demolished and major alterations were made that created one of the most outstanding residential projects of the Catalan art nouveau, or *modernista*, period. Antoni Gaudí's Casa Batlló was another building based on a renovation project. It stands on the same block as the Casa Lleó i Morera in the Eixample district, known as the "mançana de la discòrdia", or block of discord, where some of the most iconic buildings by the architects Domènech, Sagnier, Puig i Cadafalch and Gaudí vie for prominence.

As was customary in Barcelona at the time, the building consisted of rental apartments, except for the first floor, where the owners of the building – in this case the Lleó i Moreras – lived, and a shop on the ground floor, which housed the studio of the renowned photographer, Pau Audouard, who took many photographs of the interior of the apartment.

Audouard was one of the official photographers for the 1888 Barcelona Universal Exhibition and specialised in photographs of buildings and events. He moved his studio into the ground floor of the Casa Lleó i Morera in 1905, just after it had been completed. At the time, Passeig de Gràcia was becoming Barcelona's main shopping street and vying with Carrer Ferran, which had been the place to shop until then. Audouard remained there until 1915.

← Façade. Anonymous photograph, 1905. Arxiu Històric del COAC.

Elevation and section of the façade. Ink on waxed rag paper, 1903. Arxiu Municipal Contemporani de Barcelona.

Sitting room on the first floor. Photograph by Adolf Mas, c. 1902. Institut Amatller d'Art Hispànic.

Detail of the façade. Àngel Toldrà Viazo, c. 1905. Arxiu Fotogràfic de Barcelona.

The Casa Lleó i Morera: a façade that speaks to us

The Casa Lleó i Morera is currently one of the most iconic cultural landmarks of Catalonia's home-grown art nouveau movement, *modernisme*. It is located in Barcelona's Eixample district, which, at the time, was the city's new, rapidly expanding, central neighbourhood. The ornate decorative elements on the façade were made possible as a result of new bylaws that had come into effect in 1891. They gave architects absolute freedom to add galleries, balconies and balustrades to the fronts of their buildings upon payment of a levy. As the person in charge of the project, Domènech took advantage of the new regulations and hired a large team of artisans and artists who endowed the building with its high-quality decorative elements.

As soon as visitors step inside the lobby on the corner of the building, they encounter sumptuous decorations on the walls, ceiling and floor, which never fail to impress. The first flight of stairs, with its marble steps and a mosaic wall panel with floral motifs, leads to the landing on the mezzanine floor, which is richly decorated with Roman-style mosaics with geometrical motifs. The stairs lead from here to the upper floors. All the mosaics are by Lluís Bru and the walls are decorated with sgraffito-work dadoes. The arch separating the first space from the mezzanine features stone and mosaic floral motifs, including a plethora of mulberry flowers, evoking the surname of the owner (*morera* is Catalan for mulberry).

The most iconic aspect of the building is, of course, the façade. It has two picture windows on the ground floor, one on the corner and another on Passeig de Gràcia. There used to be two art nouveau-style symbolistic female figures, and nymphs suspended from large plant pots, but these have long since vanished. On the first floor, the Lleó i Morera family apartment has long picture windows overlooking the street and a rotunda on the corner, which is also decorated with six busts of female nymphs with interlinking flower garlands. There are long balconies on the second floor, with two female figures on the façade on either side of the windows. The ones on Carrer Consell de Cent are allegories of the gramophone and electricity and the ones on Passeig de Gràcia, the telephone and photography. Like the previous ones, they were made by the sculptor Eusebi Arnau. Three plaster models of the sculptures are on display at Domènech i Montaner's house and museum in Canet de Mar.

On the third floor, in addition to the twin circular balconies on the corner, there are two semi-circular balconies with circular sculptural decorations applied onto the façade, one on the corner and another on Passeig de Gràcia. Each of the columns on these balconies is surmounted by a bust of a man and a woman. According to the scholar, Manuel García Martín, they may depict members of the family: Francesca Morera, her son Albert Lleó i Morera, his wife, Olinta de Puiguriguer, and Antoni Morera i Busó, Francesca's uncle, whom she inherited the building from. On the fourth, or upper floor, there is a gallery of Gothic-style windows surmounted by pinnacles and, above it, on the corner, a *tempietto*, or circular turret.

The symbolistic female figures were made by one of the leading lights of *modernisme*, the sculptor Eusebi Arnau, who regularly collaborated with Domènech. The sculptural decorations on the balconies and balustrades, the *tempietto* and, probably, the four busts, were by Alfons Juyol, a sculptor who specialised in decorating monumental buildings. Lions and mulberry leaves, alluding to the names of the married couple who were the owners – Lleó i Morera (lion and mulberry in Catalan) – complete the decorative elements on the stone façade.

The first floor of the Casa Lleó i Morera: the integration of all the arts

The Lleó i Morera family lived on the first floor of the building. Thanks to them, one of the finest ensembles of furniture and interior decoration – from the dining room and main drawing room – of Catalan *modernisme* and European art nouveau, has survived. Many of the pieces are on display at the Museu Nacional d'Art de Catalunya.

The floor plan of the first floor reveals the characteristic layout of the apartment blocks in the Eixample. The door leading into Dr Morera's office is in the reception area and the corridor, which forms the core of the apartment, is at the side. The lintel above the door of the corridor is decorated with a sculptural grouping by Arnau depicting the Catalan lullaby,

La dida de l'infant rei (The Wet-Nurse of the Infant King). As we mentioned earlier, it alludes to the history of the Lleó i Morera family, who lost a child in infancy. The figures are rendered with great skill and subtlety. Arnau also carved another sculptural grouping depicting Saint George and the princess, a theme very much in vogue at the time that evokes the family's Catalan identity, which is also reflected in the neo-Gothic bench by the entrance. The bench was probably designed by Gaspar Homar, who was also responsible for the interior design of the entire apartment. The phrases *Pàtria, Fides, Amor* (Homeland, faith, love) and *Avant, sempre, avant* (Forward, always, forward) are carved into the benches. They are both closely linked to the Catalan poetry competition, the *Jocs Florals*, and are an example of the way Catalonia's home-grown art nouveau, *modernisme*, reclaimed the patriotic legacy of the Catalan cultural revival movement, the *Renaixença*. Next to the bench is the door leading into Dr Morera's office with its imposing desk with a Secession-style lamp and a cupboard at the back. These, along with the bench, are currently part of the collections of Barcelona's design museum, the Museu del Disseny.

The reception area leads directly into the two large sitting rooms, which overlook the street, and the gallery in the centre. These rooms showcase many of the sumptuous decorative elements designed by Domènech and executed by a skilled team of artisans and builders, under the supervision of the *ensemblier*, the interior designer and furniture maker we mentioned earlier, Gaspar Homar. (Fondevila, 1998)

The dining room is at the other end of the corridor towards the rear of the building and is decorated with eight colourful panels combining mosaics and porcelain reliefs designed by Josep Pey. They depict rural scenes, four of them inspired by family photographs. One features a landscape and the remaining three, animals and trees. The mosaics were made by Mario Maragliano, except for some of the objects and the faces and hands of the people, which are rendered in porcelain relief, lending the ensemble a realistic touch. Joan Carreras Farré carved these pieces in clay and used them to make the plaster moulds. The ceramicist, Antoni Serra, then transformed them into highly refined glazed ceramic pieces at his factory Porcellanes i Gres d'Art in 1905.

At the back of the dining room, we find the gallery, which was a characteristic feature of the apartment blocks in the Eixample. It has large stained-glass windows made by the Rigalt & Granell studio, and opens onto the interior courtyard. The servants' rooms were located on either side of the corridor and off the dining room. The entire apartment has beautiful floors, by Lluís Bru and Mario Maragliano, and the ceramic dados in the rooms were made at the Pujol i Bausis ceramics factory.

The walls of the sitting room overlooking Passeig de Gràcia were lined with wooden panels with marquetry inlays. These were also designed by Josep Pey and built at the workshop of the cabinet-maker Joan Sagarra. A sofa set between two vitrines with a marquetry panel behind it, and a writing desk were placed against two of the walls. There was also a small table and a number of chairs with and without arms. These are on display at the Museu Nacional d'Art de Catalunya in Barcelona, and the original marquetry drawings are part of the holdings of the Museu del Disseny (Vélez, 2020). The upper section of the walls was covered with floral wallpaper and the coffered ceilings featured semi-spherical low reliefs and marquetry.

There is a triangular space between the sitting room and dining room leading to the rotunda on the corner of the building. Its centrepiece is a fireplace with benches on either side. It was decorated with an *Adoration of the Magi* carved in wood by Joan Carreras, which has not survived, and enclosed on the sides by two angels made of repoussé copper and designed by Josep Pey. They are now part of the collections of the Museu del Disseny.

At the other end of the corridor, we find the characteristic gallery found in the apartment blocks in the Eixample, which opens onto the interior courtyard. It has large stained-glass windows made by the Rigalt & Granell studio. The servants' quarters were located in the centre. The entire apartment has beautiful floors by Lluís Bru and Mario Maragliano, and the ceramic dados in the rooms were made at the Pujol i Bausis ceramics factory.

The ensemble shows that Domènech i Montaner was like the conductor of an orchestra, and he has been described as such on more than one occasion. He was able to guide a rich and heterogeneous group of builders, artists and artisans to create one of the masterpieces of Barcelona *modernisme*. Marquetry, carvings, mosaics, stained glass, porcelain, wallpaper, coffered ceilings and bronzes are prime examples of the way the arts that were the trademarks of Catalonia's home-grown art nouveau, *modernisme*, could be brought together, and this building by Domènech provides more than ample proof of this.

Recognition and scorn for the building

In 1899, Barcelona City Council launched an annual competition for artistic buildings. The Casa Lleó i Morera won first prize in the seventh edition of the competition, which was held in 1906 and appraised buildings that had been completed in 1905. The prize was awarded because of the way the building integrated the different applied arts, both inside and outside: ceramics, stained glass, ironwork, mosaics… It was the first award Lluís Domènech won. In 1909 and 1913 he received two more for the Palau de la Música Catalana and Hospital de Sant Pau, which were both granted UNESCO World Heritage status in 1997.

The municipal prize consisted of placing a commemorative plaque outside the building. From 1900 onwards, the plaques were made of bronze and produced by the sculptor Andreu Aleu and the architect Bonaventura Bassegoda, in a combination of the *modernista* and Gothic styles. They were cast at the Masriera i Campins foundry in Barcelona. The plaque awarded in 1906 can still be seen on the façade on Passeig de Gràcia. At the same competition, Audouard's photographic studio won the second runner-up prize in the commercial-establishment category, which the city council had introduced in 1902.

Some parts of the building sustained damage during the Spanish Civil War. These included the *tempietto*, which was used as a machine-gun nest. A few years later, in 1943, at a time when *modernisme* was still widely disregarded, the fashion house Loewe moved into the ground floor of the building. This part of the building was seriously disfigured as the result of the addition of new shop windows. Arnau's balconies and sculptures of female figures were ripped out and smashed to pieces, although the heads were salvaged by the concierge and purchased shortly afterwards by Salvador Dalí, who placed them in the courtyard of his Theatre-Museum in Figueres.

In 1988, the architects Carles Bassó and Òscar Tusquets were commissioned to carry out a restoration project at the Casa Lleó i Morera, and were awarded the City of Barcelona prize. The project did not include the ground floor of the building, but public pressure eventually resulted in Loewe agreeing to restore it in 1992. In 2006, a restoration and conservation plan was drawn up, backed by the property developers Núñez i Navarro, who currently own the building.

The furniture from the first-floor apartment of the Casa Lleó i Morera: heritage of the city of Barcelona

Much of the furniture from the first-floor apartment is currently part of the collections of the Museu Nacional d'Art de Catalunya and the Museu del Disseny in Barcelona. However, most of the main decorative elements – walls, floors, ceilings, stained glass and metalwork – have remained in situ. (Vélez, 2020)

The furniture, lamps and a number of decorative objects were the first significant *modernista* collections to be put on show at Barcelona's art museums. After being forgotten, and even rejected, for decades, art and architecture historians brought about a *modernista* revival in the middle of the 20th century, and embarked on a series of studies, exhibitions and publications that have continued until today. Barcelona hosted two major exhibitions in 1964 and from 1969 to 1970, which not only played a strategic role in the recognition of *modernisme* by the public, but marked the "official" beginning of the *modernista* collections at the city's museums.

The director of Catalonia's art museums, Joan Ainaud de Lasarte, was the driving force behind the exhibitions. The first was entitled the *Exposición de Artes suntuarias del Modernismo barcelonès* (Exhibition of the Sumptuary Arts of Barcelona *modernisme*), which included, among its highlights, the spectacular furniture from the first-floor apartment of the Casa Lleó i Morera, which had been saved by the descendants of the family when they sold the building. This enabled Joan Ainaud to purchase these and other items between 1966 and 1967. They are now on display at the Museu Nacional d'Art de Catalunya and are considered some of the most beautiful examples of European art nouveau. The growing awareness among the public of the value of *modernisme* resulted in a series of major donations.

Shortly afterwards, Joan Ainaud was put in charge of selecting the works for the major exhibition *El Modernismo en España* (art nouveau in Spain), which was held from 1969 to 1970 in Madrid and Barcelona, and exhibited the furniture from the Casa Lleó i Morera, and other objects that were purchased at the time. The catalogue provides a good overview of the movement.

The strategy of holding two exhibitions in 1964 and 1969 was a huge success from a heritage point of view. The city's public collections began to reclaim the *modernista* heritage following acquisitions by Barcelona City Council and donations of works by some of the most outstanding *modernista* artists. From this moment on, as Joan Ainaud remembered, they never stopped growing. (Ainaud, 1990)

Today, Barcelona is considered one of the most representative cities of the art nouveau movement. Domènech i Montaner is one of the great names in groundbreaking architecture, and was able to integrate the applied and decorative arts inside and outside his buildings, transforming them, as is the case of the Casa Lleó i Morera, into a burst of colour of great quality and refinement.

Wood and mosaic decoration on the first floor.

Casa Lleó i Morera • 325

Winged dragon decorating the windows on the ground floor.

← Top of the façade.

Long balcony with female figures holding modern inventions including the camera and telephone.

Exterior and interior (right) of the round gallery.

The lion and the mulberry refer to the surnames of the owners.

→ Staircase in the entrance hall.

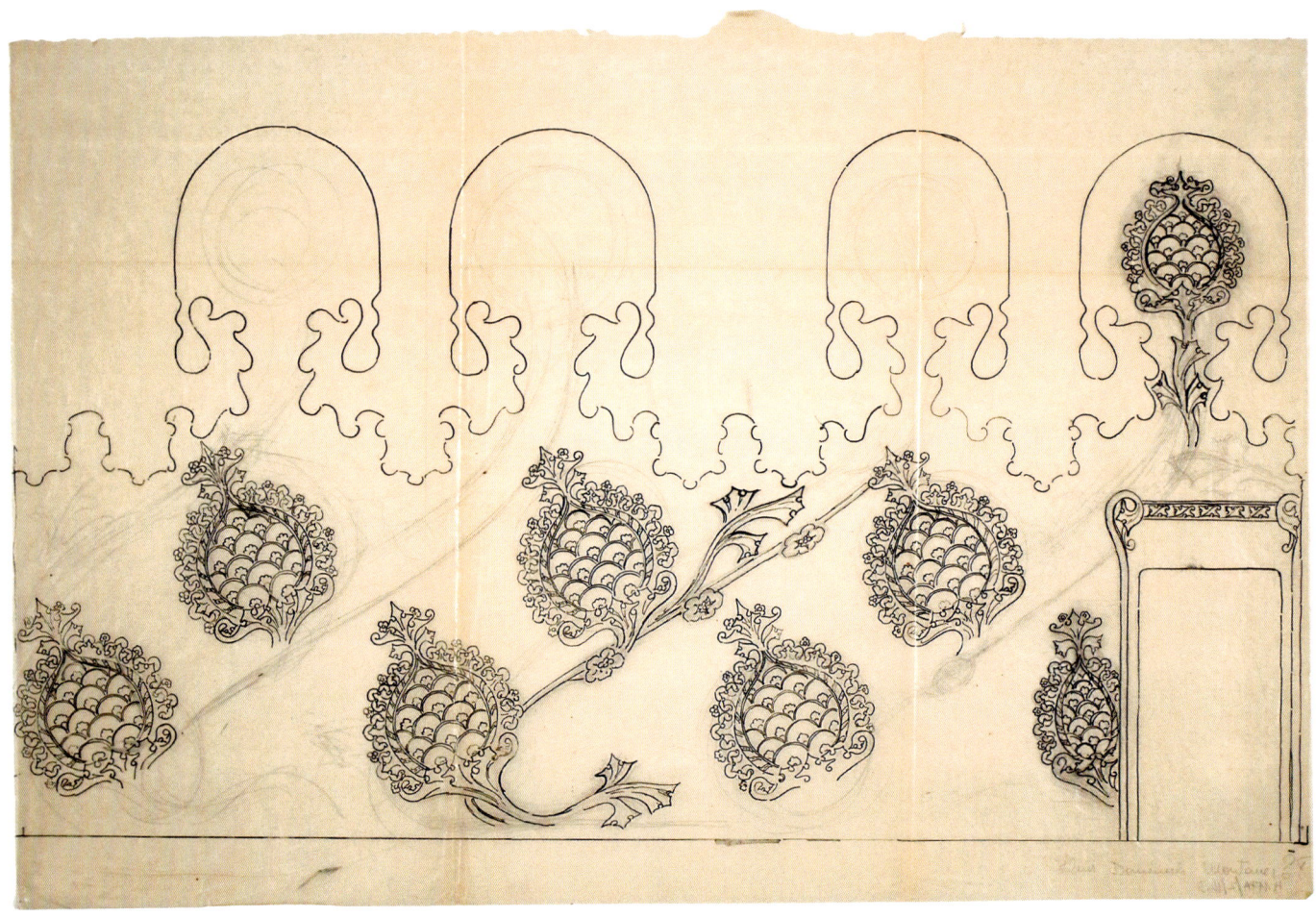

Decorative drawing of the wainscoting in the porter's lodge. Barcelona, *c.* 1904. Arxiu Històric del COAC.

→ Wainscoting on the staircase.

Spyhole in the door on the first floor.

→ Stained-glass window on the staircase.

Room overlooking Passeig de Gràcia with wooden wainscoting and walls with sgraffito-work (right).

Corridor on the first floor with sculptures by Eusebi Arnau depicting the popular lullaby, *La dida de l'infant rei*.

Sculptures by Eusebi Arnau depicting the legend of Sant Jordi (Saint George).

Casa Lleó i Morera • 341

Stained-glass windows on the stairs and detail (right) of stained glass on the first floor.

342 • Lluís Domènech i Montaner

Gallery overlooking the rear courtyard with its leaded stained glass made by the Rigalt & Granell studio.

Rooms on the first floor.

Fireplace on the first floor.

Capital by Eusebi Arnau
in the first-floor entrance hall.

← Sculpture by Eusebi Arnau depicting
the wet-nurse in the first-floor entrance hall.

Mosaics on the wainscoting in the dining room designed by Josep Pey and made by Mario Maragliano.

Palau de la Música Catalana 1905-1909

Lluís Domènech Girbau

The Palau de la Música Catalana is the most representative building of Catalonia's home-grown art nouveau movement, *modernisme*, and Lluís Domènech i Montaner's most fully developed project on every level. It is also a UNESCO World Heritage landmark.

The choir, the Orfeó Català, commissioned Domènech to design the concert hall in 1904, at the behest of its president, Joaquim Cabot, who was an active member of the political party, the Lliga Regionalista. The project was to include all the rooms required by the choir as well as a large auditorium for concert-goers.

We cannot be certain that the men and women from the Orfeó Català had a clear idea of how to fund the project, or what kind of building they wanted to erect on the complicated and irregular plot of land they had purchased. We do know that Mr Cabot was keen to bring the project to fruition. He was the only person to provide an example of the kind of building he wanted, when he sent Domènech a postcard from Geneva of the recently opened Victoria Hall, and asked him to base the Palau on this venue.

We do not know how Domènech reacted to Cabot's postcard or the ideas put forward by the musicians associated with the choir – Lluís Millet, Amadeu Vives and Francesc Matheu – or those of the composer Anselm Clavé, which were more socially engaged. Clavé preferred music by Beethoven and Wagner, which he had heard at the home of his friend, the composer Vidiella, which was the polar opposite of popular Catalan tunes.

We can deduce that Domènech decided to expand on the design his client had agreed on and make the project truly innovative, beyond the proposed models. He conveyed this sense of breaking new ground to the architecture of the Palau de la Música, regardless of whether people considered the building of good or bad quality. This approach brings to mind Otto Wagner's postal savings bank building, which was being built in Vienna in the same year Domènech received the commission from the Orfeó Català. Wagner was ten years Domènech's senior and had had to make a highly personal transition from the neoclassical style to the new attitudes embraced by his friends and students from the Secession. His architectural designs were also, undeniably, ground-breaking.

Domènech drew a great deal of inspiration from the writings of Viollet-le-Duc: "When naval architects and mechanical engineers design a ship or locomotive they do not look at the shape of ships from the time of Louis XIV or carriages; instead, they blindly follow the new guidelines and produce works with their own style and character, so that everyone can see they have a precise aim."

The location of the Palau within the urban fabric of the old town

In 1907, work began on the new thoroughfare, Via Laietana, based on the Baixeras plan, and with guaranteed funding from the Banco Hispano Colonial. For obvious reasons, when Joaquim Cabot signed the purchase deeds for the plot of land in 1904, he must have been aware of the urban development project that would soon be underway and imagined an advantageous future due to the location of his concert hall, unlike other prospective sites he had considered in the Eixample district, as Manuel García Martín (1990) explains.

Buildings that would bring in revenue to the area and make it prosperous were constructed along the front building line on the new thoroughfare. The Palau was discreetly set back from the road behind these buildings and just off the tiny square adjacent to the premises of

← Photograph by Alessandro Merletti commissioned by the printer Josep Thomas, c. 1909. Arxiu Històric Fotogràfic de l'I. E. F. C.

the veil makers' guild, the Casa dels Velers, at the end of Carrer Alt de Sant Pere. This meant that passers-by would be able to glimpse the corner of the future concert hall: a detail that did not go unnoticed by Domènech.

The building plot is the result of the fraudulent reparcelling of a piece of land, which created two new streets. One of them, now Carrer Amadeu Vives, was built adjacent to the dividing wall of the church of Sant Francesc, the only surviving remains of the convent that had burnt down in 1835. The plan that landed on the architect's desk showed a very irregular plot. The eventual boundary of the plot, which had been allotted to Lluís Domènech and his fellow architect Enric Sagnier to build on, covered an area of 1350.75 m^2, and photos of the day reveal the traces of the arches in the cloisters on the dividing wall. The ground plan clearly shows the two façades and two dividing walls in a parlous state. It would be no exaggeration to say that the plot was unworthy of such an important building.

A project for making and listening to music

By the end of 1904, Domènech must have set to work in earnest and on 13th February 1905 work began on moving the earth that would provide the architect with data about the quality and type of soil so that he could calculate the size of the foundation pads.

The plans had to be completed between 13th October, when the site was purchased, and 9th February 1905, when the plans for the project were published in *La Veu de Catalunya*, the day before the earth was excavated. The short four-month deadline required the utmost dedication from the architect, who was also at a decisive moment in his short political career. The site may have been prepared before the first stone was laid on 23rd April 1905.

The Palau de la Música project was obviously extremely complex and a paradigm of Domènech i Montaner's architectural language and, some might add, *modernisme*, which made it one of the most unique and distinctive European art nouveau landmarks. This music-making "machine" has hosted world-class performers of the calibre of Sergiu Celibidache, Maurizio Pollini, Isaac Stern, Maria Joao Pires and John Eliot Gardiner.

It is no easy task to describe the following operations and interventions. They are typical of the dialectical process which Domènech embraced, but I believe that by reconstructing the reasoning behind the project, step by step, we can understand the Palau as a logical "mental construct", akin to Johann Sebastian Bach's suites and scores.

We believe that this could at least trigger a series of interrelated decisions that define the project:

Designing a symmetrical typology of the concert hall (a good project should almost always begin from the inside), with the largest capacity and integrating audience seating and the stage. This made it necessary to fill the entire plot (1,350 m^2), fitting the floor plan of the auditorium inside the general ground plan of the site, as if defining a new one, and using the areas left over for small service areas. The decision to design a symmetrical hall was part of the architectural tradition that did not yet allow the symmetrical typologies that appeared during the modern movement. However, there are asymmetries in the outer morphology of the building.

Transforming the symmetry of the ground plan into a spatial and environmental symmetry, by creating a courtyard on the side wall of the church that gave rise to a new interior façade that let in light. The audience's perception once inside the auditorium is of being surrounded by two vast, symmetrical stained-glass windows at the sides.

The areas used by the Orfeó on a daily basis (offices, rehearsal rooms, library…) were placed on the ground floor, as stipulated in the programme. The auditorium, in contrast, was placed on the first floor, 7 metres above street level. To counteract the effects of physical fatigue the audience may have experienced to reach the first floor, Domènech designed a route via an imperial staircase filled with unusual visual resources.

Fixing the access route, which started in the lobby, on the corner of the two streets we have mentioned – Carrer Alt de Sant Pere and Carrer Amadeu Vives –

→ Laying the first stone, 23rd April 1905. Photograph by Adolf Mas. Centre de Documentació de l'Orfeó Català.

Façade of the Palau de la Música under construction. Anonymous, 1906. CEDOC.

and planning an entrance on the corner leading into the foyer, by integrating the initial flights of the imperial staircase. They are two different sequences that are connected spatially.

Favouring the basic structural concept of the building, as the typological decisions we have explained required a skeleton that would support them. The decision involved covering the auditorium, which has a 20-metre span, with metal girders that counterweigh the central force with a buttress structure at either end formed by two columns joined by an arch. The old device of the Gothic buttress is subtlely applied as it allows the wall of the façade to remain open so the stained-glass window letting in light could be placed inside.

Transforming the auditorium – tying in with the structural programme – into a light box, with stained-glass windows along the walls and in the ceiling, which bathed it in a pink light from the sides and from above. In this way, Domènech created the best atmosphere to achieve the final aim of the building: listening to music.

Finally, designing the longitudinal section of the auditorium with the basic aim of creating sightlines from each seat to the stage. The raked "shelves" in the circle and upper circle are set back creating a powerful diagonal line from the highest point of the gallery to the stage.

We would not want our sequential explanation of the most important decisions taken in the project – even though we could list more of them – to detract from the fact that it is incredibly complex and a constant crossover of ideas obtained through the classic feedback process. We have done it in this way because we were unable to find a clearer way of expressing the richness of this "music and light box on a summer's evening", as a friend defined it on a visit to the Palau.

Description of the fundamental elements

The façades were designed in accordance with the different widths of the streets around the Palau. Carrer Sant Pere Més Alt is wider, and Domènech took advantage of the perspective to make this façade a focal point and to create a feeling of depth. He achieved this by using twin pillars with arches set back from the front of the building, which acted as buttresses to the perpendicular shafts on the façade. Above them, he added, as a counterweight, busts of the composers Palestrina, Bach, Beethoven and Wagner. We can assume that the bust shown in Domènech's perspective drawing, which was intended to form a pair with the bust of Wagner, was never made due to time restraints or to reduce costs. We do not know who it would have portrayed. The façade on the long, narrow street at the side of the Palau, Carrer d'Amadeu Vives, needed to be smoother and flatter, with subtle variations compared to the other façade according to the adjacent interior space: the staircases, the auditorium and the stage. The long balcony helps enhance this effect.

The main system of columns and girders used in the structure – which is clearly shown in the photos of the building under construction – was altered in special cases, such as the introduction of fan vaults in the auditorium, thereby alleviating, mechanically and formally, the place where the large girders join the columns.

The flight of stairs leading to the upper circle is hidden, intentionally creating a double space when looked at from the side or the front, which allows us to enjoy the baroque motifs on the curved balustrades, a beautiful tribute by Domènech to so many staircases that have used this language throughout history.

The balcony in the waiting hall, now renamed the Sala Millet, makes it an interesting space. The rows of twin pillars – which also serve a structural purpose – create a spatial flow. They are all different in terms of ornamentation and the flow creates a visual distance from the façades of the building across the road – which are quite close – making good use of perceptual psychology. The waiting hall on the second floor is a very unusual space with a vaulted ceiling set on a sharp incline. The explanation for this incline lies in the fact that it mirrors the inverse incline of the raked seating, which Domènech, after building work had commenced, was forced to extend to cater to the growing number of members of the Orfeó Català.

The auditorium is the most important part of the concert hall complex. The different, interconnecting episodes that created such a special space – the elements that make it so dynamic, analogies and symbolism, the light, continuity and discontinuity and the symbiosis between structure and ornamentation – are too numerous, and difficult, to specify. However, we can look at a series of highly significant elements. The proscenium is an ironic nod to Italian-style theatre, with no front curtain. There are seats behind the stage allowing the audience to immerse themselves in the performance. This ambiguity allows the proscenium to act as a sculptural diaphragm. A circular lantern dome above the stage focuses the light on the performer, and sculptures of muses around the back of the stage bring a human scale to the composition. The stained-glass windows at the sides generate an intense, pinkish light, which plays a crucial role in the ambiance at the Palau de la Música. They provide a unifying element around the wall of the auditorium and the repeated garland motif enables us to view the three tiers of the windows as a unit, which is cut off by the floating "shelves" of the circle and upper circle. We can see that the architect took great care over the ratios of scale between the different parts of the building. The vast central lantern dome in the auditorium substantially alters the space and, in addition to letting in light day and night, penetrates the interior while floating over the audience. It is pure architecture that introduces a dynamism with its curved outline that intercepts the orthogonal grid of the structure when viewed from the ceiling.

In addition to serving their primary function, the pillars, or columns, as Domènech calls them, are the "space-makers" as a result of the circular section that creates a contrast between light and shade in the areas where the air circulates freely. The columns and their capitals are the most prominent features of the architecture at the Palau de la Música. They are a powerful, individual presence, and the most vivid example of the transformation of the most "classical" element of architecture into something primeval, like trees in the clearing in a forest. The load-bearing fan vaults above the columns are vaguely English in style, and add to the dynamic effect created by the curved lines in the ceiling and the slightly tilted garlands of lights, which are a wonderful reference to Byzantine art or a Carolingian jewel.

The sections of the ceiling above the stage are arranged radially around the central lantern dome. The ceiling is underpinned by narrow arches and pillars with a narrow space between them. They remind us of the spatial effect inside the basilica of Santa Maria del Mar, with the inimitable curve of its apse that Domènech was so fond of. The musicians' stage entrance is another brilliant detail. Instead of being mundanely domestic, as is the case in many concert halls, it is a sculptural feature that has been integrated into the proscenium.

The carpentry and woodwork at the Palau are also worthy of mention and clearly show Domènech i Montaner's use of "modern methods". The doors and windows were completed at the carpenters' workshop and fitted when the building was nearing completion. They were not cemented in and this meant that they could be reused during the refurbishment of the ground floor by the architect Òscar Tusquets in 1987. He used the doors from the former offices to build the magnificent bar in the centre of the new foyer.

Domènech's use of materials was truly groundbreaking. The brick, iron, ceramics, glass, stucco, varnished wood and paint come together to create the most elaborate language of all the architect's works, in a perfect synthesis between the construction systems and ornamentation. The ornamental elements, which received negative criticism from the proponents of the later *noucentista* movement, were produced according to a rigorous theory that is useful in order to understand what is, after all, the architectural merit of the Palau: to build an atmosphere, to create a world of images, to inextricably link poetry and music. How many elements are needed, how many interventions and how much reasoning are required to create an atmosphere that has made so many people dream and moved them to tears?

Architectural models and musical objectives

When Domènech began planning the Palau, late-romantic music was at its peak and, in 1908, the composer Richard Strauss conducted his works with the Berlin Philharmonic at the opening concert for the new home of the Orfeó Català.

The client stipulated that the auditorium should be able to host the choral concerts given by the Orfeó Català as well as orchestras who would be able to play the "finest pieces of symphonic music from around the world". This superimposition of a choir consisting of fifty female voices, fifty children's voices and a hundred male voices, with a large orchestra meant that the stage was too small, as was the case with the Victoria Hall in Geneva. Albert Schweitzer, who was at the peak of his career as an organist, worked with maestro Millet, and this led to the installation of an organ above the back of the stage, which complicated matters further. Domènech realised that the Musikverein in Vienna had the same problem. We can see this for ourselves every New Year when the bass players in the Vienna Philharmonic have to sit inside alcoves on the stage.

The debate about the size of concert halls had been going on for some time, not only for the above-mentioned reasons but because there was a need to increase the seating capacity due to the growing popularity of concert recitals. The romantic idealistic ideology had let to the creation of "friends of music" societies, or *musikfreunde*, and different cities staged musical performances on a vast scale. Hector Berlioz was obsessed with putting ten thousand performers of his music on stage, and Karl Friedrich Schinkel designed the concert hall in Berlin for the Singakademie and Leo von Klenze designed the Odeon in Munich to host large choral concerts. The English were more pragmatic and reused Paxton's Crystal Palace, which had been built for the 1851 Great Exhibition, to hold a major Handel festival in 1857 where choirs of four thousand singers performed. A purpose-built venue, the Royal Albert Hall, opened in 1871, which increased the seating capacity to the detriment of the acoustics.

When the Palau de la Música was being built, the theory of optimising acoustics was based on empirical knowledge. Around this time, the American physicist, Wallace Clement Sabine, established the concept of reverberation time and the formulas required based on room proportions. Domènech consulted the applied physics texts he had used at the School of Architecture in Barcelona. They referred to the shoe-box model, which had a rectangular base and square section, as the best proportions for a concert hall.

Domènech used three of Europe's best-known concert halls, the Musikverein in Vienna, the Concertgebouw in Amsterdam and the Gewandhaus in Leipzig, and interpolated some of their features and proportions into his project for the Palau. The Boston Symphony Hall was being built at the time and the architects McKim, Mead and White hired Sabine as their acoustics consultant. Domènech was then unaware of the existence of the symphony hall.

When Domènech was travelling in Europe between 1873 and 1874, he must have visited the Golden Hall at the Musikverein, which was designed by Theophil Edvard von Hansen and opened in 1870. They may also have told him about the new Gewandhaus that was being built by the city's cloth merchants' guild and was completed in 1884.

As far as we are aware, Domènech did not visit Amsterdam where the Concertgebouw was built between 1883 and 1888. However, we can confirm that the *Baukunde des Architeckten* (vol. II.3), which Domènech kept in his library, contains plan and section drawings comparing the three auditoria, which also detail their main physical proportions. The interpolation gives approximate measurements of 40 × 20 × 20 metres and Domènech used this as the template for taking the first decisions about the Palau we mentioned earlier.

However, an additional difficulty arose because the Orfeó Català asked him to increase the audience capacity from 2,000 to 2,500 people, when the project was already conditioned by the oddly shaped plot of land and the height restrictions stipulated by the city council. The auditoria built before the Palau could hold 1,500 people, but by the beginning of the 20th century iron girders made it possible to build longer and wider auditoria and thereby increase seating capacity (Concertgebouw, 2,206; Symphony Hall, 2,630). Domènech placed the auditorium on the first floor so that it could be more spacious and used roof trusses to raise the height.

To meet his client's conditions, Domènech had to force the parameters of width and length, at the risk of losing the ideal "reverberation conditions" he had found at the concert hall in Vienna. However, the acoustic problems at the Palau stem from the height restrictions resulting in a lower air volume of 11,000 m^3, compared to the 18,700 m^3 at the Concertgebouw and 18,750 m^3 at the Symphony Hall for a similar-sized audience.

← Elevation of the façade. Barcelona, c. 1906. Fons Domènech, Arxiu Històric del COAC.

→ Drawing of the muses at the back of the stage. Barcelona, c. 1906. Fons Domènech, Arxiu Històric del COAC.

The professor and engineer Antoni Carrión from the Polytechnic University of Catalonia has put together a study of the acoustics at theatres and concert halls in Spain, including the Palau de la Música. Carrión set a series of qualitative parameters that establish the ideal listening conditions. The main one is reverberation time. The other parameters are warmth and brilliance, decay time, sonority, acoustic intimacy, musical clarity and spatial impression. According to the study, the reverberation time at the Palau is too short for symphony music but is perfect for chamber music or choral singing, which it had been planned for initially.

In summary, we could say that Domènech drew two basic ideas from his study of European concert halls: in Vienna he saw the ingenious longitudinal section that made it possible to seat a large audience on two superimposed tiers, and, after visiting Amsterdam, he must have evaluated the symbolic and functional advantages of placing the audience behind the orchestra. The integration of performers and public, which was so successfully achieved at the Concertgebouw, is more ambiguous at the Palau, where the stage and apron are similar to Adler and Sullivan's Auditorium Theatre in Chicago.

The analysis of the acoustic aspects at the Palau could also cover the alterations that have been made to the building in recent years. However, our objective here is to look at Domènech's role in the design and layout of the building as a whole and make note of the delicate balancing act he had to perform in every aspect of the project.

There are always two orchestras playing at the Palau de la Música: the one made up of musicians with their varnished and golden instruments, and the orchestra of artisans who worked with Domènech: Eusebi Arnau, Miquel Blay, Pau Gargallo, Federico Bechini, Francesc Modolell, the stained-glass artists Rigalt and Granell, Mario Maragliano, Lluís Bru, Dídac Masana and others whose splendid notes ring out around the auditorium under the baton of the conductor who, towards the end of 1907, had grown weary of the project and left in silence vowing never to return. But everybody knows that great orchestras can play without a conductor.

Celebration of the *Jocs Florals* in 1915.
Photograph by Frederic Ballell. Arxiu Fotogràfic de Barcelona.

Opening of the Palau de la Música Catalana, 9th February 1908.
Photograph by Frederic Ballell. Arxiu Fotogràfic de Barcelona.

Miquel Blay's sculptural grouping *La Cançó Popular* It juts out from the corner of the building like a ship figurehead.

Drawing by Domènech i Montaner for the mosaic placed along the top of the main façade. Ink and watercolour on paper. Barcelona, c. 1908. CEDOC.

→ Main façade. Mosaic by Lluís Bru, an allegory of the Orfeó Català.

General view of the two façades with the corner surmounted by a turret.

Miquel Blay's sculptural grouping, *La Cançó Popular*.

Columns along the balcony on the main façade.

Foyer and foot of the imperial staircase.

Proscenium. Below the bust of Clavé, the sculptural grouping *Les Flors de Maig* (The Flowers of May), an allegory of folk music.

Proscenium. The ride of the Valkyries above twin columns framing a bust of Beethoven, an allegory of classical music.

Palau de la Música Catalana

Female figures around the back of the stage playing instruments from different cultures and eras.

Popularly known as "the muses", the figures by the sculptor Eusebi Arnau emerge from the mosaic which is the result of a collaboration between Mario Maragliano and Lluís Bru.

Ceiling of the auditorium.

Winged horse above the third tier.

Sculptural grouping *La Cavalcada de les Valquíries* (The Ride of the Valkyries).

View of the auditorium and the stage from the second tier.

← Central part of the lantern dome above the auditorium.

Casa Consol Fabra de Fuster 1908-1911

Ramon Anglada Lara · Teresa-M. Sala i Garcia

In 1908, Lluís Domènech i Montaner drew up the plans for the "Casa de Doña Consuelo Fabra de Fuster". The surname of her husband, Marià Fuster i Fuster, appears on the administrative documents because he was acting on his wife's behalf (although she owned the plot of land).

The brand-new residential block had three façades: two overlooking Passeig de Gràcia and Carrer Gran de Gràcia and a rear façade on Carrer Jesús. It was completed in 1911 and considered the most luxurious building in the city. However, Doña Consuelo only lived there for a short time due to her untimely death on 27th March 1912, at the age of just 51. The following obituary was published the next day in *La Vanguardia*:

> "One of the most illustrious and beloved women in Barcelona society departed this life yesterday after a long and painful illness. Doña Consuelo Fabra de Fuster embodied so many qualities that earned her such esteem: an affectionate manner, delicate modesty, talent and brilliant education. She, like no other, knew how to combine the duties that her social status and high rank dictate with domestic virtues and self-sacrifice, and charitable works for all manner of misfortunes".

← Photograph by Josep Domínguez, c. 1930. Arxiu Fotogràfic de Barcelona.

Clients of noble lineage

The Fabras came to enjoy a status as one of the "good families" in late 19th-century Barcelona, due to their economic power and high social standing. Camil Fabra i Fontanills, a textile magnate and the first Marquis of Alella, made the Fabra family the ideal model to follow in terms of social and moral behaviour in Catalan high society.

His work in the textile sector led him to establish closer ties with Ferran Puig i Gibert, an eminent cotton magnate who was a supplier to Fabra. In 1858, Camil Fabra married Puig i Gibert's daughter, Dolors Puig i Cerdà, and this family union would open doors for them both in the professional and political spheres. In 1866, son-in-law and father-in-law set up the Societat Puig Fabra y Compañía, which would be renamed Camilo Fabra y Compañía, Sucesores de Fernando Puig in 1882. Their political careers were also similar, and they always defended conservative and protectionist views (Velasco, 2013). Camil Fabra was a deputy in the Spanish parliament, representing the Barcelona constituency, and was made a senator for life in 1893. He was elected mayor of Barcelona that same year but resigned from his post less than three months later. On 2nd April 1889, he stood down from parliament due to his imminent ennoblement by the queen regent Maria Christina of Habsburg-Lorraine, who conferred on him the title of Marquis of Alella on 8th June 1889.

Camil Fabra i Fontanills was also a prominent art collector and patron of all manner of cultural, educational and scientific projects. Examples of the latter are his bequest that made it possible to start building the Fabra Observatory, which was continued by his children, and his many financial contributions to promoting education, such as the prizes for virtue, the *Premios a la Virtud*, awarded by the Sociedad Económica Barcelonesa de Amigos del País, which rewarded with 600 pesetas a Barcelona citizen – always a man – who had made the greatest efforts to educate his family.

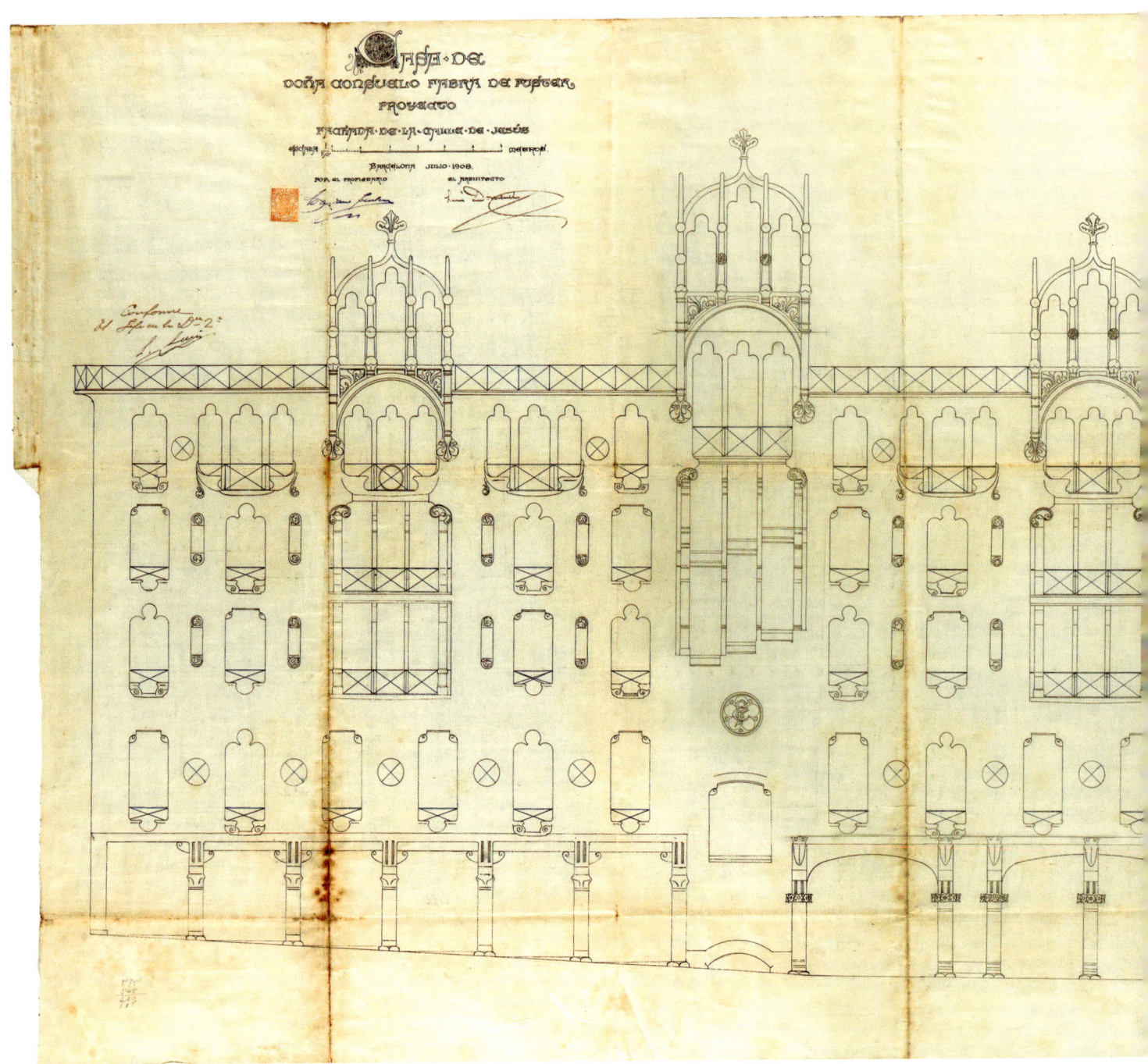

Elevation of the façade on Carrer de Jesús, 1908. Arxiu Municipal Contemporani de Barcelona.

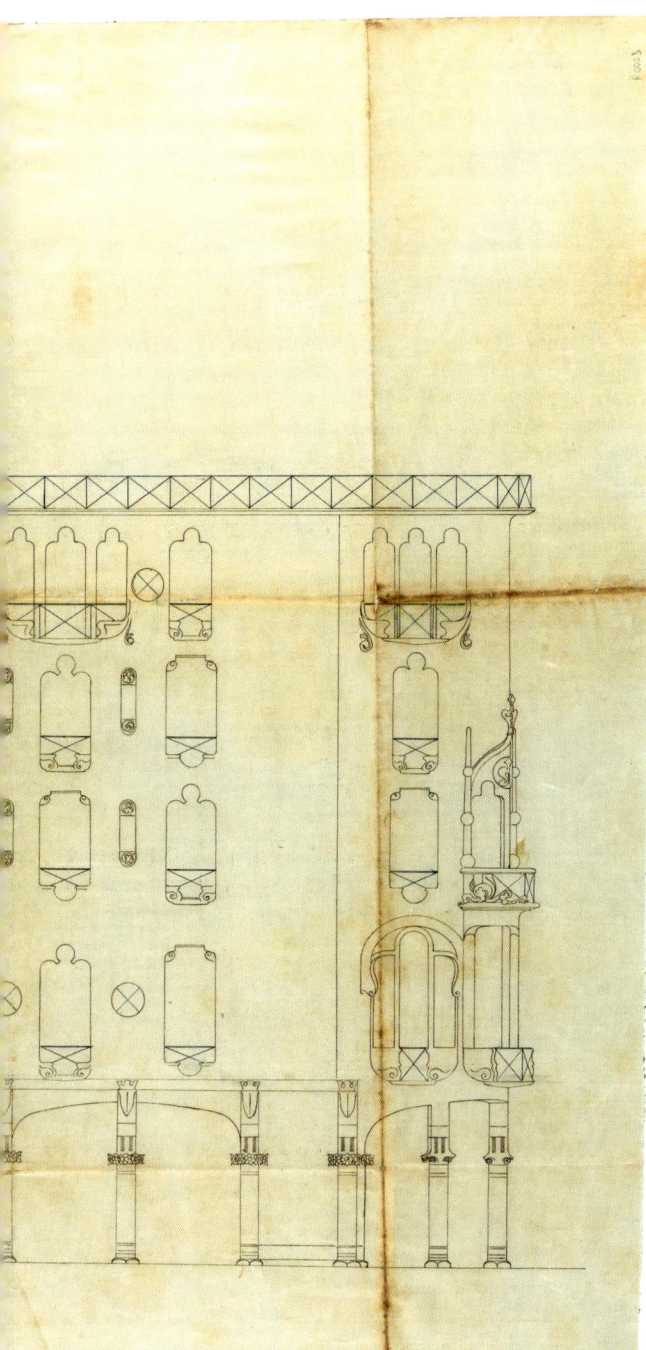

The Fabra family were defined by their constant defence of the monarchy, exemplary moral behaviour and leadership in the rules of social etiquette. In 1883, Camil Fabra wrote the treatise on the duties of high society, *Deberes de buena Sociedad*, known as the *Código Fabra*, or Fabra Code, which followed the model of detailed English tracts. It was an immediate success, and several editions were published that clarified and helped people comply with the strict codes of behaviour prevalent in Catalan high society in the late 19th and early 20th centuries. The Marquis's treatise defined the etiquette to follow when calling on people, requesting an audience, attending baptisms and weddings, observing mourning, attending balls and banquets, or the suitable times and places to go for a walk, and the company to choose, among many other aspects. The publication staunchly upheld the values of a traditional family with the man as the head of the household and the wife playing a secondary role in practically every aspect. According to Fabra, any initiative a woman engaged in that was not supervised by her husband, fiancé, brother or any other male figure, was considered negative or dangerous. According to his treatise, widows had to observe a longer period of mourning than widowers and wait longer to remarry. After every gala dinner, men and women had to retire to separate rooms where the men would smoke and discuss the political matters of the day and the women would talk about more banal subjects, as befitted their intellect.

The Marchioness of Alella, Dolors Puig i Cerdà, did not lag behind in this regard. A strong-willed woman, she often gave orders to the municipal police about ways of directing horse-drawn carriages (Masriera, 1954). Like her husband, she was also concerned about social and moral standards of behaviour. A practising Catholic, she followed his example by publishing a little book of dramatic tableaux for children entitled *Monólogos, diálogos y cuadros dramáticos infantiles para escuelas, colegios y salones*. These short plays were mostly comedies with children and young women as the main characters. They were assigned a series of negative attributes and behaviours, such as envy, greed, jealousy and lying, which needed to be dealt with and were associated with the simple fact that they were women.

The Fabra i Puigs had five children – Consuelo, or Maria de la Consolación (1861), Araceli, or María Araceli (1863), Fernando, the second Marquis of Alella (1866), Camila (1869) and Roman, the first Marquis of Masnou (1875) – and they were all educated with this ideology instilled into them.

The brothers inherited the noble titles and became the directors of the powerful Compañía Anónima Hilaturas de Fabra y Coats, which was the result of two mergers, the first in 1884 with Manuel Portabella's cotton thread company to set up the Sociedad Anónima Sucesores de Fabra y Portabella and, in 1903, with the British industrial thread manufacturer, J&P Coats. Like their father, the two brothers combined their business ventures with their political careers. This was particularly true of Ferran Fabra, the second Marquis of Alella, who had a very similar career to his progenitor, as a deputy, senator and mayor of Barcelona from 1922 and 1923 representing the pro-monarchy political party, the Federació Monàrquica Autonomista. This led to him being mercilessly criticised in the satirical press of the day.

The sisters strictly conformed to the standards of behaviour their own family had become the gatekeepers of. They followed their mother's example and were involved in numerous charitable works that would highlight their social status, which was strengthened further, after they had married, by socialising with members of their own class and their strong religious convictions.

Camila and Consol were the sisters with a more public profile. In 1909, Camila Fabra, who was Joan Vigo's widow at the time, was the president of the Women's Auxiliary Board of the first tuberculosis dispensary in Barcelona, which secured most of the funding that had enabled it to purchase a site in Sabadell where they could build a new sanatorium. Consol Fabra was a member of charitable institutions, and her aim was twofold: to ensure they complied with religious morals and to raise funds. She played a prominent role on the boards of governors of a number of charitable homes and schools, most notably the Asilo del Sagrado Corazón, where hundreds of Barcelona children from disadvantaged families were educated and fed. In 1909, Consol Fabra was asked by Queen Victoria Eugenie of Battenberg, the wife of King Alfonso XIII, to be the secretary of a board dedicated to raising funds for wounded soldiers and the families of the dead in Spain's delusional imperialist campaign in Morocco.

However, it wasn't all about charitable work. The Fabra dynasty was well acquainted with luxury and sumptuous living. The top artisans, tailors, seamstresses, jewellers, painters and sculptors worked for the family. The balls, held at the Fabra's home on Rambla de Canaletes, where the Spanish princesses were among the guests, were some of the city's most eagerly awaited events and were a good opportunity to boost the social standing of their guests. And it was here that the Fabra sisters displayed all their charms, wearing the most refined dresses and jewellery, as highlighted in the reports in the Barcelona press at the turn of the century. The fancy-dress balls in period costume became the events where Barcelona's upper classes could show off all their power. And the Fabras played an active role, as shown in Francesc Masriera's paintings of Camila, who is featured twice, once as a 17th-century lady and a woman from classical Greece; Consol, with her oriental-style clothing and wearing a veil, which is only featured in the preparatory study; and Araceli, dressed as a bride (MNAC, 1996). The four paintings took pride of place at the 1888 Barcelona Universal Exhibition, and were further proof of the family's powerful status.

Consol Fabra i Puig married Marià Fuster i Fuster on 13th December 1879. Her husband came from a liberal, bourgeois family from Palma de Mallorca, and his father, Rafel Ignasi Fuster Forteza, was the founder of the Banc de Crèdit Balear and a senator for the Balearic Islands in the Spanish parliament. The painter Antoni Fuster i Forteza was his cousin but Marià decided to practise law, although he was also an accomplished watercolourist and an active member of the arts society, the Cercle Artístic, of which he became president. He also took part in the Barcelona Universal Exhibition. He was a multifaceted, enterprising individual and went into business with the brothers Josep and Vicenç Bosch i Grau, setting up the Sociedad Bosch y Fuster which purchased and made sparkling wine (Valls, 2004). He also founded the lift manufacturers, Fuster-Fabra.

The Fuster-Fabras had six children (*Revista d'Història i Genealogia Española*): Fernando, Isabel, María Dolores, Gonzalo, Álvaro and Carlos.

The commission for a multi-family dwelling

In 1905, Consol Fabra i Puig purchased the Juncosa chocolate factory from Pere Juncosa i Font, as well as houses at numbers 2 and 4 Carrer Gran de Gràcia, with the intention of demolishing them and constructing a single building on a plot which, according to the property register, covered an area of 1,920 m². She chose the reputed architect, Lluís Domènech i Montaner, to design the building. At the time he was completing the Palau de la Música Catalana and still working on the Hospital de Sant Pau.

Domènech was commissioned in 1908, but his project came up against many administrative challenges resulting from the demolition of the buildings, including problems with the tenants on the ground floor and obtaining the necessary documents to rebuild and extend the property. Eventually, the Fuster-Fabras and their children moved into the main floor of the building in 1911.

In 1909, there was a popular uprising, known as the Tragic Week, or *Setmana Tràgica*, in Barcelona and other industrial cities in Catalonia, sparked by the call-up of reservists to fight in Morocco. Gràcia came under artillery fire and more than a thousand shells were launched. Gunshot fire was heard near the barricades at the southern end of Carrer Gran de Gràcia (by the little gardens, the Jardinets). The Casa Fabra-Fuster was under construction at the time. It stood on the frontier dividing the bourgeois and blue-collar city and building materials from the site may have been used to build the barricades. Roser Segimon, the owner of the Casa Milà, on Passeig de Gràcia, decided not to place a statue of Our Lady of the Rose on the façade for fear of anticlerical disturbances. As was to be expected, the Marquis and Marchioness of Alella remained silent when the libertarian educator from Alella, Francesc Ferrer i Guàrdia, was executed after being convicted of inciting rebellion at a legally flawed military trial.

The Casa Fabra-Fuster was Domènech's last project and he worked on it at the same time as the Palau de la Música Catalana. It was a complex and bold building, in terms of its impact on the urban landscape and sheer scale, as well as its appearance and the use of architectural language in a residential building reminiscent of the Doge's Palace in Venice. It stands on a unique plot of land, where Passeig de Gràcia and Carrer Gran de Gràcia meet. The architect designed a curvilinear corner where "the articulation of the wall is transformed into a vast gallery, one of the boldest protruding canopies of its day, and clearly marks the building's shift from one street to the other in another 'urban gesture'." (Domènech Girbau, 2018, p. 307). This means that the volumes that make up the façades are accentuated by a gallery of considerable size, with wide windows flanked by Doric columns supported by sturdy cylindrical pink-marble pillars. There are ribbed corbels above the capitals with carved swallows nesting beneath them. This ornamental motif has a special significance. In ancient Rome the swallow was a symbol of good luck and mothers believed that they carried the souls of their dead children home. During the Middle Ages, the return of the swallows every year, heralding the end of winter, was interpreted as a symbol of rebirth and spring. It is an ambivalent image and some people still say that the swallows represent the swiftness of justice, a possible allusion to the profession of the building's owner.

The design of the rear façade on Carrer de Jesús involved a "simplifying process evolving towards a purity of composition, with a series of columns where the capitals have practically disappeared and all that remain are light incisions representing geometric and plant motifs" (Bohigas, 2000, p. 43). Domènech evolved from the art nouveau style of the Casa Navàs to "a visual purity and rational style of building", in his treatment of the capitals with their carved flowers, which has become stylised at the Casa Fabra-Fuster.

Inside the house

Throughout the 20th century, the house was a test bed for architects. The hierarchy of the building is established in such a way that it can be read vertically and horizontally. We can discover what was known at the time as the "art of living" through the views outside, which are defined by the good orientation and separation of the rooms, as well as the rules of distribution.

Viollet-le-Duc's *Histoire d'une maison* appears to have had an influence on Domènech's houses, along with the treatises about the home and private life. The architect tried to protect his clients' private and social lives in his interiors, creating independent rooms based on their individual uses. Like a human geography map, spatial devices are related to the existing forms of social interaction, which define form, function and representativity, according to the roles of the members of the household.

When we analyse the way the different rooms are organised at the Casa de Consol Fabra de Fuster, we can see marked differences between the main floor and other floors, where the rental apartments were located. The building has two inner courtyards. The main entrance was designed so that carriages could pass through to the rear of the building. A monumental staircase inside led to the main floor where the rooms were distributed around a lobby: a reception area designed in the manner of a grand hall. It goes without saying that, throughout the 19th century, the hall had become a new space where people could show off their wealth, which created a *mise-en-scène*, particularly if it opened onto a grand staircase, as it allowed guests to be afforded a special welcome. This is how people entered the Casa Fabra-Fuster, where the hall, which was the public space, led into three distinct spaces: the sitting room, the tea room and the dining room, which overlooked Passeig de Gràcia. Behind them was the library, which led into the gallery. The library formed a structural axis between the two main façades, and the family's private quarters. Firstly, there was the boudoir, a small private room where the women would converse. It was followed by a family room and the main bedroom, on the corner of Carrer Major and Carrer de Jesús. Domènech added a bath and shower with a toilet, a dressing room, another shower, a ladies' dressing room, a wardrobe and two bedrooms with a sitting room, which had their own washbasins and toilets. The Fuster-Fabra's two daughters and four sons had rooms of their own, with separate areas. The staircase, where one of the lifts was located, which also led to the grand hall, separated the other bedrooms, with shared rooms in between. All the rooms were outward facing and had natural light. Curiously enough, there wasn't a billiard room or smoking room, where the men would usually gather. However, there was a "room for the master to work in" – the office– which was at the side of another administrative office, next to a "sewing room" for the women. They were all connected by a gallery. The private chapel took pride of place and formed the core of the building. It separated the maids' quarters from the rest of the house. The problem of finding a suitable location for the kitchen was an important question, underlined by the authors of the treatises on the art of living. In this case, it was located in the servants' wing and led into the "butler's pantry", which was the centre of operations, next to the larder and servants' dining room. The servants' rooms and toilets, cloakroom and ironing room were served by another lift and had their own clearly defined separate reception area.

Domènech's last building represented the pinnacle of his architectural knowledge, artistic creativity and symbolic language. It became a meditation on form, materials and ornamentation. The values of rhythm, harmony and repetition are reflected in an ornamentation that, despite its sobriety, plays with the concave and convex parts of the windows, in a manner reminiscent of a Renaissance palace. The stylised elegance of the forest of columns, inside and outside the building, is achieved with the flowers and volutes that provide it with a rhythmic sequence while highlighting the details that make up the ensemble.

The client's desire to make the Eixample more beautiful and transform Barcelona into a truly European city with monumental buildings like the one they were constructing, may explain why Domènech designed the Casa Fabra-Fuster to resemble a Venetian palazzo. The medallion carved with the owner's initials, CF, the use of strips of white stone, the Doric columns and the rhythmic flow of the different storeys on the corner, crowned by five pinnacles, give the nod to this particular style

There were four rental apartments on each storey, which did not occupy an entire floor. They had a reception area instead of a grand hall. The apartment overlooking Passeig de Gràcia is particularly striking. It had three bedrooms, a sitting room, a kitchen and offices. The main apartment had a gallery, but there wasn't a small room for taking tea, or a private chapel, library or boudoir. The main apartment had more bedrooms and offices, with their own bathrooms and toilets.

This concludes our look at the design Lluís Domènech i Montaner presented to the owners who had hired him to construct the building. Over the years, the other apartments in the building were lived in by families and were also used as offices and doctors' surgeries. In 1960, the hydroelectric power company, the Empresa Nacional Hidroelèctrica del Ribagorzana (ENHER) purchased the building. In 2004, the Casa Fabra-Fuster was converted into a luxury hotel, the Hotel Casa Fuster.

Façades overlooking the *Jardinets* and Carrer Gran de Gràcia with the curvilinear gallery on the corner.

Corner of the façade on Carrer Gran and the rear façade.

Rear façade on Carrer de Jesús.

Capital of the column underpinning the tower that accentuates the corner of the building.

→ Detail of one of the swallows' nests (the bird was a symbol of good luck in ancient Rome) decorating the capital.

Detail of the railings on the landing of the servants' stairs.

Railings on the main staircase.

The hall.

Capitals of the columns in the hall.

Capitals of the columns in the grand hall on the first floor.

As for the two original houses on Buscarons Creek, Domènech did not carry out any major interventions until the start of 1918. In anticipation of his imminent retirement from the Barcelona School of Architecture, he decided to completely renovate both houses to adapt them to the times, and especially the needs of his wife, who suffered from serious problems affecting her mobility. At the same time, it should be borne in mind that, as the years passed, Domènech had more and more grandchildren and Canet always served as the meeting point for the whole family. As his son-in-law, Francesc Guàrdia, wrote:

> "In his private life, Domènech i Montaner was even better than in the other facets of his life. He had the heart of a boy and his greatest pleasure was watching his children and grandchildren enjoy the traditional festivities, gathering them all at the table, painting shields and outfits for dances and parties they wanted to have. And he, who never yelled, liked to hear the constant hubbub and yelling of the kids at his home in Canet." (Guàrdia, 1924, p. 121)

That is why, with the help of his son Pere and his son-in-law Francesc Guàrdia, Domènech undertook the project of altering and expanding the houses on Buscarons Creek. On 20th February 1918, he applied for a building permit from Canet de Mar town council to carry out an "alteration or reconstruction of the house, raising it by a second floor in the area that did not have one, and changing the location of and adding various apertures in the facades of the existing ground and main floors".

Domènech did not demolish the original houses but kept the trapezoidal floor plan of those two, thick-walled houses, and decided to wall in the old apertures, open new windows and create doors connecting the two buildings. And like all Domènech's work, the architect designed the facades with a base, a central part and a crowning element. On the lower level, he built a plinth of natural stone that lends the building strength and at the same time, unites the three facades of the two buildings.

On the Buscarons Creek façade, Domènech designed a long balcony with three windows and carved stone elements on the first floor, and on the ground level, he placed the entrance to the house and three stone windows.

Regarding the chamfered façade of the building at the corner of Buscarons and Gavarra Creeks, the architect decided to monumentalise the narrow face by adding an imposing enclosed balcony on the first floor – which becomes the building's central axis – with floral elements and lobed arches, supported by columns with thin cylindrical shafts. And he completed the construction with grotesque elements and a decorative gable similar to the one he designed years earlier for the Gran Hotel in Palma (Mallorca).

And on the side façade of the house, on Gavarra Creek, Domènech designed a wall with round-arched windows on the ground floor and two mullioned windows on the first floor, of medieval influence.

In addition to restructuring the volume of the original construction, Domènech added a new level to the original work, with a series of windows framed with basket-handle arches alternating with false apertures sporting trefoil arches in rowlock brickwork that form a crowning frieze designed to unify the façades of the house like the plinth on the ground floor. Domènech tiled the trefoil-arched false windows in two-tone floral ceramic and finished the facade with wide eaves.

As for the interior of Can Domènech, the architect proposed a new, fully functional layout and, taking advantage of the chamfered floor plan, made sure that all the rooms had exterior openings. This is why the ground floor starts from a central corridor that distributes the rooms on either side, and this model is repeated again on the other levels of the building. The architect placed the library or reception room at the Buscarons Creek entrance to Can Domènech. The entrance corridor leads to the hall with a Catalan vaulted ceiling that, in a sense, embodies the vernacular construction tradition.

The walls of the vestibule were decorated with white tile wainscots with floral mouldings and ochre details. And, in the lobby, the umbrella stand with mirror was remarkable, attributed to Gaspar Homar and with a landscape mosaic by Mario Maragliano (Martí, 2018, pp. 124-141). Today, the room still displays the sculptural details by Arturo Mélida, who was Lluís Domènech's classmate and friend in Madrid: on one side, a lion's head that Mélida gave the architect in 1878, and on the other, in the arch separating the entrance from the hall, Domènech placed four models of the rampant lions that Mélida had modelled for the chamfered corners at the base of the monument the architect had designed in memory of the Marquis of Comillas in the Cantabrian town. In his project for the Marquis, the lions represented the strength and business ferocity of Antonio López, in the case of the house in Canet, Domènech lent them a protective character.

On the left side of the hall, Domènech designed the living room, where the family passed the time. This room was decorated with vegetable fibre wainscotting with a very simple wooden finish. In the centre of the room, Domènech built a fireplace with ceramic elements in floral relief and wood and brick details and, at the top of the flue, he integrated a plaster composition of the evangelists Saint Mark, represented by the lion, and Saint Luke, by the ox. The work, by Pau Gargallo, was the original model that was used to create the larger-scale stone sculpture that we can still see today outside the Hospital de Sant Pau. And as for the ceiling, this room still retains some pieces of cabinetry from the coffered ceiling of Casa Thomas that was partially removed when Francesc Guàrdia Vial raised the building several floors in 1912.

This room communicated with Maria Roura's room. She had been sleeping on the ground floor of the house for years due to her mobility problems. Domènech wished to make the distribution functional, hence the toilet, the kitchen and the dining room were just next to it. In fact, the dining room of the Domènech house was one of the noblest rooms, in which is a noteworthy, large exposed-brick fireplace, the upper part of which has a plaster proof of the pontifical coat of arms at the entrance gateway to the Comillas Seminary, the work of Eusebi Arnau. The Jesuit monogram can be seen on the coat of arms, and is crowned with a tiara and the pontifical keys. As custodians of the coat of arms, Domènech added two heralds dressed in medieval garb, on which are inscribed the year, 1892, and the name Leo XIII. (Sama, 2015, pp. 54-81)

On the facing around the fireplace, we can see some excellent lustreware tile samples that the architect had used years before to clad the exterior of the Comillas seminary church and the entrance gateway to the pontifical compound. It should be borne in mind that Domènech was one of the people behind the revival of lustreware in Catalonia and one of those who most contributed, through his studies, to raising appreciation of Hispano-Moresque work, to the point that, in 1887, he travelled to Manises with Antoni Gaudí to learn more about the lustreware technique.

For the production of the Comillas ceramic pieces – which were made by Pau Pujol of the Pujol i Bausis factory and Josep Ros of La Ceramo in Valencia –, Domènech and Gallissà designed the four evangelists: the angel representing Matthew, the eagle John, the bull Luke and the lion Mark, with a very oriental, linear outline. This evangelist iconography is combined with polychrome yellow, blue and gold-lustre ceramics and semi-spherical lustreware "buttons" containing the Jesuit monogram. (Sama, 2015, pp. 54-81)

As for the joinery in the room, the wall of the fireplace originally had wainscotting of walnut boards crowned with a bas-relief frieze with repeating floral motifs, identical to those that can also be seen on the main floor of Casa Thomas in Barcelona. And the dining room ceiling in the Casa Domènech was also decorated with some cabinetry pieces from the original coffered ceiling of the stairwell in the Casa Thomas.

On the first floor, the architect distributed five bedrooms and a bathroom, which he lined in white tiles measuring 20×20 and polychrome pieces with floral elements. As for the area around the bathtub, it was faced with bevelled white tiles measuring 10×20 alternating with green tiles with an incised rosette. And on the upper floor – which had six more rooms –, Domènech maintained the same layout and also projected another bathroom clad in floral tiles from Pujol i Bausis' wainscot number 19 and white tiles measuring 20×20 combined with an incised rosette in toasted wheat colour.

To facilitate access to the second floor, the architect opened a double-level stairwell and designed a narrow, twisting staircase leading to the second floor in which he integrated a plaster model of a female figure that Eusebi Arnau sculpted for the balcony balustrade of the Casa Matilde Serrallés on Carrer Fontanella in Barcelona. At the top, he opened a large skylight to let light flood all the floors, which he surrounded with plant-motif cabinetry by the Viladevall brothers, which was also left over from the ceiling above the Casa Thomas stairwell.

Casa Domènech is Lluís Domènech i Montaner's final work as an architect, but it is also the place he decided to spend the last years of his life in his old age, with his wife, children and grandchildren; surrounded by all of the sculpture, cabinetry and ceramics trials from his most singular buildings, as if Domènech had attempted to bring together, in a very personal space, the three pillars that had lent his life meaning: familial love, his passion for architecture and his love of Canet de Mar.

Can Rocosa. Cockerel outside the café and restaurant.

Can Rocosa and Casa Domènech • 405

Main façade of Can Rocosa.

→ Casa Domènech.

Gallery at the Casa Domènech.

Can Rocosa.
Model for the Casa Lleó i Morera, alluding to the telephone.

Casa Domènech. Model for the fireplace at the seminary in Comillas.

Can Rocosa. Lluís Domènech i Montaner's self-designed drawing table.

Chronology and catalogue of works
(Source: Fundació Lluís Domènech i Montaner)

1884. Sgraffito-work at the Ateneu in Canet de Mar.

Field	Year	Events
Biography	1849	He is born on 30th December
Biography	1870	He graduates in science from Barcelona University
Politics	1870	He joins Jove Catalunya
Biography	1873	He graduates as an architect on 13th December from the Madrid School of Architecture
Biography	1873	Death of his father, Pere Domènech Saló
Biography	1875	He marries Maria Roura
Teaching	1875	Interim professor at the Barcelona School of Architecture
Work	1876	He designs Anselm Clavé's tomb with Josep Vilaseca
Work	1876	He refurbishes the church of Sant Gervasi with Josep Vilaseca
Work	1876	Refurbishment of Maria Montaner's apartment block, Barcelona
Work	1877	He develops the project for the Institucions Provincials d'Ensenyament with Josep Vilaseca
Culture	1878	He publishes *En busca de una arquitectura nacional*
Work	1878	Torre Simon. Barcelona
Culture	1879	He publishes *Reforma de Barcelona*
Culture	1879	He publishes *Caràcters propis de l'Arquitectura catalana á través de diferentas épocas y estils artistichs*
Culture	1879	He publishes *El Claustre del Monestir de Sant Cugat del Vallès*
Work	1879	Montaner i Simon publishing house, Barcelona
Work	1880	Casa Domènech, Barcelona
Culture	1881	He is appointed judge for the poetry competition, the *Jocs Florals*
Work	1881	Casa Font i Torres, Barcelona
Work	1884	Ateneu in Canet de Mar
Politics	1885	Presentation of the *Memorial de Greuges* – a report defending the interests of Catalonia – to King Alfonso XII
Culture	1886	He publishes the first volume of *Historia General del Arte*
Work	1887	Ledger stone for Lluís Domènech i Roura

Work	1887	Café and Restaurant for the Barcelona Universal Exhibition
Work	1888	Gran Hotel Internacional, Barcelona
Work	1888	Refurbishment of Barcelona City Hall
Politics	1888	President of the Lliga de Catalunya
Politics	1888	First manifesto presented to the queen regent
Work	1889	Palau Montaner, Barcelona
Work	1889	Refurbishment of the Pontifical Seminary in Comillas
Work	1889	Casa Roura, Canet de Mar
Work	1889	Monument to the Marquis of Comillas
Work	1889	Refurbishment of the Casa Dolors Rabassa, Barcelona
Work	1890	Casa Maria Montaner, Barcelona
Politics	1891	President of the Unió Catalanista
Politics	1892	He presides over the assembly that approved the draft statute for self-government, the *Bases de Manresa: Bases per a la Constitució Regional Catalana*
Culture	1892	He publishes *La reforma de Barcelona resolta pel sentit comú*
Work	1893	He redesigns the cemetery in Comillas
Work	1893	Casa Agustí, Badalona
Work	1894	Project for the Monument to Jaume II el Dissortat (James the Unlucky)
Culture	1895	President of the *Jocs Florals* (1st Sunday in May). He publishes his speech *Jochs Florals de Barcelona*
Work	1895	Josep Thomas' house and workshop, Barcelona
Work	1895	Refurbishment of the Casa de l'Ardiaca, Barcelona. Letterbox (1902)
Work	1896	Farmàcia Duran, Barcelona
Culture	1897	He publishes *Arquitectura moderna de Barcelona*
Work	1897	Institut Pere Mata, Reus
Politics	1898	He contributes to and signs the 2nd manifesto for the queen regent

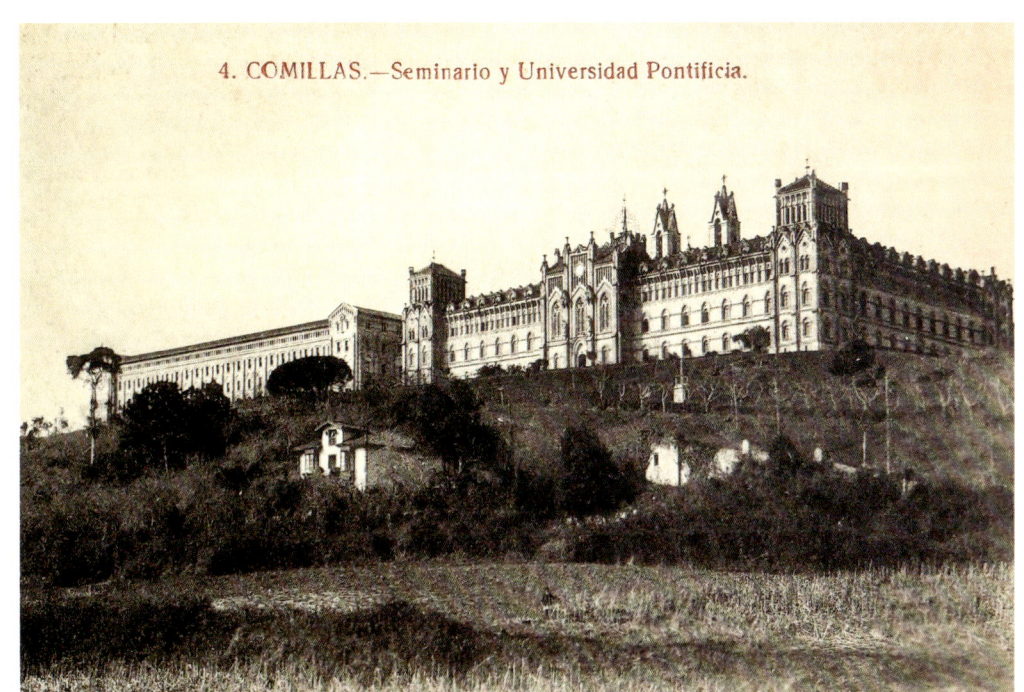

1889. Refurbishment of the Pontifical Seminary. Postcard of the Pontifical Seminary and University of Comillas. M. Solís, c. 1900. Courtesy of Rossend Casanova.

1888. Refurbishment of Barcelona City Hall.

1893. Casa Agustí. Badalona.

1896. Farmàcia Duran. Barcelona.

1902. Casa Lamadrid. Barcelona.

1903. Monument to Doctor Robert. Barcelona.

Culture	1898	President of the Ateneu Barcelonès, opening address
Work	1898	Joaquin del Piélago's family tomb, Comillas
Politics	1898	Message to the queen regent
Teaching	1899	He is appointed tenured professor at the Barcelona School of Architecture
Culture	1899	President of the Ateneu Barcelonès
Work	1899	The fountain, the Fuente de los Tres Caños, Comillas
Work	1900	Fàbrica Jover, Serra i Cia., with Domènech Roura, Canet de Mar
Work	1900	Project for the theatre-circus in Reus
Teaching	1900	He is appointed director of the Barcelona School of Architecture
Work	1900	Refurbishment of the interior of the Fonda España, Barcelona
Work	1900	Castle of Santa Florentina, Canet de Mar
Work	1900	Crypt at Santa Florentina, Canet de Mar
Work	1900	Casa Rull, Reus
Culture	1900	He publishes *Los jarrones hispano-árabes*
Work	1901	Casa Navàs Blasco, Reus
Politics	1901	Deputy in the Spanish parliament in Madrid
Teaching	1901	First scientific field trips
Work	1902	Creu de Pedracastell, Canet de Mar
Work	1902	Laying of the first stone at the Hospital de Sant Pau, Barcelona
Work	1902	Casa Lamadrid, Barcelona
Politics	1903	He is re-elected deputy to the Spanish parliament
Work	1903	Gran Hotel, Palma
Work	1903	Casa Lleó i Morera, Barcelona
Culture	1903	President of the Ateneu Barcelonès
Culture	1903	He writes *Antoni Ma Gallissà en l'intimitat*

Work	1903	Monument to Doctor Robert
Culture	1904	President of the Ateneu Barcelonès
Politics	1904	He publishes *Fivallers de guardarropia*
Politics	1904	He leaves the Lliga Regionalista
Teaching	1904	Trip to the Romanesque heritage in Pallars
Teaching	1904	Trip to the Romanesque heritage in the Cerdanya
Work	1905	Margenat chapel, Reus
Politics	1905	His term as a deputy comes to an end and he ceases to play an active role in politics
Work	1905	Palau de la Música Catalana, Barcelona
Teaching	1905	Director of the Barcelona School of Architecture
Culture	1905	He writes the introduction to *Història de l'Art Romànic a Catalunya*
Teaching	1905	Trip to the Romanesque heritage in the Empordà
Teaching	1905	Trip to the Romanesque heritage in Ripoll, Berga and La Garrotxa
Teaching	1905	Trip to the Romanesque heritage in Roussillon
Work	1905	Refurbishment of the ramblers' association building, the Centre Excursionista de Catalunya, Barcelona
Work	1905	Redevelopment of Gran Vía Pedro el Grande, Barcelona
Work	1905	Refurbishment of the Masia Rocosa, Canet de Mar
Work	1906	Mausoleum-Pantheon of Jaume I, Tarragona
Culture	1906	Lecture on Barcelona's acropolis and the columns on Carrer de Paradís
Work	1907	Interior decoration of the Casa Francesc Macià, Lleida

1906. Mausoleum-Pantheon of Jaume I. Tarragona.

Chronology • 419

Work	1908	Project for the pantheon of the Princes of Aragon, Tarragona
Work	1908	Casa Consol Fabra de Fuster, Barcelona
Work	1908	He is involved in the redevelopment of Via Laietana, Barcelona
Work	1909	Font de Rubinat library, Reus
Culture	1909	He publishes *L'arquitectura romànica a Catalunya*
Teaching	1909	He publishes *En defensa de l'Escola d'Arquitectura*
Work	1909	Cinema Kursaal
Work	1910	Tombs of Domènech i Montaner and Josep Montaner Vila, Canet de Mar
Culture	1911	President of the Ateneu Barcelonès
Work	1911	Casa Gasull, Reus
Obra	1911	Refurbishment of the façade of the Casa Llopis Borràs, Reus
Work	1912	He designs the cooperative winery, the Celler Cooperatiu, in Espluga de Francolí, with Pere Domènech i Roura
Obra	1912	Font Montaner (Font Montells) tomb, Canet de Mar
Work	1913	Refurbishment of the Casa Solà-Morales, Olot
Obra	1913	Monument to Joan Maragall, Barcelona
Obra	1914	Project for the Reial Acadèmia de Medicina, Barcelona
Obra	1915	Project for the Exhibition of Electrical Industries
Culture	1916	He publishes the book *Poblet*
Work	1918	Casa Domènech, Canet de Mar
Teaching	1919	He retires from the Barcelona School of Architecture
Culture	1921	He joins the Acadèmia de Bones Lletres de Barcelona
Culture	1922	He publishes *Armorial Historich de Catalunya. Desde els seus origens fins al s. XVI*
Biography	1923	He dies on 27th December 1923

→ 1913. Casa Solà-Morales. Olot.

Bibliography

AINAUD DE LASARTE, J. "Les exposicions del Modernisme de 1964 i de 1969-1970", In: *El Modernisme* (2 vol.) – Barcelona 1990. Barcelona: Lunwerg; Olimpíada Cultural Barcelona 92, 1990. pp. 17-25.

ALCALDE, S. "La capella-panteó de la família Margenat de Reus. Una obra funerària de Domènech i Montaner". *Domenechiana: revista del Centre d'Estudis Lluís Domènech i Montaner* (2014), nos. 2-3, pp. 165-174.

ALCALDE, S. "La Casa Rull (1900-1902). La primera obra residencial de Lluís Domènech i Montaner a la ciutat de Reus". *Domenechiana: revista del Centre d'Estudis Lluís Domènech i Montaner* (2014), no. 4, pp. 6-28.

ALCALDE, S. "Els projectes no construïts de Lluís Domènech i Montaner per a la societat El Círcol de Reus. La reforma de l'escala d'accés al primer pis del Círcol (1899) i el Teatre Circ (1900)". *Domenechiana: revista del Centre d'Estudis Lluís Domènech i Montaner* (2015), no. 6, pp. 142-155.

ALCALDE, S. [et al.]. *Lluís Domènech i Montaner (1849-1923). Obra arquitectònica raonada*. Vol. 1. Canet de Mar: Centre d'Estudis Lluís Domènech i Montaner, 2016.

ALCALDE, S. [et al.]. *Lluís Domènech i Montaner (1849-1923). Obra arquitectònica raonada*. Vol. 2. Canet de Mar: Centre d'Estudis Lluís Domènech i Montaner, 2017.

ALCALDE, S. [et al.]. *Lluís Domènech i Montaner. El llegat arquitectònic a la ciutat de Reus*. Canet de Mar: Centre d'Estudis Lluís Domènech i Montaner, 2017.

ALCALDE, S. [et al.]. *La Casa Domènech de Canet de Mar. L'arquitectura íntima de Domènech i Montaner*. Canet de Mar: Centre d'Estudis Lluís Domènech i Montaner, 2019.

ALONSO ORTIZ, L.; CAMPUZANO RUIZ, E. *Lluís Domènech i Montaner en Comillas*. Santander: Fundació Lluís Domènech i Montaner, 2015.

ÁLVAREZ, Félix (2015). Interview given at the Fundació Antoni Tàpies on 2nd February.

AMADÓ, R.; DOMÈNECH, L. "Fundación Tàpies». *El Croquis* (1991), no. 46, pp. 92-105.

AMADÓ, R.; DOMÈNECH, L. "La Fundació Antoni Tàpies, Barcelona, 1986-1988". In: *Documentos de arquitectura 7*. Almeria: Colegio Oficial de Arquitectos de Andalucia Oriental, 1988.

AMENÓS i MARTÍNEZ, L. "Les arts del ferro al servei de l'arquitectura modernista". *Butlletí de la Reial Acadèmica Catalana de Belles Arts Sant Jordi* (2011), no. 25, pp. 121-148.

Anglada Camarasa al Gran Hotel. Redescobrir una època. Barcelona, Fundació La Caixa, 1993.

ANGLADA LARA, R. "Del Código Fabra als quadres dramàtics de la marquesa d'Alella". *Revista Alella* (2021), no. 374, pp. 46-49.

ANGLADA LARA, R.; ESTANYOL i CASALS, E. "L'etiqueta social a la Barcelona del segle XIX". *COMeIN, Revista dels Estudis de Ciències de la Informació i de la Comunicació* (2015), no. 42.

ARAMBURU-ZABALA, M.Á.; SOLDEVILLA ORIA, C. *Arquitectura de los indianos en Cantabria (Siglos XVI-XX)*. Santander: Ediciones de la Librería Estudio, 2007.

ARNAVAT, A. "Reus 1900, segona ciutat de Catalunya. Un passeig pel tombant de segle". In: *Reus 1900. Segona ciutat de Catalunya*. Reus: Ajuntament de Reus; La Caixa, 1998.

ARNAVAT, A. [et al.] *La Casa Navàs de Lluís Domènech i Montaner*. Reus: Pragma, 2006.

ARNAVAT, A. "Domènech i Montaner a Reus". In: FONTBONA, F. (dir.). *Patrimoni monumental de Catalunya. Del Renaixement al segle XX*. Barcelona: Enciclopèdia Catalana, 2013.

ARNÚS, M. *Comillas. preludio de la Modernidad*. Madrid: Electa, 1999.

ARNÚS, M. *Comillas. Preludio de la Modernidad*. Sant Lluís (Menorca): Triangle Postals, 2004.

Arxiu Municipal Administratiu (AMA), Barcelona. File no. 31.256.

Arxiu Municipal Administratiu (AMA), Barcelona. File no. 345.528.

B [onaventura] P [ollés]. "Hotel de Mme. Ivette Guilbert en París. Arquitecto M. Xavier Schoelkopf". *Arquitectura y Construcción* (1901), no. 109, pp. 268-269.

BANCELLS, C. *Sant Pau, hospital modernista*. Barcelona: Nou Art Thor, 1988. (Terra Nostra, 13).

BASSEGODA, J. "Discurs pronunciat a la inauguració de l'exposició homenatge a Vilaseca el 15 de maig de 1910". *Anuario de la Asociación de Arquitectos* (1911), pp. 248-249.

BASSEGODA i AMIGÓ, B. "In memoriam. Gaudí". *La Vanguardia* [Barcelona] (14th March 1929), pp. 7-8.

BASSEGODA NONELL, J. "El dietari de Lluís Domènech i Montaner (febrer-novembre de 1893)". *Butlletí de la Reial Acadèmia Catalana de Belles Arts de Sant Jordi* (1993-1994), nos. 7-8, pp. 51-104.

BELLVER POISSENOT, L. *La editorial Montaner i Simon (1868-1981). El esplendor del libro industrial ilustrado (1868-1922)* [doctoral thesis]. Barcelona: Departament d'Història de l'Art, Universitat de Barcelona, 2017.

BENET, R. "Notes biogràfiques de Josep Llimona". *Butlletí dels Museus d'Art de Barcelona* (1934), no. 35.

BERMEJO LORENZO, C. *Arte y arquitectura funeraria. Los cementerios de Asturias, Cantabria y Vizcaya (1787-1936)*. Oviedo: Universidad de Oviedo, 1998.

BLETTER, R. H. *El arquitecto Josep Vilaseca i Casanovas. Sus obras y dibujos*. Barcelona: La Gaya Ciencia, 1977.

BOHIGAS, O. "Vida i obra d'un arquitecte Modernista". In: *Domènech i Montaner. Any 2000*. Barcelona: Col·legi d'Arquitectes de Catalunya, 2000. pp. 25-50.

BORJA-VILLEL, M.J. "La Fundació Antoni Tàpies». In: *Fundació Antoni Tàpies*. Barcelona: Fundació Antoni Tàpies, 1990.

BORONAT i TRILL, M.J. *La política d'adquisicions de la Junta de Museus, 1890-1923*. Barcelona: Publicacions de l'Abadia de Montserrat, 1999.

BRAVO, I.; CARBONELL, J. À.; DOÑATE, M. *Els Masriera: Francesc Masriera, 1842-1902, Josep Masriera, 1841-1912, Lluís Masriera, 1872-1958*. Barcelona: Museu Nacional d'Art de Catalunya; Proa, 1996.

BRU i TURULL, R. "Lluís Domènech i Montaner i el japonisme: dels esgrafiats del Cafè Restaurant (1888) als de la Fonda España (1903)". *Domenechiana: revista del Centre d'Estudis Lluís Domènech i Montaner* (2019), no. 14, pp. 18-41.

CABANA, F. *Fàbriques i empresaris. Els protagonistes de la Revolució Industrial a Catalunya*. Vol. 4. Barcelona: Fundació Enciclopèdia Catalana; Diputació de Barcelona, 2001.

CABAÑAS MORENO, M. P. *Joan Miró, el camino del arte*. Madrid: Encuentro, 2013.

CARBONELL, S.; CASAMARTINA, J. *Les fàbriques i els somnis. Modernisme tèxtil a Catalunya*. Terrassa: Centre de Documentació; Museu Tèxtil, 2002.

CARBONELL, S. "Arquitectes, decoradors i clients. El Modernisme tèxtil a quatre mans: Lluís Domènech i Montaner, Ricard de Capmany, Gaspar Homar i els Tayà". *Datatèxtil* (2014), no. 31, pp. 40-51.

CASANOVA, R. "Els referents estilístics de Lluís Domènech i Montaner i les seves confluències al Museu de la Història". *Matèria: revista internacional d'Art* (2001), no. 1, pp. 231-242.

CASANOVA, R. *El Castell dels Tres Dragons. De Cafè-restaurant a Museu de Zoologia (1887-2000)* [doctoral thesis]. Barcelona, Universitat de Barcelona, 2002.

CASANOVA, R. "Antoni Maria Gallissà i el mite del Castell dels Tres Dragons". In: *El Modernisme a l'entorn de l'arquitectura*. Barcelona: L'Isard, 2002.

CASANOVA, R. "Lluís Domènech i Montaner, a la recerca de la ceràmica moderna". *Millars: Espai i historia* (2002), no. 25, pp. 155-174.

CASANOVA, R. "Publicidad pre-modernista a 30 metros de altura". In: *Tradición y modernidad: la cerámica en el Modernismo. Actas del IX Congreso de la Asociación de Ceramología celebrado en Esplugues de Llobregat, 29-31 octubre 2004*. Barcelona: Universitat de Barcelona, 2006, pp. 71-80.

CASANOVA, R. *El castell dels tres dragons*. Barcelona: Museu de Ciències Naturals, Institut del Paisatge Urbà i la Qualitat de Vida, 2009.

CASANOVA, R. " El Taller del Castell dels Tres Dragons. Història d'un mite assimilat". *Domenechiana: Revista del Centre d'Estudis Lluís Domènech i Montaner* (2019), no. 15, pp. 8-25.

CASANOVA, R. *Estudi de diversos elements de la Fundació Antoni Tàpies de Barcelona* [unpublished].

CASELLAS, R. "Segunda exposición del Círculo de San Lucas". *La Vanguardia* [Barcelona] (26th May 1895), p. 4.

CASTELLANO, P. "La primera gran indústria del llibre: les editorials Espasa, Salvat i Montaner i Simon". In: VÉLEZ, P. [ed.]. *L'exaltació del llibre al Vuitcents. Art, indústria i consum a Barcelona*. Barcelona: Biblioteca de Catalunya, 2008.

CID, D.; SALA, T.-M. *Las casas de la vida*. Barcelona: Ariel, 2021.

CIRICI, A. *El arte modernista catalán*. Barcelona, Aymà, 1951. pp. 203-204.

COSTA MARTÍNEZ, R. "El polémico viaje de Eduardo Dato a Cataluña en mayo de 1900". *Espacio, tiempo y forma. Revista de la Facultad de Geografía y Historia* de la UNED (2018), no. 30, pp. 167-187.

COTONER, M.L. "La Biblioteca "Arte y Letras", primera aproximación". *Quaderns. Revista de traducció* (2002), no. 8, pp. 17-27.

DALY, C. *L'Architecture privée au XIXe siècle sous Napoléon III*. Paris: Morel et Cie, 1864.

DOMÈNECH GIRBAU, L. "La plenitud: funció i símbol". In: *Lluís Domènech i Montaner i el director d'orquestra*. Barcelona: Fundació Caixa de Barcelona, 1989. pp. 164-166.

DOMÈNECH GIRBAU, L.; FIGUERAS i BURRUL, L.; DOMÈNECH i AMADÓ, R. *Lluís Domènech i Montaner i el director d'orquestra*. Barcelona: Fundació Caixa de Barcelona, 1989.

DOMÈNECH GIRBAU, L. *El Palau de la Música Catalana*. Barcelona: Lunwerg, 2000.

DOMÈNECH GIRBAU, L. *Domènech i Montaner. Un home universal*. Barcelona: La Magrana, 2018.

DOMÈNECH i MONTANER, L. "Caràcters propis de l'arquitectura catalana á través de diferentes époques y estils artístichs II". *Butlletí de l'Associació d'Excursions Catalana* (1879), no. 7, pp. 94-97.

DOMÈNECH i MONTANER, L.; VILASECA, J. *Antecedentes del pleito contencioso-administrativo que contra la Diputación Provincial de Barcelona siguen los arquitectos José Vilaseca y Luis Domenech en reclamación de indemnización de perjuicios por los acuerdos de venta de los terrenos del instituto*. Barcelona: Impremta La Renaixensa, 1889.

DOMÈNECH i MONTANER, L. "De com se pot fer lo Museu de la Historia á Barcelona". *La Renaixensa* (1892), Vol. 2, no. 4, pp. 1661-1663.

DOMENECH i MONTANER, L. "Antonio Ma Gallissà". *Arquitectura y Construcción* (1903), no. 131. pp. 164-171.

DOMÈNECH i MONTANER, L. "L'Antoni Ma Gallissà en l'intimitat". *La Veu de Catalunya* [Barcelona] (21st May 1903), no. 1,556, pp. 3-4.

DOMÈNECH i MONTANER, L. "Records". *La Ilustració Catalana* (1905), no. 167, pp. 498-502.

DOMÈNECH i MONTANER, L. "Pròleg". In: SERRA i FONT, M. *Canet en l'Avenir. Orientacions a seguir*. Canet de Mar: Tip. Hospici Prov., 1914.

DOMÈNECH i MONTANER, L. "Reforma de Barcelona" (1879) and "La reforma de Barcelona resolta per sentit comú" (1892). In: BORRÀS, M.L. *Lluís Domènech i Montaner, Escrits polítics i culturals. 1875-1922*. Barcelona: La Magrana, 1991.

Domènech i Montaner. Any 2000. Barcelona: Col·legi d'Arquitectes de Catalunya, 2000.

DOMÈNECH i MONTANER, L. *Epistolari Lluís Domènech i Montaner* (Carles Sàiz i Xiqués, ed.). Canet de Mar: Els 2 Pins, 2013.

DOMÈNECH ROURA, P. "El Castillo de Santa Florentina". *Pedracastell* (1948), no. 30.

DURAN TORT, C. "La Renaixença, defensora del dret civil català", Revista de llengua i dret, no. 37, (September, 2002), pp. 191-212

DURAN TORT, C. "L'àguila emprèn el vol. D'un fris de La Renaixensa a símbol ideològic (1876-1910)". *Butlletí de la Reial Acadèmia Catalana de Belles Arts de Sant Jordi* (2015), pp. 93-111.

ESQUINAS GIMÉNEZ, N. *Josep Llimona i el seu taller* [doctoral thesis]. Barcelona: Universitat de Barcelona, 2015.

FABRA i FONTANILLS, C. *Deberes de buena sociedad*. Barcelona: Librería de Antonio J. Bastinos Editor, 1883.

FARRÉ, C. [et al.]. *Passat i present del Gran Hotel*. Barcelona: Fundació La Caixa, 1993.

FIGUERAS, L. [et al.]. *Lluís Domènech i Montaner i el director d'orquestra*, Fundació Caixa de Barcelona, exhibition catalogue, Barcelona, 1990.

FIGUERAS, L.; MANADÉ, M. "Línea, modelos y función de la cerámica en la obra del arquitecto Modernista Lluís Domènech i Montaner". In: *Tradición y modernidad. La cerámica en el modernismo. Actas del Congreso celebrado en Esplugues de Llobregat, 29-31 octubre 2004*. Barcelona: Universitat de Barcelona, 2006. pp. 99-114.

FONDEVILA, M. (coord.). *Gaspar Homar: Moblista i dissenyador del modernisme*. Barcelona: Museu Nacional d'Art de Catalunya; Fundació La Caixa, 1998. pp. 19-41.

FREIXA, M. "El projecte per a l'edifici de les Institucions Provincials d'Ensenyament. Lluís Domènech i Montaner i Josep Vilaseca i Casanovas en els primers anys de professió". In: *Domènech i Montaner any 2000*. Barcelona: Col·legi Oficial d'Arquitectes de Catalunya, 2000.

FREIXA, M. "La escultura funeraria en el modernismo catalán". *Fragmentos* (1984), no. 3, pp. 41-54.

FREIXA, M. "La 'Historia General del Arte' de l'editorial Montaner i Simón en el context de la Renaixença". *II Simposi Lluís Domènech i Montaner. Ponències*. Canet de Mar: Centre d'Estudis Domènech i Montaner, 2020. pp. 11-27.

FREIXA, M. *El Modernismo en España*. Madrid: Cátedra, 1986.

FUCHSHUBER, G. *L'edifici de la Fundació Antoni Tàpies*. Barcelona: Sapic, 1992.

GARCÍA LLANSÓ, A. "La colección de D. Ramon de Montaner". *La Vanguardia* [Barcelona] (6 June 1898), no. 5438, p. 4.

GARCIA-MARTIN, M. *La Casa Lleó i Morera*. Barcelona: Catalana de Gas, 1988.

GARCÍA-MARTÍN, M. *L'Hospital de Sant Pau*. Barcelona: Gas Natural, 1990.

GARCÍA-MARTÍN, M. *Comillas modernista*. Barcelona: Gas Natural, 1993.

GARNIER, C.; AMMANN, A. *L'habitation humane*. Paris: Hachette, 1892.

GIL, N. *El taller de vitralls modernista Rigalt, Granell i Cia. (1890-1931)* [doctoral thesis]. Barcelona, Universitat de Barcelona, 2013.

GONZÁLEZ MORENO-NAVARRO, J. L. "Domènech i la raó higienista". A GIRÁLDEZ FERNÁNDEZ, P. (ed.) *Les Avantguardes entre segles (XIX-XX): nous problemes, nous materials, noves solucions*. Barcelona: Patrimoni 2.0 Editors, 2015.

GONZÁLEZ PORTO, J. M. Letter to Joan Estelrich, Barcelona, 30th January 1950.

GUÀRDIA i VIAL, F. "Lluís Domènech i Montaner (nota necrològica)". *Anuario Asociación de Arquitectos de Cataluña* (1924), [n.n.], pp. 117-121.

GUITART, B. "Don Luís Doménech i Montaner". *Arquitectura* (1924), no. 57, pp. 4-10.

HOMS, N. "L'antiga editorial Montaner i Simon (1879-1881). El passat fabril de la Fundació Antoni Tàpies". *Domenechiana: revista del Centre d'Estudis Lluís Domènech i Montaner* (2015), no. 5, pp. 8-33.

HORRACH ESTARELLAS, B. *Aprediendo de la balearización. Mallorca, un laboratorio internacional del turismo de masas y de conformación de los destinos turísticos litorales* [doctoral thesis]. Barcelona: Universitat Politècnica de Catalunya, 2015.

INFIESTA, J.M. [et al.]. *Josep Llimona y Joan Llimona. Vida y obra*. Barcelona: Nuevo Arte Thor, 1977.

I. P. M. de Reus [ed.]. *Instituto Pedro Mata de Reus*. Reus, 1929.

J. C. and R. "Notes artistiques. Saló Parés. Segona Esposició del Circol Artístich de Sant Lluch". *La Veu de Catalunya* [Barcelona] (19th May 1895), no. 20, pp. 236-237.

La Vanguardia, 22nd June 1898, p. 4.

LANUZA, A. *Comillas. Apuntes Históricos, Noticias varias y reseña de la permanencia de SS. MM. Y AA. en aquella villa*. Santander: Imp. y Lit. de J. M. Martínez, 1881.

LAPLANA, J.; PALAU-RIBES O'CALLAGHAN, M. *La pintura de Santiago Rusiñol. Obra completa*. Barcelona: Mediterrània, 2004.

LLANAS, M. *El llibre i l'edició a Catalunya: apunts i esbossos*. Barcelona: Gremi d'Editors de Catalunya, 2001.

LLANAS, M. *L'edició a Catalunya: el segle XIX*. Barcelona: Gremi d'Editors de Catalunya, 2004.

LLANAS, M. *L'edició a Catalunya: el segle XX (fins a 1939)*. Barcelona: Gremi d'Editors de Catalunya, 2005.

LLANAS, M. *L'edició a Catalunya: el segle XX (1939-1975)*. Barcelona: Gremi d'Editors de Catalunya, 2006.

LLANAS, M. *Sis segles d'edició a Catalunya*. Vic / Lleida: Eumo Editorial / Pagès Editors, 2007.

Lluís Domènech i Montaner. Madrid: Colegio Oficial de Arquitectos de Madrid, 1981.

MAESTRE QUETGLAS, J. "Cambios de uso del patrimonio: la recuperación del Gran Hotel de Palma de Mallorca". In: *La multiculturalidad en las Artes y en la Arquitectura. XVI Congreso Nacional de Historial del Arte*. Las Palmas de Gran Canaria: Gobierno de Canarias; Anroart, 2006. pp. 125-132.

MALEXECHEVERRÍA, I. *Bestiario Medieval*. Madrid: Siruela, 1986.

MARCH BARBERÀ, J. [et al.]. *Institut Pere Mata de Reus*. Reus: Pragma, 2004.

MARIN SILVESTRE, I. *Eusebi Arnau Mascort*. Barcelona: Infiesta, 2006. (Gent Nostra).

MARLÍ, Enric i Albert (2010): Interview given at the Fundació Antoni Tàpies on 12th February.

MARTÍ, G. "Les llars de foc dissenyades per Lluís Domènech i Montaner". *Domenechiana: revista del Centre d'Estudis Lluís Domènech i Montaner* (2014), nos. 2-3, pp. 144-164.

MARTÍ, G. "La col·laboració de l'escultor Miquel Blay en l'obra de Lluís Domènech i Montaner". *Domenechiana: revista del Centre d'Estudis Lluís Domènech i Montaner* (2017), no. 9, pp. 8-43.

MARTÍ, G. "El paraigüer de la Casa Domènech". *Domenechiana: revista del Centre d'Estudis Lluís Domènech i Montaner* (2018), no. 13, pp. 124-141.

MARTÍ, G.; ALCALDE, S. "El projecte per a la Via de Pere el Gran. La ciutat ideal de Lluís Domènech i Montaner". *Domenechiana: revista del Centre d'Estudis Lluís Domènech i Montaner* (2022), no. 21, pp. 9-45.

MARTÍ, G.; SÀIZ, C. "La Casa Lleó i Morera de Lluís Domènech i Montaner (1903-1905). Un model d'habitatge burgès». In: *Domenechiana: revista del Centre d'Estudis Lluís Domènech i Montaner* (2014), no. 4, pp. 152-199.

MARTÍN, M. "Monumento histórico-artístico nacional : grave deterioro arquitectónico del Hospital". *Destino Política de Unidad Barcelona* (1979), no. 2158, pp. 18-19.

MARTORELL i TERRATS, J. "La arquitectura moderna: I. La estética. II. Las obras". *Catalunya: revista literària quinzenal* (1903), no. 18 , pp. CCXLI-CCLVIII.

MARTORELL i TERRATS, J. "La arquitectura moderna: I. La estética. II. Las obras". *Catalunya: revista literària quinzenal* (1903), no. 24, pp. DLXI-DLXXVII.

MAS GIBERT, X. "L'empremta històrica i cultural de Lluís Domènech i Montaner a Canet de Mar". *Domenechiana: revista del Centre d'Estudis Lluís Domènech i Montaner* (2013), no. 1, pp. 146-158.

MAS GIBERT, X. "Iniciativa i participació en el folklorisme a Canet de Mar. L'aportació de Domènech i la seva família a la reactivació de les festes populars". *Domenechiana: revista del Centre d'Estudis Lluís Domènech i Montaner* (2017), no. 10-11, pp. 140-171.

MAS GIBERT, X. "Del que ens va arribar de Lluís Domènech i Montaner a través de la seva família". *Domenechiana: revista del Centre d'Estudis Lluís Domènech i Montaner* (2019), no. 15, pp. 100-115.

MAS GIBERT, X. "Les creus domenequianes de Pedracastell". In: SERRA, M. *La Creu de Pedracastell*. Canet de Mar: Centre d'Estudis Lluís Domènech i Montaner, 2022.

MASRIERA i ROSÉS, L. *Mis memorias. La sociedad de Barcelona vista desde un mostrador a últimos del siglo pasado*. Barcelona: Dalmau y Jover, 1954.

MIRALLES, F.; ARGULLOLL, R.; HERNÁNDEZ, N. *Joaquim Mir. Antològica 1873-1940*. Barcelona: Obra Social Fundació "la Caixa", 2009.

«Miscelánea. Bellas Artes. Barcelona. Salón Parés». *La Ilustración Artística* (1895), no. 699, p. 362.

Modernisme. Art, tallers i indústries. Barcelona: Fundació Catalunya La Pedrera, 2015.

MONCADA, J. *Dante, S.A.* [unpublished novel, courtesy of Rosa Maria Moncada].

MONEDERO PUIG, M. *José Llimona*. Madrid: Nacional, 1966.

MORALES SARO, M.C. "Paraísos de mármol. La imagen del ángel en la escultura funeraria modernista". *Cuadernos de Arte e Iconografía* (1989), no. 4, pp. 377-83.

OLIVER, M. dels S. *Illa Daurada I. La ciutat de Mallorques. Viatge a Mallorca segons del Lluís Vidal, mallorquí de professió*. Barcelona: Biblioteca Popular l'Avenç, 1906.

ORTIZ DE LA AZUELA, J. *Comillas. Notas para su historia*. Madrid: Establecimiento Tipográfico de Fortanet, 1902.

P. del O. "Crónica". *La Esquella de la Torratxa* [Barcelona] (24th May 1895), no. 854, pp. 322-324.

PADILLA, J.I.; VILA, J.M. *Ceràmica medieval i postmedieval: circuits productius i seqüències culturals*. Barcelona: Universitat de Barcelona, 1998.

PERMANYER, L. "La casa y el obrador de Thomas". *La Vanguardia* [Barcelona] (6th December 1988), p. 7.

PIFARRÉ YAÑEZ, D. *Els esgrafiats del Modernisme a Barcelona. Obres i repertoris ornamentals* [doctoral thesis]. Barcelona: Universitat de Barcelona, 2015.

PONS i GURI, J.M. *Origen del municipi de Canet de Mar. Versió tramesa per Marià Serra*. Canet de Mar: Els 2 Pins, 1999.

PONS i PONS, D. *Miquel dels Sant Oliver i l'Ateneu Barcelonès* [audio file]. Barcelona: Ateneu Barcelonès, 2014.

PONS, M.; RIPOLL, M.I. (coord.). *Joan Alcover, Miquel Costa i Llobera i els llenguatges estètics del seu temps*. Barcelona: Publicacions de l'Abadia de Montserrat, 2007.

PUIG i CADAFALCH, J. "Don Lluís Domènech i Montaner». *Hispania* (1902), no. 93, pp. 539-557.

PUIG i CERDÀ, D. *Monólogos, diálogos y cuadros dramáticos infantiles para escuelas, colegios y salones*. Barcelona: Librería de Antonio J. Bastinos Editor, 1909.

QUINEY, A. *Hermenegildo Miralles, arts gràfiques i enquadernació*. Barcelona: Biblioteca de Catalunya, 2005.

RAMON GRAELLS, A. "De la idea a la ciutat». In: DOMÈNECH GIRBAU, L. (ed.). *El Palau de la Música Catalana de Lluís Domènech i Montaner*. Barcelona: Lunwerg, 2000.

RAMON GRAELLS, A. "L'Hospital de Sant Pau". In: *Domènech i Montaner any 2000*. Barcelona: Col·legi d'Arquitectes de Catalunya, 2000.

RAMON GRAELLS, A. "L'Hotel Internacional de Lluís Domènech i Montaner: arquitectura moderna i nacional". *Biblio 3W: Revista Bibliográfica de Geografía y Ciencias Sociales* (2012), Vol. 17, no. 966.

REYERO, C.; FREIXA, M. *Pintura y escultura en España, 1800-1910*. Madrid: Cátedra, 1995.

RODRÍGUEZ GUTIÉRREZ, B. "Noticias de la Biblioteca 'Arte y Letras' (Barcelona, 1881-1898)". In: *Análisis de la literatura ilustrada del XIX*. Biblioteca Virtual Miguel de Cervantes, 2010 [online].

RODRÍGUEZ LLERA, R. "Comillas, paisaje cultural". *Espacio, Tiempo y Forma. Serie VII, Historia del Arte* (2005-2006), no. 18-19, pp. 237-279.

ROGENT, F. *Arquitectura moderna de Barcelona*. Barcelona: Parera Editor, 1897.

ROSSELLÓ, M. *La Casa Escofet. Mosaics per als interiors, 1886-1900-1916*. Escofet 1886. Barcelona: Universitat Politècnica de Catalunya; Escofet, 2009. pp. 20-21.

ROVIRA, J. "Lluís Domènech i Montaner en la memòria dels canetencs". *Domenechiana: revista del Centre d'Estudis Lluís Domènech i Montaner* (2015), no. 5, pp. 130-137.

ROVIRA, J. "Domènech i Montaner. Vinculacions canetenques". *Domenechiana: revista del Centre d'Estudis Lluís Domènech i Montaner* (2020), no. 17, pp. 206-213.

RUSKIN, J. "La lámpara de la Memoria". In: RUSKIN, J. *Las siete lámparas de la arquitectura*. Barcelona: Stylos, 1987. pp. 167-185.

SADURNÍ VIÑAS, A. *Diccionari d'artistes vigatans*. Vic: Publicacions del Col·legi de Sant Miquel dels Sants, 2008.

SÀIZ i XIQUÉS, C. "Antoni Samarra i la seva producció artística a Canet de Mar". *El Sot de l'Aubó* (2007), no. 22, pp. 21-33.

SÀIZ i XIQUÉS, C. *Lluís Domènech i Montaner (1848-1923). El llegat arquitectònic, polític i cultural a Canet de Mar*. Canet de Mar: Els 2 Pins, 2008.

SÀIZ i XIQUÉS, C. "Ramon de Montaner i Vila (1832-1921). Aproximació biogràfica del primer Comte de la Vall de Canet". *El Sot de l'Aubó* (2008), no. 25, pp. 3-8.

SÀIZ i XIQUÉS, C. "Ricard de Campmany i Roura». *El Sot de l'Aubó* (2008), no. 26, pp. 3-11.

SÀIZ i XIQUÉS, C. "La casa Domènech de Canet de Mar (1918-1919). La darrera obra modernista de Lluís Domènech i Montaner". *El Sot de l'Aubó* (2011), no. 35, pp. 12-20.

SÀIZ i XIQUÉS, C. "Els decorats de Lluís Domènech i Montaner per a l'obra Judith de Welp". *El Sot de l'Aubó* (2011), no. 36, pp. 14-17.

SÀIZ i XIQUÉS, C. "L'arquitectura funerària de Lluís Domènech i Montaner. El llegat modernista dels cementiris de Canet de Mar, Comillas, Barcelona i Reus". *El Sot de l'Aubó* (2011), no. 38, pp. 19-23.

SÀIZ i XIQUÉS, C. "L'altre Lluís Domènech i Montaner. Disseny, arts gràfiques i projectes editorials". *El Sot de l'Aubó* (2012), no. 40, pp. 17-26.

SÀIZ i XIQUÉS, C. "L'arquitectura de Lluís Domènech i Montaner a Canet de Mar". In: *Empremtes. Lluís Domènech i Montaner a Canet de Mar*. Canet de Mar: Ajuntament de Canet de Mar, Casa Museu Lluís Domènech i Montaner, 2013. pp. 65-67.

SÀIZ i XIQUÉS, C. "L'Ateneu de Canet de Mar. Una obra primerenca de Lluís Domènech i Montaner (1884-1885)". *Domenechiana: revista del Centre d'Estudis Lluís Domènech i Montaner* (2013). no. 1, pp. 70-89.

SÀIZ i XIQUÉS, C. "La torre Simon (1878) de la vila de Gràcia. El primer projecte arquitectònic de Lluís Domènech i Montaner". *El Sot de l'Aubó* (2013), no. 43, pp. 13-22.

SÀIZ i XIQUÉS C. "Casa Domènech". In: BALCELLS, C. *Joies del Modernisme Català. Espais interiors*. Barcelona: Enciclopèdia Catalana, 2014. pp. 406-409.

SÀIZ i XIQUÉS, C. "El Castell de Santa Florentina. Lluís Domènech i Montaner i *la restauració en estil* de l'antiga Casa Forta de Canet". *Domenechiana: revista del Centre d'Estudis Lluís Domènech i Montaner* (2014), nos. 2-3, pp. 102-130.

SÀIZ i XIQUÉS, C. "La Casa Roura de Canet de Mar i els tallers de producció artesanal del Castell dels Tres Dragons. El primer modernisme de Lluís Domènech i Montaner". *Domenechiana: revista del Centre d'Estudis Lluís Domènech i Montaner* (2015), no. 6, pp. 8-53.

SÀIZ i XIQUÉS, C. "De la primitiva fortalesa medieval a l'actual Castell de Santa Florentina. Mil anys d'història a la Vall de Canet". *Trobada d'Entitats de Recerca Local i Comarcal del Maresme* (2015), no. 9, pp. 13-37.

SÀIZ i XIQUÉS, C. "Lluís Domènech i Montaner i la reforma de la Fonda Espanya de Barcelona (1899-1903)". *Domenechiana: revista del Centre d'Estudis Lluís Domènech i Montaner* (2016), no. 7, pp. 9-57.

SÀIZ i XIQUÉS, C. "La masia Rocosa i la Casa Domènech de Canet de Mar. L'arquitectura íntima de Lluís Domènech i Montaner". *Domenechiana: revista del Centre d'Estudis Lluís Domènech i Montaner* (2016), no. 8, pp. 56-123.

SÀIZ i XIQUÉS, C. *Lluís Domènech i Montaner i les Bases de Manresa. A la recerca de la Constitució catalana perduda*. Canet de Mar: Centre d'Estudis Lluís Domènech i Montaner, 2017.

SÀIZ i XIQUÉS, C. *Domènech i Montaner i la vertebració de la Catalunya autònoma. Una biografia política*. Canet de Mar: Centre d'Estudis Lluís Domènech i Montaner, 2019.

SÀIZ i XIQUÉS, C. "L'arrelament de Lluís Domènech i Montaner a Canet de Mar". *El Sot de l'Aubó* (2019), no. 67, pp. 9-14.

SÀIZ i XIQUÉS, C. "La decoració artística de l'Ateneu de Canet de Mar. Mitologia, religió i catalanisme". *Domenechiana: revista del Centre d'Estudis Lluís Domènech i Montaner* (2020), no. 17, pp. 8-37.

SÀIZ i XIQUÉS, C. "L'obertura de la Via Laietana i el projecte d'annexió dels carrers de la ciutat antiga (1914)". *Domenechiana: revista del Centre d'Estudis Lluís Domènech i Montaner* (2022), no. 21, pp. 46-78.

SÀIZ i XIQUÉS, C.; ALCALDE, S. *La Casa Roura de Domènech i Montaner 1889-1892*. Canet de Mar: Centre d'Estudis Lluís Domènech i Montaner, 2018.

SÀIZ i XIQUÉS, C.; ARCAS, F. "Higienisme, urbanisme i modernitat en el Canet de Mar d'inicis de segle XX. La influència de Lluís Domènech i Montaner en els polítiques del Dr. Marià Serra i Font". *Domenechiana: revista del Centre d'Estudis Lluís Domènech i Montaner* (2022), no. 21, pp. 46-78.

SALA, T.-M. "Tallers i artífexs en el Modernisme". In: *El Modernisme*. Barcelona: Olimpíada Cultural Barcelona 1992, 1990. pp. 259-268.

SALA, T.-M. *El Modernisme*. Manresa: Angle, 2008.

SALINÉ PERICH, M. *El mosaic modernista a Catalunya (1888-1929) de la mà de Lluís Bru i Salelles i l'obra de Lluís Domènech i Montaner* [doctoral thesis]. Barcelona: Universitat de Barcelona, 2015.

SALMERÓN, P.; TERREU GASCÓN, M. "Els Hospitals de la Santa Creu i de Sant Pau. El projecte original de Lluís Domènech i Montaner (I)". *Domenechiana: revista del Centre d'Estudis Lluís Domènech i Montaner* (2014), no. 2-3, pp. 7-41.

SALMERÓN, P.; TERREU GASCÓN, M. "L'oficina d'obres de l'Hospital de Sant Pau". *Domenechiana: revista del Centre d'Estudis Lluís Domènech i Montaner* (2018), no. 12, pp. 90-103.

SAMA GARCÍA, A. *Gaudí y la arquitectura de la Renaixença en Comillas* [doctoral thesis]. Madrid: Universidad Complutense, 2011.

SAMA GARCÍA, A. "Esplendor indiano: arte y magnificencia en Comillas bajo el mecenazgo de los López". *Moneda única* (2012), no. 116, pp. 94-96.

SAMA GARCÍA, A. "El cementerio marino. Arquitectura funeraria de Domènech i Montaner en Comillas". *Arte y Ciudad: Revista de investigación* (2012), no. 1, pp. 43-88.

SAMA GARCÍA, A. "El cementerio marino: arquitectura funeraria de Domènech i Montaner en Comillas". *Domenechiana: revista del Centre d'Estudis Lluís Domènech i Montaner* (2013), no. 1, Canet de Mar, pp. 90-132.

SAMA GARCÍA, A. "El homenaje marino. Monumento a Antonio López en Comillas". *Arte y Ciudad: Revista de investigación* (2013), no. 4, pp. 7-48.

SAMA GARCÍA, A. "Las puertas de metal de Lluís Domènech i Montaner en la Universidad Pontifícia de Comillas. Recuperación y esplendor de las artes de Vulcano". *Domenechiana: revista del Centre d'Estudis Lluís Domènech i Montaner* (2014), no. 2, pp. 90-132.

SAMA GARCÍA, A. "El homenaje marino. Monumento a Antonio López en Comillas". *Domenechiana: revista del Centre d'Estudis Lluís Domènech i Montaner* (2014), no. 4, pp. 72-112.

SAMA GARCÍA, A. "El reflejo dorado. La cerámica de Lluís Domènech i Montaner en el Seminario de Comillas". *Domenechiana: revista del Centre d'Estudis Lluís Domènech i Montaner* (2015), no. 6, pp. 54-81.

SAMA GARCÍA, A. "Escultura decorativa y zoología simbólica. El artesonado del Seminario de Comillas". *Domenechiana: revista del Centre d'Estudis Lluís Domènech i Montaner* (2015), no. 8, pp. 8-55.

SAMA GARCÍA, A. "La memoria del agua. La fuente de los Tres Caños en Comillas". *Domenechiana: revista del Centre d'Estudis Lluís Domènech i Montaner* (2017), nos. 10-11, pp. 110-139.

SAMA GARCÍA, A. "Bronce funerario. La lauda sepulcral de Lluís Domènech i Montaner para la capilla-panteón de Comillas". *Domenechiana: revista del Centre d'Estudis Lluís Domènech i Montaner* (2021), nos. 19-20, pp. 150-201.

Santiago Rusiñol (1861-1031). Barcelona: Museu d'Art Modern, Museu Nacional d'Art de Catalunya, 1998.

SAUNIER, C. "L'hôtel de Mme. Yvette Guibert". *L'art Décoratif* (1901), no. 29, pp. 190-197.

SAZATORNIL RUIZ, L. *Arquitectura y desarrollo urbano de Cantabria en el siglo XIX*. Santander: Universidad de Cantabria; Colegio Oficial de Arquitectos de Cantabria; Fundación Marcelino Botín, 1996.

SEGUÍ AZNAR, M. *La arquitectura modernista en Baleares*. Palma de Mallorca: Corc, 1975.

SEGUÍ AZNAR, M. *El Modernisme en les Illes Balears*. Palma: Govern de les Illes Balears, 2000.

SEGUÍ AZNAR, M. *La arquitectura del ocio en Baleares. La incidència del turismo en la arquitectura y el urbanismo*. Palma: Lleonard Muntaner, 2001.

SERRA FONT, M. (ed.). *Canet en l'Avenir. 1913 Orientacions a seguir* [preface by Lluís Domènech i Montaner]. Canet de Mar: Biblioteca Canetenca, 1915.

SERRA i FONT, M.; CLASCÀ M. de; UMBERT, I. *Dietari del Dr. Marià Serra i Font. Canet de Mar 1880-1926*. Canet de Mar [Barcelona: Àrea de Cultura], 2006.

SERRA i PAGES, R. "Lluís Domènech i Montaner (1850-1923)". *Butlletí de la Reial Acadèmia de Bones Lletres* (1926), no. 6, p. 391.

SERRACLARA i PLA, M.T. *Casa Fuster culmina el Eixample*. Barcelona: Ajuntament de Barcelona, Institut del Paisatge Urbà, 2008.

SOLÉ, E. (15th August 1897): *La Frontera. Periódico Ilustrado defensor de los intereses de Camprodón y del Distrito*, year II, no. 14.

SOLER MORADELL, J. "Ascendència canetenca de Lluís Domènech i Montaner (II)". *Domenechiana: revista del Centre d'Estudis Lluís Domènech i Montaner* (2014), no. 2-3, pp. 186-193.

SOLER MORADELL, J.; ALCALDE, S. "L'ascendència Domènech de Lluís Domènech i Montaner". *Domenechiana: revista del Centre d'Estudis Lluís Domènech i Montaner* (2015), no. 6, pp. 136-141.

STAFFE, B. *Usages du monde. Règles de savoir-vivre dans la société moderne*. Paris: Victor Havard éd., 1896.

SUBÍAS PUJADAS, M.P. "Pujol i Bausis, una empresa cerámica en el modernismo". In: *Tradición y modernidad: la cerámica en el Modernismo. Actas del IX Congreso de la Asociación de Ceramología celebrado en Esplugues de Llobregat, 29-31 octubre 2004*. Barcelona: Universitat de Barcelona, 2006.

SUBIAS PUJADAS, M.P. *Pujol i Bausis centre productor de ceràmica arquitectònica a Esplugues de Llobregat*. Esplugues de Llobregat: Ajuntament d'Esplugues de Llobregat, 1989.

SUBIRACHS i BURGAYA, J. *L'escultura del segle XIX a Catalunya: del romanticisme al realisme*. Barcelona: Publicacions Abadia de Montserrat, 1994.

TÀPIES, M. "Introducció". In: Fundació Antoni Tàpies. Barcelona: Fundació Antoni Tàpies, 2004.

TÀPIES, Miquel (2011): video about the sculpture *Mitjó* (Sock, model, 1991; sculpture, 2010), Fundació Antoni Tàpies, Barcelona.

TARRÉS PUJOL, J. "Josep Thomas i la Sociedad heliográfica española: orígens de les impressions en fotogravat a l'Estat". *Revista Cartòfila* (2007), no. 26, pp. 21-25.

TERREU GASCÓN, M. "Els Hospitals de la Santa Creu i de Sant Pau. El projecte original de Lluís Domènech i Montaner (II)". *Domenechiana: revista del Centre d'Estudis Lluís Domènech i Montaner* (2015), no. 5, pp. 96-129.

TERREU GASCÓN, M. (ed.). *Hospital de la Santa Creu i Sant Pau: el projecte i l'execució*. Barcelona: Fundació Privada Hospital de la Santa Creu i Sant Pau, 2022.

THOMPSON, J. D. & GOLDIN, G. *The hospital: a social and architectural history*. New Haven: Yale University Press, 1975.

Tradición y modernidad: La cerámica en el modernismo. Actas del IX Congreso de la Asociación de Ceramología celebrado en Esplugues de Llobregat, 29-31 octubre 2004. Barcelona: Universitat de Barcelona, 2006.

TRENC BALLESTER, E. *Les arts gràfiques de l'època modernista a Barcelona*. Barcelona: Gremi d'Indústries Gràfiques de Barcelona, 1977.

TSCHUDI MADSEN, S. *Sources of Art nouveau*. Oslo: Aschehoug, 1957.

UN AFICIONAT. "L'Hospital Clínich" *La Veu de Catalunya. Diari Català d'avisos, noticias y anuncis* [Barcelona] (9th September 1900), no. 1.

VALENTI, C.; RISTORTO, M. "Bestiarios medievales e imaginario social". *Scripta Nova* (2015), nos. 8-11, pp. 13-24.

VALLS JUNYENT, F. "Les trifulgues amb el xampany dels fabricants de l'Anís del Mono". *Estudis d'història agrària* (2004), no. 17, pp. 939-956.

VELASCO FABRA, G. J. *La familia de Camilo Fabra y Fontanills, marqués de Alella, durante el siglo XIX en España*. Madrid: Letraclara, 2013.

VÉLEZ, P. "Les arts decoratives en la Historia del Arte de l'editorial Montaner i Simon". In: VÉLEZ, P. (coord.). Art de Catalunya = Ars Cataloniae. *Arts decoratives, industrials i aplicades*. vol. 11. Barcelona: L'Isard, 2000. pp. 198-199.

VÉLEZ, P. "Les 'biblioteques' il·lustrades, una nova visió de l'esteticisme". *D'Art* 1987, no. 13, pp. 201-212.

VÉLEZ, P.; FREIXA, M. [et al.]. *El modernisme, cap a la cultura del disseny*. Barcelona: Museu del Disseny de Barcelona, Ajuntament de Barcelona, 2020.

VÉLEZ, P. *L'exaltació del llibre al vuitcents. Art, indústria i consum a Barcelona*. Barcelona: Biblioteca de Catalunya, 2008. pp. 103-104.

VÉLEZ, P. *La col·lecció Josep Roca i Alemany*. Barcelona: Ajuntament de Barcelona, 1989. (Catàleg del Museu de les Arts Gràfiques, 1).

VILASECA, J.; DOMÈNECH L. "Lo monument á Clavé". *La Renaixensa* (1875), no. 10, pp. 341-346.

VILLAR, P. *Barcelona, ciutat de cafès*. Barcelona: Ajuntament de Barcelona; Viena Edicions, 2013.

VIOLLET-LE-DUC, E. *Histoire d'une maison*. Paris: J. Hetzel et Cie, 1873. (Bibliothèque d'Éducation et Récréation).

YEGUAS i GASSÓ, J. (ed.). *Llibre Ver del Convent de Bellpuig*. Tàrrega: Arxiu Històric Comarcal de Tàrrega, 2003. (Ardèvol, 5).

Published by:
Triangle Postals S.L. and Ajuntament de Barcelona
Editorial and Publishing Council of the City of Barcelona

Communication Director:
Pilar Roca i Viola

Editorial Services Director:
Núria Costa Galobart

Direcció de Serveis Editorials
Ajuntament de Barcelona
Passeig de la Zona Franca, 66
08038 Barcelona
Tel. 93 402 31 31
barcelona.cat/barcelonallibres

Collection:
"Barcelona, Architecture and Urban Planning",
curated by **Carme Ribas**

Every possible procedure has been taken in order to identify the ownership of the editor's rights. Any accidental error or omission notified to the editor in writing, will be amended in future editions.

No part of this book may be reproduced or used in any form or by any means – including reprography or information storage and retrieval systems – without the written permission of the copyright owners.

Editorial director, Triangle Postals
Ricard Pla

Editors
Mireia Freixa, Josep Liz, Pere Vivas

Text
© **Ramon Anglada Lara**
Historian and documentalist, CRAI Technical Processing Unit, Barcelona University.

© **Rossend Casanova**
Doctor of Art History.

© **Lluís Domènech Girbau.**
Doctor of Architecture. President of the Lluís Domènech i Montaner Foundation.

© **Mireia Freixa**
Emeritus professor, Barcelona University. Third vicechair, Fundació Lluís Domènech i Montaner.

© **Enric Granell**
Professor, Department of Theory and History of Architecture (ETSAB-UPC).

© **Núria Homs**
Conservator, Fundació Antoni Tàpies.

© **Maria Manadé Palau**
Art historian. Secretary, Fundació Lluís Domènech i Montaner.

© **Jordi March Barberà**
Art historian.

© **Gemma Martí**
Conservator and restorer of moveable assets and coordinator, Centre d'Estudis Lluís Domènech i Montaner and co-curator of Domènech i Montaner Year

© **Xavier Mas i Gibert**
Writer and historian. Researcher on the research team, Centre d'Estudis Lluís Domènech i Montaner.

© **Antoni Ramon**
Professor, Department of Theory and History of Architecture (ETSAB-UPC).

© **Carles Sàiz i Xiqués**
Professor of History and Heritage, UNED Barcelona. President, Centre d'Estudis Lluís Domènech i Montaner.

© **Teresa-M. Sala i Garcia**
Tenured professor of Art History, Barcelona University. Member of the Fundació Lluís Domènech i Montaner.

© **Antonio Sama**
Assistant professor, Madrid Complutense University.

© **Clàudia Sanmartí Martínez**
Architect. Co-curator of Domènech i Montaner Year 2023.

© **Pilar Vélez**
Doctora in Art History. Member of the Reial Acadèmia Catalana de Belles Arts de Sant Jordi and the Fundació Lluís Domènech i Montaner.

Photographs
© **Pere Vivas**

© **Hans Hansen** (pp. 243, 244, 245, 246, 247, 248, 249)
© **Ricard Pla** (pp. 132, 133, 370, 371, 416b)
© **Joan Colomer** (pp. 209, 210)
© **Oleguer Farriol** (p. 313)
© **Biel Puig** (p. 306)
© **Jordi Puig** (p. 416)

Archive photographs
Arxiu Casa Navàs
Arxiu Fotogràfic Centre Excursionista de Catalunya (AFCEC)
Arxiu Fotogràfic de Barcelona
Arxiu Històric de la Ciutat de Barcelona
Arxiu Històric del Col·legi d'Arquitectes de Catalunya
Arxiu Històric de l'Hospital de la Santa Creu i Sant Pau
Arxiu Municipal Contemporani de Barcelona
Arxiu Municipal de Barcelona
Arxiu Municipal de Reus
CEDIM/Fons Jordi Domènech Arnau
Centre de Documentació de l'Orfeó Català (CEDOC)
CIVA Collections, Brussels
The Glasgow School of Art
Institut Amatller d'Art Hispànic. Arxiu Mas
Museu del Disseny de Barcelona
Institut d'Estudis Fotogràfics de Catalunya / Fons Merletti
Museu Nacional d'Art de Catalunya, Barcelona 2023

Production director
Mercè Camerino

Coordinator
Malva Calzado

Translation
Mark Waudby
Catalina Girona (pp. 7-21, 49-57, 219-223, 237-241, 401-405)

Graphic design
Joan Barjau

Printed by
Agpograf

Printed in Barcelona, 10-2023

Legal deposit: Me 786-2023

ISBN: 978-84-8478-995-6

Triangle Postals, SL
Sant Lluís, Menorca
Tel. +34 971 15 04 51
www.triangle.cat

Acknowledgments:

Anna Ribas
Berenguer Vidal (CEC)
Biblioteca Pare Gual i Pujadas de Canet de Mar
Carme Hosta
Casa Navàs
Casa Museu Lluís Domènech i Montaner de Canet de Mar
Castell de Santa Florentina
CEDIM
Cubiñá
Estanislau Vidal-Folch - Delegació del Govern a Catalunya
Família Padró de Capmany
Fundació Antoni Tàpies
Fundació Hospital de la Santa Creu i Sant Pau
Fundació La Caixa - Caixaforum Palma
Fundació Lluís Domènech i Montaner
Hereus de Jaume Ribera Llopis
Hotel Casa Fuster
Hotel España
Institut Municipal Reus Cultura
Institut Pere Mata
Josep Maria Antràs
Lina Ubero. Museu de Ciències Naturals de Barcelona
Marta Saliné
Museu del Disseny de Barcelona
Núñez i Navarro
Núria Homs
Palau de la Música Catalana
Pere Xirau. Ajuntament de Canet
Rossend Casanova
Silvia Fernández - 6Q Restaurant

In collaboration with: